DATE DUE

STAFF DEVELOPMENT

STAFF DEVELOPMENT

Eighty-second Yearbook of the National Society for the Study of Education

PART II

By
THE YEARBOOK COMMITTEE
and
ASSOCIATED CONTRIBUTORS

Edited by
GARY A. GRIFFIN

Editor for the Society
KENNETH J. REHAGE

19 NSSE 83

Distributed by THE UNIVERSITY OF CHICAGO PRESS ● CHICAGO, ILLINOIS

The National Society for the Study of Education

Founded in 1901 as successor to the National Herbart Society, the National Society for the Study of Education has provided a means by which the results of serious study of educational issues could become a basis for informed discussion of those issues. The Society's two-volume yearbooks, now in their eighty-second year of publication, reflect the thoughtful attention given to a wide range of educational problems during those years. A recently inaugurated series on Contemporary Educational Issues includes substantial publications in paperback that supplement the yearbooks. Each year, the Society's publications contain contributions to the literature of education from more than a hundred scholars and practitioners who are doing significant work in their respective fields.

An elected Board of Directors selects the subjects with which volumes in the yearbook series are to deal, appropriates funds to meet necessary expenses in the preparation of a given volume, and appoints a committee to oversee the preparation of manuscripts for that volume. A special committee created by the Board performs similar functions for the Society's paperback series.

The Society's publications are distributed each year without charge to more than 3,000 members in the United States, Canada, and elsewhere throughout the world. The Society welcomes as members all individuals who desire to receive its publications. For information about membership and current dues, see the back pages of this volume or write to the Secretary-Treasurer, 5835 Kimbark Avenue, Chicago, Illinois 60637.

The Eighty-second Yearbook includes the following two volumes:

Part I: *Individual Differences and the Common Curriculum*
Part II: *Staff Development*

A complete listing of the Society's previous publications, together with information as to how earlier publications still in print may be obtained, is found in the back pages of this volume.

Library of Congress Catalog Number: 82-62382
ISSN: 0077-5762

Published 1983 by
THE NATIONAL SOCIETY FOR THE STUDY OF EDUCATION

5835 Kimbark Avenue, Chicago, Illinois 60637
© 1983 by the National Society for the Study of Education

First Printing, 6,500 Copies

Printed in the United States of America

Officers of the Society
1982-83

(Term of office expires March 1 of the year indicated)

HARRY S. BROUDY

(1985)
University of Illinois, Champaign, Illinois

LUVERN L. CUNNINGHAM

(1984)
Ohio State University, Columbus, Ohio

ELLIOT W. EISNER

(1983)
Stanford University, Stanford, California

JOHN I. GOODLAD

(1983)
University of California, Los Angeles, California

A. HARRY PASSOW

(1985)
Teachers College, Columbia University, New York, New York

RALPH W. TYLER

(1984)
*Director Emeritus, Center for Advanced Study in the Behavioral Sciences
Stanford, California*

KENNETH J. REHAGE

(Ex-officio)
University of Chicago, Chicago, Illinois

Secretary-Treasurer

KENNETH J. REHAGE

5835 Kimbark Avenue, Chicago, Illinois 60637

The Society's Committee on Staff Development

GARY A. GRIFFIN

(Chairman)
Research and Development Center for Teacher Education
University of Texas at Austin
Austin, Texas

R. LINDEN COURTER

Continuing Education Office
San Diego City Schools
San Diego, California

KENNETH R. HOWEY

College of Education
University of Minnesota
Minneapolis, Minnesota

JOSEPH VAUGHAN

Teaching and Instruction
National Institute of Education
Washington, D.C.

BEATRICE A. WARD

Research and Development Division
Far West Laboratory for Educational Research and Development
San Francisco, California

Associated Contributors

JOHN I. GOODLAD

Graduate School of Education
University of California, Los Angeles
Los Angeles, California

JUDITH E. LANIER

College of Education
Michigan State University
East Lansing, Michigan

JOHN R. MERGENDOLLER

Research and Development Division
Far West Laboratory for Educational Research and Development
San Francisco, California

vii

GARY G. PRICE

School of Education
University of Wisconsin
Madison, Wisconsin

STUART C. RANKIN

Office of Research, Planning, and Evaluation
Detroit Public Schools
Detroit, Michigan

THOMAS A. ROMBERG

School of Education
University of Wisconsin
Madison, Wisconsin

PHILLIP C. SCHLECHTY

School of Education
University of North Carolina
Chapel Hill, North Carolina

LOIS THIES-SPRINTHALL

School of Education
Saint Cloud State University
Saint Cloud, Minnesota

NORMAN A. SPRINTHALL

Department of Counselor Education
North Carolina State University
Raleigh, North Carolina .

WILLIAM J. TIKUNOFF

Research and Development Division
Far West Laboratory for Educational Research and Development
San Francisco, California

BETTY LOU WHITFORD

School of Education
University of Louisville
Louisville, Kentucky

Acknowledgment

As Gary A. Griffin, editor of this volume, points out in his introductory chapter, significant developments have taken place since the publication in 1957 of the Society's Fifty-sixth Yearbook entitled *In-Service Education for Teachers, Supervisors, and Administrators.* The principles that guided the preparation of that yearbook still appear to have considerable validity and applicability in today's schools. Yet the context in which staff development is now undertaken is characterized by new dimensions. The present volume explores these dimensions and illuminates the issues that must be faced if staff development efforts are to result in the strengthening and improvement of our schools.

The Society is deeply grateful to Professor Griffin, to the Committee that worked with him in the preparation of this volume, and to the several authors who have contributed chapters. We believe that the analysis of issues presented here, and the several examples of staff development efforts in quite different settings, will provide a valuable basis for considering in depth a pervasive and continuing problem of the educational scene. We are very pleased to have this volume as Part 2 of our Eighty-second Yearbook.

KENNETH J. REHAGE
Editor for the Society

Table of Contents

Part One

The Contexts of Staff Development

Part Two

Case Studies of Staff Development

Part Three
Conclusions

CHAPTER I

Introduction: The Work of Staff Development

GARY A. GRIFFIN

The functions of this introductory chapter are fourfold. First, the timeliness of a yearbook on staff development in schools is discussed from several vantage points including professional, organizational, and societal ones. Second, the premise that staff development is a central function of school maintenance and improvement is advanced. Third, staff development as work is argued from a set of overarching premises which emerge, in large part, from subsequent chapters in this yearbook. The chapter concludes with a brief introduction to the remainder of the volume.

Why Consider Staff Development?

There appears to be little argument that schools, particularly those in the public sector, are in serious difficulty. That difficulty has manifested itself as concern for quality education,[1] debate regarding what schools can and cannot accomplish,[2] confusion over what schooling should and should not make present to students,[3] competition among differing claims about the most appropriate delivery of instruction,[4] sharp disagreements regarding the most appropriate governance and decision-making structures,[5] and the overall ability (intellectual and institutional) of the schools to contribute significantly to the quality of citizens' lives in a less than static society.[6] The problematic nature of schools in our present cultural milieu appears not to be an arguable issue among thoughtful educators and sensitive observers.

What *is* arguable, in some settings, is how to act upon the problems associated with the schools. Policy makers provide guidelines, regulations, and compliance procedures that are designed, it is assumed, to promote certain conceptions of schooling. Local and national special interest groups lobby in organized and less formal ways for inclusion

1

or exclusion of curriculum content and pedagogical practices. Teacher organizations bargain for certain privileges and responsibilities related to matters various. School boards and chief school officers select from an often bewildering array of options those "solutions" to problems which seem to carry promise for moving schools toward some positive ends. It is of concern to many of us that these and other well-intentioned activities appear to have little impact on business as usual.

Staff development programs, it seems to some, hold the promise of creating a means of problem amelioration potentially more effective than many of the panaceas which have been and continue to be put forward. The term "staff development" is open to many definitions and interpretations. For the purposes of this chapter, staff development means any systematic attempt to alter the professional practices, beliefs, and understandings of school persons toward an articulated end. It is important to acknowledge the presence of the words "school persons" as opposed to the more typical use of the word "teachers." By definition, staff development involves all of those persons who make up the organizational entity called the school. This includes administrators, supervisors, teachers, support personnel, and any others who work toward the accomplishment of the mission of the schools they serve.

The global definition above, along with its attendant qualifications, is in large measure different from the perspective usually taken when one speaks of "teacher in-service education." Although that label has its appropriate and valued usage, it *locates* professional growth unilaterally and does not acknowledge that teachers are only one part of a complex and often misunderstood system of interaction. Staff development, on the other hand, acknowledges that what is to be accomplished and with whom can be considered more comprehensively.

A variety of positions can be used to support the timeliness of a yearbook on staff development at this point in history. Twenty-five years have passed since the publication of the last yearbook of the National Society for the Study of Education that specifically treated programs aimed at the continuing education of school persons.[7] Those years have been marked by at least four phenomena which, directly or indirectly, provide substantial foundations for rethinking both school improvement and professional growth.

First, the knowledge bases regarding the characteristics of effective schooling practices have increased dramatically during the past decade. We are considerably more sanguine about the relation of certain specific teaching behaviors to pupil outcomes.[8] The school culture has received rigorous research attention and the result has been the specification of certain institutional regularities that are associated with school effectiveness.[9] Our understanding of how adults (school people, in this instance) learn has grown to the point that we can begin to predict what strategies will be most appropriate for increasing school-related knowledge and skill.[10] Thus, the content and process dimensions of school change and improvement through working with school professionals are more solidly supported than in past years.

Second, research attention has been paid to staff development efforts in recent years with the result that there is now a hint of predictability built into the efforts.[11] Admittedly, the research efforts are still in an exploratory period and the findings are often confounded by methodological and conceptual problems. There is, however, a growing body of evidence to suggest that certain approaches to professional development are, all things considered, more potentially powerful than others.

Third, the expectations for schools held by members of the society are being expressed with greater clarity and with more vehemence. After moving through the period of antischool social rhetoric, during which calls for deschooling society were often met with relatively unbridled enthusiasm, the place of the school, for most of the citizenry, appears to continue to be well established. Of course, whether or not the current school crises will cause a return to the mind-set of "throw the scoundrels out" is a moot point. Nevertheless, schools *are* in place in the country and there appears to be an increasing bent toward improving the schools rather than replacing them with some other untested teaching-learning instrument. This condition can be seen as influential upon the establishment of carefully conceptualized strategies for changing schools, in this instance the enactment of staff development programs.

Fourth, and closely aligned with certain of the arguments already cited, the state of schools as social institutions is such that change is seen as essential by most (and often disparate) groups in the society.

As noted above, the schools, despite their relatively entrenched roles in the culture, are in crisis. And, many would argue, what better means to respond to the crisis than to provide ways for persons in the process to grow and understand and change? Again, staff development programs can be conceived of as the most potentially effective means to promote growth, understanding, and change.

Staff development, then, can be considered as a timely topic for debate and consideration by school people in that programs now (a) can be based more dependably upon accumulated knowledge regarding effective school practices, (b) can be planned according to conceptions of practice with some limited predictability in terms of outcomes, (c) can be responsive to constituent and client concerns about the character and effects of schools, and (d) are believed by many to be the most appropriate means to act upon schools in crisis.

Staff Development and School Maintenance and Improvement

The school as a social system has received increased attention during the past fifteen years. This attention has been systematic and rigorous inquiry on the one hand and informal and propositional speculation on the other. The research efforts have allowed students of schooling to understand the institution better from sociological, political, economic, and organizational perspectives in addition to more typical curricular and instructional ones. The less formal observations, often politically motivated, have resulted in speculations and hunches about why and how schools work or do not work.

Despite the wide range of modes of inquiry, from the methodologically rigorous through the narrowly self-interested, there has emerged a widely held consensus that schools tend to be closed systems, peopled by well-meaning but often relatively uninformed semiprofessionals, guided by ambiguous and sometimes conflicting goals, and organized loosely around an ill-defined technical core.[12] These conclusions have pointed toward a variety of school-improvement activities which differ from the more historically typical "improvement by mandate." Most of these activities are considerate of the person in the process and are rooted in a conception of staff development as an appropriate school improvement strategy.

Schiffer has argued that the progressive era of education ushered in the notion that school improvement programs should focus upon cooperative and system-wide strategies for change rather than the more traditional treatment of teachers as persons who must somehow be helped to overcome deficits in knowledge and skill.[13] She acknowledges that although the focus of staff development may have changed, the practices, when examined carefully, remained the same. This conclusion, in terms of staff development, is closely aligned with that of Sarason[14] and Goodlad and Klein[15] regarding the school culture and educational innovations respectively.

The present volume, in many instances, illustrates the point that old school practices die hard. However, it also provides evidence that new configurations of staff development purpose and activity have emerged and, further, provides evidence that the growing sensitivity to the relation of the school person and the school organization can result in a positively empowered group of educational workers. This point of view, although seldom stated explicitly, is pervasive in current thinking regarding staff development.

There is in the staff development literature an implicit tension between staff development for the purpose of changing schools and staff development for school maintenance ends. This yearbook, to a degree, reflects that state of ideological tension but, as might be expected, tends toward the presentation of ideas and practices that can be used to the advantage of those persons concerned with *changing* schools.

It can be argued that there has been an unwarranted (and largely unproductive) emphasis upon altering or changing school conditions at the expense of creating and maintaining stability. Stability, it could be argued, is necessary for personal psychological and organizational health. Although the argument has a certain appeal, especially in times when social volatility is more the rule than the exception, students of the school culture have become all too familiar with the school conditions which, with little or no manipulation, appear to inhibit change and promote stasis. These conditions are acknowledged, if not described in full detail, throughout the yearbook.

It is important that the reader be assured that the descriptions and proposals regarding staff development presented herein were selected because of an apparent match between widely desired school consequences and the features of these descriptions and proposals. The realities of schooling, teaching, and learning are not absent from the

discussions. And, certainly, the proposition that attention to thoughtful maintenance of organizational and personal stability is a necessary
condition for planned change has not been ignored by the authors of
the yearbook chapters.

The Work of Staff Development

The contributors to this volume were urged to consider several
issues as they prepared their chapters. For the first section, dealing
with broadly conceptualized contexts of staff development, the realities of the people and the settings were suggested as the chief criteria
for inclusion or exclusion of ideas and practices. For the second
section, which contains descriptions of actual cases of staff development, chief among the issues was attention to what can (or did)
actually happen in the conduct of staff development efforts. These
emphases have resulted in what might be called "real world" depic-
tions rather than the more usual untested and untried but somehow
believed-to-be-true propositions that have characterized much of the
writing on staff development.

This perceptive, but often distanced, examination of staff development activities may lead the reader to minimize the importance of what
can be called the work of staff development. Although it can be
inferred from each of the chapters that someone or some group of
persons was guiding, monitoring, and otherwise leading the efforts
under examination, the nature of the leadership is not explicit. For this
reason, the following brief discussion is presented as a means to make
more present several orientations to *doing staff development* which,
individually or severally, sparked and maintained the work of school
improvement.

STAFF DEVELOPMENT AND SCHOLARSHIP

It is an unfortunate truism that school persons are often so caught
up in the "dailiness" of schooling that sustained attention to conventional scholarship is neither a significant feature of professional life nor
a valued personal developmental activity.[16] Alternately, it is argued
that scholars are so divorced from the practice-bound conventions of
schooling that they cannot be trusted to comment validly on schools
or the persons in them. This tension is described explicitly in the

chapter by Lanier and is implicit in the strategy reported by Tikunoff and Mergendoller.

What emerges as a vital link between the scholar and the practitioner, as acknowledged in this volume, is the need for knowledge by each party of the work and the ideological perspectives of the other. Throughout the yearbook there are instances illustrating the benefits that can (or should) accrue to the persons who make conscious and deliberate efforts to understand school phenomena from different and often newly discovered orientations. This mutuality of interest and inquiry would result, at least nominally, in persons who could be described as practitioner-scholars and scholar-practitioners.

This is not to argue the desirability of role reversal. It is, however, a proposal intentionally designed to widen the lenses through which school practices are examined. A limited understanding of the practices and possibilities of schooling is too often the consequence of a limited vision. Acceptance of the responsibility to inquire broadly, analyze perceptively, and reflect thoughtfully is at the center of the scholarly activity proposed here.

STAFF DEVELOPMENT AND PROBLEM SOLVING

Testimony to the contrary aside, the persons charged with staff development in schools appear most often to be working on the assumption that their principal contributions to the operation of schools is the recognition of and action upon problems in the school environment. The problems may be curricular (for example, the lack of an adequate plan for conducting instruction in a multiethnic setting), instructional (for example, the difficulties associated with making decisions about the best means of communicating the basic skills), organizational (for example, the most appropriate configuration of subject areas and student groups in a time of diminishing resources), or any other set of difficulties common to providing school-bound opportunities for pupils.

The problem-solving orientation to staff development is most commonly situation-specific. That is, a staff development activity is planned and implemented as the result of a perceived need in the setting at a particular time. Many school persons call this practice "putting out fires." Indeed, certain of the practices reported in this yearbook emerged as consequences of needs to act upon immediate and pressing problems.

What also can be seen in the subsequent chapters is a thoughtful and systematic attention to providing structures for problem solving that can be applied not only to a condition in need of immediate attention but also to similar situations which, given the nature of providing schooling, will more than likely arise in the future. This conceptualization of problem solving, a present- *and* future-oriented activity, can be a significant departure for many concerned with doing the work of staff development.

STAFF DEVELOPMENT AND INTERINSTITUTIONAL RELATIONS

A characteristic of schools which has been given both research and speculative attention is the relative isolation of institutions providing similar, or essentially compatible, services.[17] The chapters which follow, in many instances, provide evidence to suggest that the effort necessary to promote and maintain institutional alignment in terms of purpose, activity, and product is well invested.

The typical working *on* schools by higher education institutions is countered in several of the cases described herein by an orientation toward working *with* schools. The consequences of this refocused institutional relationship appear to be of benefit to most, if not all, parties. There are, of course, both historical and current reasons for the persistence of the "expert" status conferred upon colleges and universities in relation to elementary and secondary schools. What the illustrations in this yearbook provide testimony for, however, is the set of positive consequences which can accrue to both institutions if this orientation toward organizational relationships is altered.

The difficulty of promoting institutional relationships which depend upon trust, mutuality of interest, shared governance, and realignment of institutional purposes is, of course, enormous and should not be underestimated. The work necessary to reshape typical configurations involves more than expressions of good will. It demands a sense of the shape and texture of an organization, a consideration of probably only vaguely perceived possibilities, a diligent attention to institutional regularities which could hinder or promote desired ends, a giving up of often long cherished means of doing one's job, and a willingness to listen to both surface and subtext messages. But, as certain of the chapters which follow suggest, the work of creating institutional realignments can be powerful means toward accomplishing staff development objectives.

STAFF DEVELOPMENT AND INTERPERSONAL RELATIONS

All of the chapters in this yearbook give specific attention to the people in the process of staff development. Although this attention would seem to be a requisite for strategies designed to introduce and monitor change in *people*, such has not always been the case. Two dramatic, and very different, reactions to school improvement efforts designed less around people than around conceptions of bureaucracy are action research of the 1940s[18] and the group process efforts of the 1960s and early 1970s.[19] Although too loosely organized and implemented to be called movements, both sets of intentions and practices were attempts to provide a surround for school change and improvement which involved not just policy makers but potential users of the changes.

The work of staff development, as described in this volume, is people-centered as well as idea-driven. The value of that work is explicit and public. The difficulty of that work is often dramatic. The outcomes of that work are axiomatic when considering human organizations. Yet, the presence of that work frequently is less obvious than the more technological aspects of staff development.

Consider, for example, the so-called models for staff development and school change which have been promoted in recent years. The stages or steps in the models most often are based upon and rooted in assumptions about functions with little attention to who, under what conditions, and with what costs, carries them forward. Words such as *planning, implementation, diffusion,* and *evaluation* dot the schema. Under the words, however, there exist the too often implicit assumptions about who is to do the planning, implementing, diffusing, and so on. The lack of precise attention not only to the who but also to the why and the how can be considered a major flaw in many staff development proposals. The chapters which follow demonstrate the utility of correcting this condition.

This section has considered the work of staff development from several perspectives which may be less visible in the subsequent chapters than is desirable. The intention here is to offer some attention to the ways that staff development can be focused and accomplished. Naturally, there are alternate and complementary modes of doing staff development, such as concentration upon staff development and change *qua* change, staff development and management, administration, evaluation, staff development as promotion of organizational mission and function, and so on. The dimensions of staff development work here, however, are presented as a set of possible organizing concepts for this volume and are not meant to be universally inclusive.

Organization of the Yearbook

The yearbook includes four sections of unequal proportions. This first chapter introduces the volume and attends to issues related to doing staff development in school settings. The next section, consisting of four chapters, focuses upon the contexts of staff development. Context here is broadly conceptualized so as to include (a) discussion of the adult learner in the chapter by Norman Sprinthall and Lois Thies-Sprinthall, (b) John I. Goodlad's consideration of the school as the unit for conducting staff development, (c) analysis of the nature of the larger school system as it influences the conduct of staff development in the chapter by Phillip Schlechty and Betty Lou Whitford, and (d) descriptions of staff development practices, in the chapter by Kenneth Howey and Joseph Vaughan, as they have been and are being carried forth. Case studies of staff development programs follow. These case studies illustrate the variety of purposes, practices, and ideologies which can be put into place to provide growth opportunities for school persons. Judith Lanier describes a long-term and emergent set of interrelated activities with particular attention given to pedagogical change on the part of both teachers and teachers of teachers. Thomas Romberg and Gary Price examine an attempt to use curriculum change as the driving force underlying staff development. Beatrice A. Ward and Linden Courter provide a description of the difficulties and accomplishments encountered in a large urban school system when massive curricular and instructional change was introduced. The section concludes with the presentation by William J. Tikunoff and John Mergendoller of an intervention designed to involve teachers and other school persons in research and development activities in order to promote professional growth and school improvement. The yearbook concludes with a set of preliminary propositions that I have derived from preceding chapters and which, when considered interactively, could be used to guide staff development inquiry and practice, and a consideration by Stuart Rankin of the utility of the content of this volume for school persons involved with doing the work of staff development.

FOOTNOTES

1. Robert Benjamin, *Making Schools Work* (New York: Continuum Publishing Corp., 1981).

2. Harold H. Punke, *Mythology in American Education* (Danville, Ill.: Interstate Printers and Publishers, 1981).

3. Maxine Greene, "Public Education and the Public Space" (Presidential address at the annual meeting of the American Educational Research Association, New York, March 1982).

4. Bruce R. Joyce, Clark C. Brown, and Lucy Peck, *Flexibility in Teaching* (New York: Longman, 1981).

5. Donna Shalala, "Politics for Education: An Idea Whose Time Has Come" (Paper delivered at the annual meeting of the American Educational Research Association, New York, March 1982).

6. Carl Bereiter, "Structures, Doctrines, and Polemical Ghosts: A Response to Feldman," *Educational Researcher* 11 (May 1982): 22-27.

7. Stephen M. Corey, Chairman, *In-service Education for Teachers, Supervisors, and Administrators*, Fifty-sixth Yearbook of the National Society for the Study of Education, Part I (Chicago: University of Chicago Press, 1957).

8. For detailed discussions of the research on teaching effectiveness, see Thomas L. Good, *Research on Teaching: What We Know and What We Need to Know* (Austin, Texas: The Research and Development Center for Teacher Education, The University of Texas at Austin, 1981) and Susan Barnes, *Synthesis of Selected Research on Teaching Findings* (Austin, Texas: The Research and Development Center for Teacher Education, The University of Texas at Austin, 1981).

9. Michael Rutter, Barbara Maughan, Peter Mortimore, Janet Ouston, and Alan Smith, *Fifteen Thousand Hours: Secondary Schools and Their Effects on Children* (Cambridge, Mass.: Harvard University Press, 1979).

10. Norman Sprinthall and Lois Thies-Sprinthall, "Educating for Teacher Growth," in *Alternate Perspectives for Program Development and Research in Teacher Education*, ed. Gary A. Griffin and Hobart Hukill (Austin, Texas: The Research and Development Center for Teacher Education, The University of Texas at Austin, 1982), pp. 17-58.

11. Gary A. Griffin, Robert Hughes, Jr., and Jeanne Martin, *Knowledge, Training, and Classroom Management* (Austin, Texas: The Research and Development Center for Teacher Education, The University of Texas at Austin, 1982).

12. These organizational properties of schools are convincingly presented in Seymour B. Sarason, *The Culture of the School and the Problem of Change* (New York: Allyn and Bacon, 1971); Sam Sieber and David Wilder, *The School and Society* (New York: Free Press, 1973); Matthew B. Miles, *Innovation in Education* (New York: Teachers College Press, 1964); and Amatai Etzioni, *The Semi-Professions and Their Organizations* (New York: Free Press, 1969).

13. Judith Schiffer, *School Renewal through Staff Development* (New York: Teachers College Press, 1980).

14. Sarason, *The Culture of the School and the Problem of Change*.

15. John I. Goodlad, M. Frances Klein, and Associates, *Looking Behind the Classroom Door* (Worthington, Ohio: Charles A. Jones, 1974).

16. Gary A. Griffin, "School-based Interactive Research and Development on Teaching: Some Recurring Themes," *IR&DT Newsletter* 1, no. 2 (1978): 1-4.

17. Miles, *Innovation in Education*.

18. Alice Miel, *Changing the Curriculum: A Social Process* (New York: Appleton-Century Crofts, 1946).

19. John B. P. Shaffer and M. David Alinsky, *Models of Group Therapy and Sensitivity Training* (Englewood Cliffs, N.J.: Prentice-Hall, 1974).

Part One
THE CONTEXTS OF STAFF DEVELOPMENT

CHAPTER II

The Teacher as an Adult Learner: A Cognitive-Developmental View

NORMAN A. SPRINTHALL AND LOIS THIES-SPRINTHALL

Introduction

One of the most important omissions by the discipline of psychology has been the lack of theory for adulthood. As a result, educational programs in general and preservice and in-service teacher education programs in particular have been created and carried out without a substantive knowledge base. In this chapter, we will outline a series of recent theoretical advances that may form a promising theoretical framework for addressing the problem of teacher development from the perspective of the teacher as an adult learner. We will briefly review and critique previous conceptual frameworks. This will be followed by a brief review of recent theory and research that supports the growing importance of a cognitive-developmental viewpoint. Current theory and implications for teacher development programs will form the conclusion of the chapter.

Critique of Previous Models of Adulthood

As the disciplined study of human behavior, psychology has not provided a viable theory of adult growth. A common conclusion is that psychology has provided an increasingly detailed account of the process of normal and abnormal child development and a growing body of knowledge about adolescence, yet there is a dearth of information concerning adult growth. For years a major characterization of adulthood has been that of adults recapitulating their Freudian and neo-Freudian stages of childhood. In other words, adult growth was largely the process of understanding the intrapsychic march of the libido through the oral, anal, and phallic erogenous zones. The goal of such theory and practice was to enable adults to come to terms with neuroses and milder forms of mental illness. From such a psychoanalytic perspective there was to be one further benefit. From the study of the neurotic, we could understand the process of healthy adult growth. In assuming that human beings are basically reactive rather than proactive, we end up with a view that at best we can only accommodate to the early intrapsychic determinants. In other words, the major pattern of growth for adults is set by the age of six. After that point, humans are essentially reactive and accommodative. Such determinism does not square with the human condition as we have come to know it. Such a preoccupation by psychoanalytic psychology also has not illuminated the process of adult growth. Not only is the psychoanalytic view overly deterministic, but it also has not yielded a viable model for education or indeed reeducation.

Therapy was regarded as the treatment of choice, the royal road to comprehending one's own intrapsychic struggle. The journey of the id, ego, and superego could be traveled only in the company of a psychotherapist who would serve as guide, transference object, uncoverer, and interpreter. Anything less was bound to fail.

Unfortunately, little research data are available to support the psychoanalytic claims. In an exhaustive review of longitudinal studies with children, Kohlberg, LaCrosse, and Ricks came to starkly pessimistic conclusions: "Put bluntly, there is no research evidence indicating that clinical treatment of emotional symptoms during childhood leads to predictions of adult adjustment. . . . The best predictors of the absence of adult mental illness are the presence of forms of personal competence and ego maturity during childhood."[1]

Two other conceptual frameworks have been employed by psychology vis-à-vis adulthood. The assessment tradition in psychology provided the trait and factor approach and the operant conditioning school of Skinner provided the positive reinforcement view. It is important to note their assumptions, even though neither really competed with the predominant psychoanalytic world view.

Born out of World War I and subsequent vocational questions, the trait-factor method assumed that personality vectors stabilized some time during late adolescence. At that point, using the then new technique of paper-pencil inventories, young adults could be matched to occupations in a scientific manner. With measured interests, aptitudes, and personality profiles the idea of adult development was direct. Fit the person to the job and happiness (if not growth) would follow. Fortunately (or unfortunately) young adults possessed more potentialities that the testers could assess. Witness the hundreds of trait and factor studies done with teachers that have added up to nothing.[2] The trait-factor approach hailed as the hard-headed empirical approach to adult psychology failed its own empirical test. The static information from psychological inventories did not provide a basis for understanding or promoting adult development.

Finally, the Skinnerian tradition essentially went to the other extreme. Differences in thinking and processing emotions, in understanding ourselves as persons, are all just epiphenomenal—meaningless mentalistic conceptions. Such concepts have no basis in the real world of behavior. All we need is a theory of operant conditioning that says: find the appropriate reinforcer and the problem of adult development is solved.[3] A young black box or an old black box can be conditioned with equal facility, as long as we know the appropriate reinforcers. Thus, appropriate skills can be emitted on call through the ABAB paradigm. Operant behavior is essentially random under normal conditions (A). Applying reinforcement principles under condition (B) shapes and directs our behavior. This system has not been tried out in complex systems with normal adults (with the exception of the fantasy in *Walden Two*) but has been employed with mental hospital populations (token economies), with so-called "retarded" groups and other "subcultural" or minority populations, prisoners, runaway adolescents, and others. Generally, the assumptions of behavior modification become highly controversial when applied to such majority populations as adolescents or adults. The amount of control and the need for absolute systematic application of positive reinforcement create technological as well as philosophical problems. And as the majority populations become aware of such concerns, the employment of such global token economies is increasingly questioned. In addition, basic assumptions of the S-R approach apparently reduce the complexity of the human condition to such a low level that most educators and psychologists would probably agree with Allport's description of the total behavioristic approach as so bereft vis-à-vis the human condition that it could only be epitomized as "threadbare or even pitiable."[4]

The three most common models of adulthood essentially have

yielded an inadequate knowledge base for adult development theory. As a result, in the absence of adequate theory, practical applications become more like random trial and error, rather than planned and sequential educative experiences.

Toward a Cognitive Developmental Framework

A promising alternative conception is emerging for adult development in general and for teacher career development specifically. In this section we shall detail some of the theoretical tenets and research findings that may point the way to significant directing constructs for teacher development.

In the tradition of John Dewey and buttressed by recent work by contemporary theorists on a variety of developmental domains, we wish to call attention to a broadly based and growing theoretical consensus as directing constructs for teacher education. The propositions are indeed direct. Cognitive developmental theory assumes:

1. All humans process experience through cognitive structures called stages—Piaget's concept of schemata.

2. Such cognitive structures are organized in a hierarchical sequence of stages from the less complex to the more complex.

3. Growth occurs first within a particular stage and then only to the next stage in the sequence. This latter change is a qualitative shift—a major quantum leap to a significantly more complex system of processing experience.

4. Growth is neither automatic nor unilateral but occurs only with appropriate interaction between the human and the environment.

5. Behavior can be determined and predicted by an individual's particular stage of development. Predictions, however, are not exact.

A large body of empirical investigations scattered widely through the literature have supported these propositions but will not be reviewed here.[5] We will present, however, a review of the work from a variety of developmental domains that are appropriate for general human development as well as for teacher development specifically. Table 1 presents a description of the best known theorists and the segments or domains of human growth on which they have concentrated their efforts.

Certainly the most familiar domain in the table is the work of Piaget, who has charted the process of cognitive growth during

TABLE 1

DOMAINS OF DEVELOPMENTAL STAGES

Theorist	Piaget (1963)	Kohlberg (1969)	Loevinger (1966)	Hunt (1974)	Perry (1969)
Domains	Cognitive	Value/Moral	Ego/Self	Conceptual	Epistemological/Ethical
Stages	Sensori-Motor	Obedience-Punishment (1)	Presocial Impulsive	Unsocialized Impulsive	
	Preoperational	Naively Egotistic (2)	Self-protective	Concrete Dogmatic	
	Concrete	Social Conformity (3)	Conformist	Dependent Abstract	Dualist
	Formal Substage I	Authority Maintaining (4)	Conscientious		Relativist
	Formal Substage II	Principles Reasoning (5 and 6)	Autonomous	Self-directed Abstract	Committed-Relativist

childhood and adolescence. Essentially his framework provides a means for understanding how persons understand the physical world of time, space, and causality.[6] Kohlberg's work has focused on a related domain of the process of value development, namely, how individuals think about moral decision making.[7] Loevinger's work, employing the concept of ego development, examines how one understands one's own "self" and one's relationship to other people.[8] Both Hunt[9] and Perry[10] have examined development in terms of epistemology, the process of understanding what learning is, what knowledge is, and the role of the individual as a learner.

There is no single cognitive-developmental theory that is superordinate. Rather, given the emergent nature of research efforts literally scattered over the globe, the current state of the art reveals small clusters of researchers working independently and in relative isolation. This gives a sense of partial overlap and at times a sense of relativistic frustration that inhibits the creation of an overall synthesis. Such coordinated research efforts may lie in the future; at present, we have a series of very loosely connected and mostly idiographic efforts. The main point is that such work provides a means of understanding the process of human growth through a variety of domains. As a result, we can specify with some precision the content of development as well as the sequence.

Do Developmental Stages Make a Difference?

Another way to phrase this question is to ask the Dewey proposition, Should education be designed to promote cognitive development? In other words, if humans move from less complex stages to more complex levels does it mean anything? Or, are developmental stages indicators of differences in reasoning and thinking yet not related to the real world of action? Greene makes the point rather vividly. During the Nazi occupation of France, the villagers of Le Chambon responded ethically and concretely by saving refugees. They did more than reason; they acted.[11]

The evidence supporting the relationship between stages and different behaviors is not quite as dramatic as for the Chambonnais in Greene's example, but it is consistent. Recent studies have indicated that for adults in general, stages of psychological maturity did predict successful functioning in adult life using multiple indicators of success. Success was defined quite broadly to include not only career success, but also indices such as allocentrism (empathy toward others), the ability to symbolize experience, and the ability to act in accordance with a disciplined commitment to humane values. This is an important point. Success is not defined simply as economic gain. Thus, we can make the general claim that adults at more complex stage levels function in more humane and democratic modes than those at less complex stages.[12]

If cognitive-developmental stage predicts differential functioning for adults in general, then what about adults in the helping professions, especially teachers? Are the helping professions a specific instance of the same generalization? Recent studies of physicians by Candee clearly indicate that M.D.'s at more complex stages of cognitive and moral development (in this case measured by the Kohlberg domain) function more democratically with patients than their lower-stage colleagues, even though the two groups did not differ on traditional measures of academic achievement.[13] The more developmentally complex doctors were more empathic, flexible, and responsive in enlisting the patients as colleagues in the service of their own treatment plan.

The doctors who processed moral judgment issues at less complex levels were more rigid, authoritarian, and perceived patients as fitting highly simplified cultural stereotypes. Similar findings were reported in studies of physicians (N = 348) by Sheehan, who reported a positive correlation of .57 between indices of psychological and moral development and humane physician competencies similar to Candee's criteria.[14] Such a correlation was quite remarkable given the narrow range of the sample with respect to age, intelligence, grade point average, and academic ability.

Silver's study of school principals, in this case measuring development with Hunt's system, indicated significant differences in perceived leadership style in accord with developmental level.[15] She found that principals who score at more complex levels on Hunt's estimate of conceptual development were perceived by their teachers as more flexible in problem solving, more responsive, less rigid, and less authoritarian. In other words, a pattern of functioning was found that was highly congruent with that found for Candee's and Sheehan's physicians and for Heath's adults in the studies previously noted.

Studies of teachers are both more numerous and equally supportive of the general thesis. For example, studies by Hunt and Joyce reach highly confirmatory findings.[16] Teacher behaviors consistently associated with high conceptual level scores are described as flexible, responsive, adaptable, empathic. Such teachers employ different levels of structure according to pupil needs, use a wide variety of teaching "models" in their classrooms, are "indirect," and "read and flex" with pupils. In short, high conceptual level teachers perform in the classroom in a manner that fits closely with clusters of behaviors associated with effective teaching.

This is particularly important to underscore. Gage has recently noted that there is a consistent scientific base for the art of teaching.[17] His quite elegant meta-analysis indicates that the "know-nothing" view of teaching effectiveness is neither valid nor fashionable. He provides a systematic review of research suggesting very strongly that a high ratio of indirect teaching to direct teaching (I/D ratio) in the Flanders sense is positively associated with pupil gain. In thirteen of the sixteen studies reviewed under his conservative rules the measure of effectiveness was the I/D ratio. He concluded that teacher indirectness was highly significant as a causal factor in pupil achievement. He further indicated that particular elements of the Flanders categories were noteworthy. For example, the use of teacher praise and accepting pupil ideas were positively related to positive attitudes and achievement by pupils, while criticism and disapproval were negatively correlated. In other words, indirect teaching is consistently associated with pupil gain and is a major characteristic of psychologically mature, high conceptual level teachers. We should add that such indirect teaching is still expressed as a ratio. Such teachers do use direct modes, and can employ both aspects of structure (the Joyce dualism of prescribing environments and task complexity). The main point is that developmentally complex teachers make such decisions based on the pupils' needs and current functioning, as Joyce says, "to pull the student toward greater capacity but not overstress his or her capabilities."[18]

Further confirmation of the developmental hypotheses of developmental stage as a predictor of teacher effectiveness was indicated by a substantial study by Walter and Stivers.[19] Their measure of Eriksonian stage of identity formation in a large-sample study (N= 319) was the single most powerful predictor of success in student teaching. The identity index was an estimate of ego-stage maturity, a concept similar to Stage Four in the Loevinger system noted in table 1. A stepwise multiple R indicated the Identity Index score accounted for 11 percent (r = .33) and was by far the most relevant variable. Including four additional factors, such as grade point average, intelligence quotient, and the verbal and quantitative scores on the Scholastic Aptitude Test, increased the multiple R to .41. A separate analysis by sex indicated that the Eriksonian measure was particularly potent in predicting effective versus ineffective performance by males. The range of scores on the Identity Diffusion Index was greater for males than females. Male students demonstrating a lack of psychological maturity on this measure were particularly ineffective in employing "higher-order" teaching skills.

In specific regard to student teacher supervision, Thies-Sprinthall found a significant relationship between the quality of the supervisor evaluation and cognitive-developmental level. Using a combined measure of developmental level (Hunt plus Kohlberg), the higher-stage supervisors were more accurate in judging the quality of performance in student teaching than their lower-stage colleagues. In fact, it was quite troubling to find that lower-stage supervisors tended to rate higher-stage student teachers most inaccurately.[20]

All these studies point toward the same conclusion. The samples differ widely, the research methods varied, and the instruments themselves were dissimilar to a degree. However, in each situation different aspects of cognitive development were the focus of different studies. Some used Hunt's theory and conceptual level tests; others used Kohlberg's theory and either the Moral Judgment Interview or other measures of moral development; still others employed the Loevinger theory and her Sentence Completion Test. Regardless of these specific differences, however, the overall results were highly similar, namely, that persons judged at higher stages of development function more complexly, possess a wider repertoire of behavioral skills, perceive problems more broadly, and can respond more accurately and empathically to the needs of others.

Hunt has termed this the "New Three R's"—responsiveness, reciprocality, and reflexivity—or a person's ability to "read and flex" with pupils.[21] Kohlberg refers to the process as the ability to take roles, to place one's self empathically in the shoes of another, and to make decisions according to principles of democracy and justice.[22] Loevinger denotes higher-stage functioning as the ability to tolerate stress, to attend to the least compelling stimulus, to process decisions according to democratic principles, and to perceive questions from an objective "third-party" perspective.[23] Other theorists such as Heath and Perry employ somewhat differentiated concepts; Heath's psychological maturity includes both rationality and allocentrism,[24] while Perry's advanced stages are referred to as the process of "commitment in relativism."[25] At an abstract level, however, there are basic similarities across all developmental domains. Loevinger has stated the truism that all developmental theories must positively correlate, while Sullivan and others have made the point empirically with moderate positive correlations in the .4 to .6 range between Hunt's, Kohlberg's and Loevinger's measures of different constructs.[26] Thus we cannot specify exactly the nature of the interrelationship across the domains. There is, however, a similarity in terms of basic assumptions. Also, the research studies indicate that higher-stage functioning on one or a number of these measures does predict to important real world behaviors.

One final point should be made on cognitive-developmental stage as a predictor. Schalock has most recently suggested that the Beginning Teacher Evaluation Studies (BTES) may point the way to establish functional clusters comprehending effective monitoring, systematic feedback, planned explanations, and clear goal statements.[27] These complex behaviors, highly similar to Hunt's "Three R's," clearly imply the need on the part of teachers to act allocentrically, to attend when necessary to the least compelling stimulus, to symbolize experience—in short, the characteristics of higher-stage functioning by adults.

Can Adults Develop?

If we have established a consistent relationship between developmental stage and performance in complex human interaction, then may we assume that adults can develop, grow, move, and change in order to improve in the level of functioning? Or, does cognitive-developmental theory eventually join hands with trait-factor psychology and assume stabilization by late adolescence or at least early adulthood? Certainly a most common assumption about adults is the no-growth, no-change hypothesis. Major new information, however, points in two directions. First, the conception of adulthood as a period of slow cognitive-developmental degeneration is invalid. Second, the stability of functioning during adulthood may well be the result of inadequate stimulating interaction. Adults do not regress cognitively, and it may be possible to restart the developmental motor, so to speak, to nurture further growth. These are major new assumptions that merit careful examination.

Baltes and Schaie have been the two researchers most responsible for revising our common conceptions of aging. Their careful studies have shown the so-called decline in IQ to be a myth.[28] Even a most conservative interpretation indicated that three major intellectual factors (inductive reasoning, spatial ability, and verbal ability) actually show slight increases in capacity well into middle age. In fact, the only areas of consistent decline were the speed of visual and auditory perception and short-term memorization. In the important areas of problem solving, generalization, and concept formation there was no decline until after retirement age. In a serious effort to eliminate our erroneous folk wisdom and a negative self-fulfilling prophecy concerning aging, Baltes and Schaie suggest replacing the degeneration hypothesis with the concept of plasticity, that is, adults can learn new abilities and improve old abilities. New research, they point out, is generally supportive of the notion of plasticity.[29] Rather than decline, then, adults even under current conditions demonstrate slight increases in important capacities and at worst stabilization. However, such stability reflecting what is does not have to remain as what ought to be. The plasticity hypothesis means that under certain learning conditions adults may continue to increase in levels of cognitive-developmental maturity. While Baltes and Schaie have examined intellectual capacities and problem solving in general, other researchers have just started examining direct cognitive-developmental variables.

Bart, a Piagetian researcher, has found that about 30 percent of adults in general reach some aspect of a stage of formal thought, and those are only in modern technological societies that require formal operations.[30] However, this base rate does not mean that growth potential is not possible. In a carefully presented argument, Bart reaches the opposite conclusion. Adult education could be designed to foster growth. In fact, Piaget himself forecast such a possibility. He noted that in occupations such as carpenter, locksmith, or mechanic, the artisans could learn hypothetical reasoning vis-à-vis their own field.[31] Similarly, lawyers and doctors can (and hopefully do!) learn formal thought in their own field even though their thinking in other realms might be concrete. "For young people studying law—in the field of juridical concepts and verbal discourse, their logic would be far superior to any form of logic they might use when faced with certain problems in the field of physics that involve notions they certainly once knew but have long since forgotten."[32] As a result it comes as no surprise to find Piaget advocating serious research on formal operations during adulthood. Picking up this idea, Mertens suggests that we pursue it directly in teacher education. She calls for the idea of a formal operational teacher, since at that level the teacher can process alternative ideas, and generate and test out different hypotheses in teaching children.[33]

In the area of moral judgment the most recent longitudinal findings from Kohlberg also support the general framework. Although his sample has not shown dramatic changes, there was almost a 10 percent increase in principled (Stage Five) reasoning between the adults at age twenty-one and the same adults at age thirty-six. Also, legalistic, inner-directed (Stage Four) reasoning improved by 31 percent during the same interval.[34] Such growth at the two highest empirically demonstrated Kohlberg stages is modest, yet does suggest a potential direction for positive growth.

Hunt points to these same generalizations, based on his long-term studies of stages of conceptual development, especially of teachers. The evidence is such that an adult's current level of functioning, from a stage framework, should never be viewed as a permanent classification. The present level is a person's preferred style. Hunt uses the term "modifiability" to denote the possibility of promoting growth during adulthood.[35]

A key point in this new view of adult plasticity is that the minimal growth reported has occurred almost randomly. There have been no carefully planned and executed long-term studies specifically designed to stimulate adult growth. A major factor documented in studies of children and adolescents indicates most clearly that developmental growth is not unilateral. There is no magical unfolding of potential. Rather, growth depends upon appropriate interaction with the environment. A responsive learning atmosphere is a necessary condition to promote development. In the case of adult teachers it would be hard to conclude that they experience the requisite learning interactions. Lengthy studies of preservice teachers have reported the psychonoxious effects of the supervision of student teachers.[36] The picture for in-service education is even more discouraging. In a massive national survey Howey, Yarger, and Joyce found little evidence that in-service education was anything but a brief and relatively mindless experience for most teachers.[37] Hunt was less kind. He characterized it as entertainment rather than education, and bad entertainment at that.[38]

What this means is quite direct. Adult growth is certainly possible. Much work is obviously required. We will next summarize what is known about the process, also noting the very recent nature of this work.

Promoting Developmental Growth

The problem of developmental education is essentially a problem of creating learning experiences that meet the old dictum of starting where the learner is and then providing interaction which will stimulate growth to the next highest stage in the sequence.

The developmental assumption of interaction holds that effective teaching involves the process of "matching" and "mismatching" environments according to the developmental level of the learner. Thus developmentally immature persons would interact best in a highly structured environment, with rule/example/rule teaching, short-term rewards, low ambiguity as to expectations, and so forth. The opposite would hold for psychologically mature learners. And indeed Hunt has shown that pupils at his less complex stages of conceptual development do achieve academic gains with rule/example/rule teaching, while his higher-stage pupils thrived with a more inductive approach.[39] He did not test out the effect directly upon the pupils' stage of development. However, his work clearly implied that effective programs could have a direct impact upon the level of cognitive-developmental stage functioning.

A series of studies have been conducted with high school pupils and college students with the stage of cognitive development as the dependent variable. These studies conducted over the past decade, summarized by Sprinthall and by Parker,[40] indicate that modest but consistent positive changes take place in stage growth, but only under particular instructional conditions. This means that stage can be modified as a result of specific educational interventions. Pupils can move "up" within a stage or from one stage to the next in the sequence as the outcome of what has been called deliberate psychological education.

These studies also show the importance in Hunt's frame of reference of "matching" and "mismatching." The entry-level characteristics of the pupils (for example, their stage of development prior to treatment) interacted with the intervention. An analysis of within treatment-group differences demonstrated that the amount of structure and the amount of role-taking experience produced gains with sub-groups of students clustered at specific stages. For example, classes teaching peer counseling techniques and theory to high school students produced developmental growth for students at Loevinger and Kohlberg stage three, but not for those higher or lower. Such a program appeared too structured and too controlled for the higher-stage pupils, and too unstructured and too complex for the lower-stage pupils. This is similar to a reanalysis of programs for college students.[41] Hedin's study, however, was the first to vary task and structure systematically for a high school class according to three entry-level stage clusters of pupils. Her work demonstrated that it is possible to stimulate developmental growth for all students in a high school class through systematic variation of social role-taking process and content.[42]

. Of course, that single study does not prove the point. The sample size was relatively small—an intact high school class—and replication is requisite. However, it may point the way to more studies with a deliberately differentiated curriculum according to initial stage characteristics of the learners. The overall effect of the Hedin study was highly congruent with the prior studies. The experimental groups as a whole always demonstrated positive gains on developmental indices while control and quasi-control groups always remained essentially unchanged. Thus there is support for the general proposition as to the "modifiability" of developmental stage. What we now need to work out are more careful instructional prescriptions that can be tried out and evaluated with other populations to learn more about the limits and opportunities for matching learning environments according to stage characteristics.

If the above studies indicate what may be possible for secondary pupils and college students in general, what about research on educational programs for preservice and in-service teachers? At the moment, there is the least amount of research in this area.

Admittedly the idea of targeting programs toward cognitive developmental level is controversial. Even such an innovator as Joyce seems ambivalent over such a prospect. He suggests that we concentrate on teaching teachers to acquire a broader repertoire of teaching skills, which are then "on call," rather than attempting to modify the conceptual developmental level.[43] Yet, at least theoretically and based on some of his own research, it appears that the higher conceptual level teachers would be the ones who could not only master the variety of models of teaching but, and most importantly, could *choose* the model that would best fit with particular students. Without the ability to "read and flex" in the Hunt sense, we do not know if the teacher would call on the appropriate model to enhance student growth.

There are a few recent studies that provide initial support for the contention that teacher education programs can focus on cognitive-developmental stage as a target. With preservice teachers Hurt and Sprinthall[44] and Glassberg and Sprinthall[45] have tried out programs over one term designed to raise the stage of development. The gains were modest but consistent. The experimental groups improved on stage scores (the measures of Loevinger and Kohlberg plus clinical measures) while controls remained unchanged. Also, appropriate higher-order teaching skills improved. All these studies employed multiple measures for the dependent variable. Similarly, at the in-service level the message was less clear but still important to note. In a first trial by Sprinthall and Bernier, the results were equivocal.[46] In a second tryout by Oja and Sprinthall, the results were slightly more promising.[47] A moderate size sample of thirty-six in-service teachers improved on estimates of psychological maturity and skills as a result of a six-week summer session followed by one term of supervised practice in their own schools.

A pilot study by Thies-Sprinthall also achieved positive outcomes in affecting the developmental stage and behavior of a small sample of in-service supervising teachers. In that study (N=10), eight of the experienced teachers improved on both higher-order teaching and a combined index of Hunt and Kohlberg estimates of stage development.[48]

To be sure, none of these studies can be considered definitive, yet as a group they provide evidence to support the contention that professional education can be organized to promote development.

Toward an Instructional Model

On the basis of the initial cognitive-developmental studies, what do the findings suggest as to procedures? In other words, what is the content and process of programs designed to promote both stage growth and skill acquisition? Generally the guidelines are emergent. Each of the first generation programs followed a formative evaluation cycle so that information from one study provided the basis for subsequent improvement. Thus the overall scheme is still in the initial phase of development. It is possible, however, to draw up some tentative guidelines as a means of illustrating important components.

1. Growth toward more complex levels of cognitive-devel-

opmental functioning appears to be most influenced by placing persons in *significant role-taking experiences.* A substantial difference is to be noted between role playing (simulation, games, fantasy trips, and the like) and actual role taking. In the latter case, the person is expected to perform a new and somewhat more complex interpersonal task than his or her own current preferred mode. The experience is direct and active, as opposed to vicarious and indirect. For example, with teenagers, role taking may involve a pupil in actually learning to counsel a peer, or teaching junior high pupils, or co-teaching in a nursery school. For preservice and in-service teachers, role taking may involve teaching counseling skills or supervision skills, or employing new teaching "models." The concept of cross-role training or role taking for teachers seems valid—namely, that educating professionals through direct yet multiple professional roles may act as a stimulus to growth.

2. A second consideration concerns the *qualitative aspects* of such experience-based role taking. Obviously, as Dewey noted long ago, major differences are inherent in what anyone can learn from experience. From an experiential point of view, working at the Rub-A-Dub-Dub Car Wash may not be equivalent to teaching a blind retarded child to swim. What we need to chart is the learning potential implicit in particular kinds of role-taking experience that are neither beyond the reach nor below the grasp of an individual learner. Role taking could be a significant educative *or* miseducative activity depending upon the calibration or the experiential "match."

Developmental stage differences imply major differences in the initial ability to take roles. For example, in some of the school studies it was clear that the developmentally less mature junior high pupils could not work effectively in a relatively unstructured preschool. On the other hand, children in the same age-and-stage range could work effectively in a more highly structured cross-age teaching assignment in a traditional elementary school. Based on clinical evidence, it appears that teachers at modest conceptual level stages have difficulty understanding and accepting why they could employ common counseling techniques for small-group instruction for mainstreamed classes. Such a role-taking experience may not be appropriate, at least at the outset, for these teachers. Also the Thies-Sprinthall study suggested quite clearly that supervising teachers at modest levels of development experienced substantial difficulty in relating effectively with student teachers functioning at higher stages.

3. In addition to "real" experience, we see a genuine need for *careful and continuous guided reflection*. Again, in a Deweyan sense, unexamined experience misses the point. An inordinate commitment to this concept appears required to make it work. Apparently the general educational enterprise rarely teaches anyone how to reflect upon real experience. Vocabulary for reflection seems to vary from the minimal to the nonexistent. In a series of secondary schools, most teenagers seemed to believe that "wow," "sad," and "dynamite" represented the complete thesaurus for human emotions! If preservice or in-service teachers are asked to keep a journal, the results are usually meager at best. As a stimulus to growth, teaching how to ask questions, how to examine experience from a variety of views, and so forth, seem at least equal to providing real experience. Naturally, there are always some in each group who, for whatever reason, are reflective; yet for the majority, structured reflection seems requisite to promote rigorous examination.

4. Balance is needed between the real experience and discussion/reflection/teaching. Research with teenagers indicates that tremendous amounts of experience do not have greater impacts than more modest amounts. In a peer-teaching program, tutoring two or three hours per week proved as effective as ten to twelve hours in affecting the level of psychological maturity, as long as a weekly seminar was provided. Without the guided reflection, no discernable effect was evident in volunteer tutors. *Guided integration* appears essential.

5. Programs need to be *continuous*. Rarely will a single three-credit course provide a sufficiently in-depth experience to produce significant change. The follow-up studies by Howey, Yarger, and Joyce noted earlier clearly document the ineffectiveness of brief, episodic, weekend-type learning.[49] The time for significant change probably should extend over at least a one-year period. In one of our projects we found that grouping or clustering teachers by school building made it more possible to provide continuous supervision on-site when teachers were asked to transfer their newly learned teaching models to their own classrooms. Many theorists in the past have written of the relative isolation of classroom teachers. Such an environmental factor may indeed influence why so little new learning transfers. Without continu-

ity during both the acquisition and transfer phase, new instructional techniques may be placed quickly into desk drawers, atop new curriculum guides. As a result, both new techniques and new content quietly gather dust.

6. Since developmental stage growth represents by definition functioning at a new and more complex level, instruction needs to provide for both *personal support* and *challenge*. The general role of the leader must include, at a minimum, the ability to model a variety of teaching practices. By itself, such modeling probably will not be enough. A key Piagetian concept is that development involves the process of upsetting or upending one's current stage (and state of equilibrium), thereby creating dissonance or a state of equilibration. The person attempts to incorporate the new into the old without really changing the old.

New learning, in a developmental sense, requires that we actually give up old, less adequate, more concrete, less empathic, more stylized systems of thought and action. The stability that a less adequate stage may offer can often become an extremely well-entrenched barrier to change. Any effective instructional model must offer major personal support as a direct part of the instruction, not as an indirect service or adjunct "therapy." Separating the person from "old learning" may be similar to the grieving process, at least for some. In any case, our work with in-service teachers convinces us that significant professional development is often painful.

7. Since cognitive developmental theory has emerged only recently as a major organizing concept, much work remains, especially at the *assessment level*. There are, however, a series of available instruments that can be used both in predictive studies where cognitive stage is an independent or predictor variable and in studies of intervention where a program is designed to impact cognitive stage as a dependent variable. There are assessment methods for each domain represented in table 1. For example, levels of moral judgment can be estimated from answers to standard moral dilemmas using the Moral Judgment Interview Scoring Manual,[50] or in a more objective manner through the Defining Issues Test created by Rest.[51] Similarly, Loevinger's theory of ego stages can be assessed through her thirty-six-item Sentence Completion Test, rated according to her training manual.[52] The Eriksonian test of identity stage, a concept analogous to a

transition from Loevinger's stage three to four, can be assessed through a sixty-item objective check list, the work of Constantinople.[53] In their manuals, both Hunt and Perry describe methods for rating answers to open-ended questions.[54]

Generally we have found it advisable to employ more than one measure for either predictor or intervention research. In this way the outcomes partly cross-validate each other. Also, and by far most importantly, the outcome information can become the basis for readjusting a program designed for intervention. In fact, when these programs were first tried out over a decade ago, the assessment instruments indicated quite clearly that our initial attempts failed.[55] As well, the data base indicated the kinds of change we needed to make in order for the program to work. Thus the assessment procedures can become a means of formative evaluation especially for research of the treatment type.

Summary

In this chapter we have presented the case for a cognitive-developmental approach for the career development of teachers. We see the framework as providing a solid theoretical basis for understanding the process of growth. Also, following Dewey, we see the possibility of creating programs to stimulate developmental growth. We do not see it as a fallacy to suggest that if we know (tentatively) what development *is* then we may also know what education *ought* to be. The evidence strongly supports the assumption that developmental stage predicts qualitatively different levels of human behavior in complex tasks. The evidence on the second point is less clear but suggests that it may be possible to refine programs to the point where stage growth may be stimulated. We should add that current work at both the Far West Laboratory[56] and at Michigan State University[57] seems to parallel at least some of these ideas for promoting growth of in-service teachers. The focus of on-site, collaborative education, which gradually increases the complexity of teacher perception, seems congenial with elements of the cognitive-developmental approach. It is also clear that much work needs to be done before anything like an articulated education program for teacher development would be ready for implementation on a major scale. To build a cumulative base in theory and research is still the most pressing need facing the profession. The ideas presented here may serve as a first step in that process.

FOOTNOTES

1. Lawrence Kohlberg, Jean LaCrosse, and David Ricks, "The Predictability of Adult Mental Health from Childhood Behavior," in *Handbook of Child Psychopathology*, ed. Benjamin Wolman (New York: McGraw-Hill, 1971), pp. 1271-84. Also, the generic effectiveness of psychotherapy as treatment for adults remains problematic. As recently as 1980 a special commission for the American Psychological Association reported only that "hard facts" were possible but presumably still needed to establish validity. See "ITA Report Says 'Hard Facts' Possible on Psychotherapy," *APA Monitor* 11 (December 1980): 1.

2. The most recent review of innumerable descriptive research studies, which have yielded so little, can be found in Del Schalock, "Research on Teacher Selection," *Review of Research in Education*, ed. David Berliner (Washington, D.C.: American Educational Research Association, 1979), chap. 9.

3. B. Fred Skinner, *Science and Human Behavior* (New York: Macmillan, 1953).

4. Gordon W. Allport, *The Person In Psychology* (Boston: Beacon, 1968), p. 70.

5. Piaget's studies are easily the most numerous in support of his stages of growth. Flavell has summarized the validity of his contributions as "nothing short of stupendous, both quantitatively and qualitatively." See John Flavell, "Stage-Related Properties of Cognitive Development," *Cognitive Psychology* 2 (October 1971): 421-53. Kohlberg, Hunt, Loevinger, and Perry validated their own work in a series of original studies, many of which have been subsequently cross-validated by other researchers. For reviews of each basic view, the reader is referred to: Jean Piaget, *Psychology of Intelligence* (Paterson, N. J.: Littlefield Adams, 1963); Lawrence Kohlberg, "Stage and Sequence: The Cognitive-Developmental Approach to Socialization," in *Handbook of Socialization*, ed. David Goslin (Chicago: Rand McNally, 1969), pp. 347-80; Jane Loevinger, "The Meaning and Measurement of Ego Development," *American Psychologist* 21 (March 1966): pp. 195-206; David Hunt, *Matching Models in Education* (Toronto: Ontario Institute for Studies in Education, 1974); and William Perry, *Forms of Intellectual and Ethical Development during the College Years* (New York: Holt, Rinehart and Winston, 1969).

6. Piaget, *Psychology of Intelligence.*

7. Kohlberg, "Stage and Sequence."

8. Loevinger, "The Meaning and Measurement of Ego Development."

9. Hunt, *Matching Models in Education.*

10. Perry, *Forms of Intellectual and Ethical Development during the College Years.*

11. Maxine Greene, "Toward the Concrete: An Approach to Moral Choosing," *Moral Education Forum* 5 (Spring 1980): 2.

12. Douglas Heath, *Maturity and Competence* (New York: Gardner, 1977).

13. Dan Candee, "Role Taking, Role Conception and Moral Reasoning as Factors in Good Physicians Performance," *Moral Education Forum* 2 (Winter 1977): 14-15.

14. John T. Sheehan, "Moral Judgment as a Predictor of Clinical Performance" (Paper presented at the Conference on Research in Medical Education, Washington, D.C., 1978).

15. Paula Silver, "Principals' Conceptual Ability in Relation to Situation and Behavior," *Educational Administration Quarterly* 11 (Autumn 1975): 49-66.

16. David Hunt and Bruce Joyce, "Teacher Trainee Personality and Initial Teaching Style," *American Educational Research Journal* 4 (May 1967): 253-59.

17. N. L. Gage, *The Scientific Basis for the Art of Teaching* (New York: Teachers College Press, 1978).

18. Bruce Joyce and Marsha Weil, *Models of Teaching* (Englewood Cliffs, N.J.: Prentice Hall, 1980), p. 478. Given much of the recent research suggesting that direct instruction in the Rosenshine sense is the new preferred mode of instruction, it may appear that such statements noted above are in conflict. There are two general aspects. As we have indicated, a flexible teacher can employ direct as well as indirect methods. In fact, Hunt's research has shown that for low conceptual level students, high-structured direct instruction is clearly the method of choice. See Hunt, *Matching Models in Education*, p. 46.

A second point, which Good has mentioned, is that even such direct instruction is probably only appropriate for growth in basic skills in mathematics and reading: "I have questioned its relevancy for other subject areas (for example, social studies) and do not feel that it is *the* preferred general instructional model." See Thomas Good, "Research on Teaching," in *Exploring Issues in Teacher Education: Questions for Future Research*, Publication No. 7003, ed. Gene Hall, Shirley Hord, and Gail Brown (Austin, Texas: Research and Development Center for Teacher Education, 1980), p. 66. In fact, most recent evidence from the National Assessment of Educational Progress does underscore the point. Under conditions of direct instruction in basic skills of reading and mathematics the scores are improving in the early elementary grades. However, comprehension scores in reading and problem-solving scores in mathematics are declining. This could suggest that less directive and greater inquiry approaches could be the method choice at that point. The research on cognitive development has shown, as we have noted, that teachers functioning at more complex levels possess the flexibility to adjust method to student need.

19. Shirley Walter and Eugene Stivers, "The Relation of Student Teachers' Classroom Behavior and Eriksonian Ego Identity," *Journal of Teacher Education* 38 (November-December 1977): 47-50.

20. Lois Thies-Sprinthall, "Supervision: An Educative or Miseducative Process?" *Journal of Teacher Education* 31 (July-August 1980): 17-20.

21. David Hunt, "Teachers' Adaptation: 'Reading' and 'Flexing' to Students," in *Flexibility in Teaching*, ed. Bruce Joyce, Clark Brown, and Lucy Peck (New York: Longmans, 1980), chap. 4.

22. Kohlberg, "Stage and Sequence."

23. Loevinger, "The Meaning and Measurement of Ego Development."

24. Heath, *Maturity and Competence.*

25. Perry, *Forms of Intellectual and Ethical Development during the College Years.*

26. Edmund Sullivan, George McCullough, and Mary Stager, "A Developmental Study of the Relationship between Conceptual, Ego, and Moral Development," *Child Development* 41 (June 1970): 399-411.

27. Schalock, "Research on Teacher Selection," pp. 383-85.

28. Paul Baltes and Warner Schaie, "On the Plasticity of Intelligence in Adulthood and Old Age," *American Psychologist* 31 (October 1976): 720-25.

29. Ibid., p. 722.

30. William Bart, "Piagetian Cognitive Theory and Adult Education" (Paper presented at the Adult Education Research Conference, University of Minnesota, Minneapolis, 1977).

31. Jean Piaget, "Intellectual Evaluation from Adolescence to Adulthood," *Human Development* 15 (January 1972): 1-12.

32. Ibid., p. 10.

33. Donna Mertens, "Formal Level of Functioning: A Scientific Phenomenon?" (Paper presented at the annual meeting of the American Educational Research Association, New York, 1977).

34. Lawrence Kohlberg, *Meaning and Measurement of Moral Development* (Worcester, Mass.: Clark University Press, 1979).

35. Hunt, *Matching Models in Education.*

36. Studies conducted over the past decade have regularly reported the negative impact of the student teaching experience. In general, student teachers end up as more rigid, more authoritarian, and less sensitive to pupil needs at the conclusion of their training. See Thies-Sprinthall, "Supervision," for a review of these studies.

37. Kenneth Howey, Sam Yarger, and Bruce Joyce, *Improving Teacher Education* (Washington, D.C.: Association for Teacher Education, 1978).

38. David Hunt, "In-Service Training as Persons-In-Relation," *Theory Into Practice* 17 (Autumn 1978): 239-44.

39. Hunt, *Matching Models in Education*, p. 46.

40. Norman A. Sprinthall, "Psychology for Secondary Schools: The Saber-Tooth Curriculum Revisited?" *American Psychologist* 35 (May 1980): 336-47; Clyde Parker, *Encouraging Development in College Students* (Minneapolis, Minn.: University of Minnesota Press, 1978).

41. Carol Widick and Debra Simpson, "Developmental Concepts in College Instruction," in *Encouraging Development in College Students*, ed. Parker, pp. 27-59.

42. Diane Hedin, "Teenage Health Educators: An Action Learning Program to Promote Psychological Development" (Doct. diss., University of Minnesota, 1979).

43. Joyce and Weil, *Models of Teaching.*

44. B. Lance Hurt and Norman A. Sprinthall, "Psychological and Moral Development for Teachers," *Journal of Moral Education* 6 (January 1977): 112-20.

45. Sally Glassberg and Norman A. Sprinthall, "Student Teaching: A Developmental Approach," *Journal of Teacher Education* 31 (March 1980): 31-38.

46. Norman A. Sprinthall and Joseph Bernier, "Moral and Cognitive Development of Teachers," *New Catholic World* 221 (July-August 1978): 179-84.

47. Sharon Oja and Norman A. Sprinthall, "Psychological and Moral Development for Teachers," in *Value Development . . . as the Aim of Education*, ed. Norman A. Sprinthall and Ralph L. Mosher (Schenectady, N.Y.: Character Research Press, 1978), pp. 117-34.

48. Lois Thies-Sprinthall, "Promoting the Conceptual and Principled Thinking Level of the Supervising Teacher," Research Report, mimeographed (St. Cloud, Minn.: (St. Cloud State University, 1980).

49. Howey, Yarger, and Joyce, *Improving Teacher Education.*

50. Kohlberg, *Meaning and Measurement of Moral Development.*

51. James Rest, "Judging the Important Issues in Moral Dilemmas—An Objective Measure of Development," *Developmental Psychology* 10 (July 1974): 491-501.

52. Jane Loevinger and Ruth Wessler, *Measuring Ego Development* (San Francisco: Jossey-Bass, 1970).

53. Anne Constantinople, "An Eriksonian Measure of Personality Development in College Students," *Developmental Psychology* 1 (July 1969): 357-72.

54. David Hunt, JoAnn Greenwood, Joyce Noy, and Nancy Watson, *Assessment of Conceptual Level: Paragraph Completion Method* (Toronto: Ontario Institute for Studies in Education, 1973); Perry, *Forms of Intellectual and Ethical Development during the College Years.*

55. Norman A. Sprinthall, "A Curriculum for Secondary Schools," *School Counselor* 20 (May 1973): 361-69.

56. William Tikunoff and Beatrice Ward, *Effective Teacher Education Programs* (San Francisco: Far West Laboratory for Educational Research and Development, 1979). Their intensive classroom observations have convinced them that in-service teachers generally fall into one of three stages which Tikunoff refers to as "mythologists," "mechanics," and "causal thinkers." There is a notable similarity to Hunt's three stages, which he calls As, Bs, and Cs.

57. Lee Shulman and Judith Lanier, "The Institute for Research on Teaching," *Journal of Teacher Education* 28 (July-August 1977): 44-49.

CHAPTER III

The School as Workplace

JOHN I. GOODLAD

The hypothesis with which I begin is becoming increasingly popular. It is that the individual school is the key unit on which to focus for effecting improvement within the formal educational system. In this chapter, I first examine the strength of this hypothesis, concluding that it can be defended only on heuristic grounds. That is, it is unproved but valuable for research. However, since proof is so elusive, especially in matters of education, and the need for educational improvement so pressing, we cannot afford to stand idle waiting for the slow accumulation of knowledge. Consequently, if strong arguments for the hypothesis can be put forward—stronger, let us say, than for extant alternatives—then we would be well advised to consider its implications for staff development. This I also attempt to do.

The School as the Unit for Improvement

There are at least three different kinds of arguments for the proposition that the individual school is the most viable unit for effecting educational improvement. The first draws on empirical research—controlled comparisons of alternatives, for example. The second is somewhat tautological, drawing repeatedly on evidence of what goes on in schools: what now goes on has gone on for some time; therefore it is good. The third argument involves ordered reasoning: better reasons can be mustered for this rather than that.

The first kind of argument can be dismissed quickly. The research necessary to a strong affirmation of the school-based postulate simply does not exist. Both scholars and practitioners cite references adding up to a rather substantial list in arguing for the school as the locus for change. But, on checking these sources, one finds the best of them to be rationales for dealing with the school from the perspective of the

36

hypothesis, not evidence regarding its validity. Books by House,[1] Wise,[2] and Sarason[3] are, in part, excellent examples of this genre.

Although research conducted by the Rand Corporation often is cited as though it were the final, decisive piece in the fabric of evidence, one finds that this, too, is mostly in the genre of educational change strategies. Some approaches to effecting innovations, for example, appear to be more efficacious than others.[4] The importance of dealing with the total culture of the school, emerging as a conclusion from research on change, tells us only *that*.[5] It leaves us short, however, of being able to conclude that the individual school is, for example, a *more* promising place to begin a process of educational change than is the office of the district superintendent.

My work with the League of Cooperating Schools often is cited in support of the proposition that the school is the key unit for educational improvement. My colleagues and I began with this as a hypothesis that I had cited earlier[6] and developed a change strategy based on its implications.[7] After six years of working with the eighteen schools in the League, the hypothesis became for me virtually a principle basic to improving the quality of life in schools and, as a concomitant (I assumed), the quality of certain outcomes. But my conclusions pertained to the conditions under which schools might become more effective, satisfying places. My belief in the importance of focusing on schools as a vital element in seeking to improve the quality of the formal educational system increased. But my colleagues and I did not provide the research evidence some people believe exists to support the individual school as the most viable unit for effecting educational improvement. Some people believe that abolishing schools, not seeking to improve them, would be the most significant step in securing the education our people and this country require now and in the future.

Turning to the second of the three lines of argument identified earlier, we certainly do not commonly behave as though the school is the right and natural focus for educational improvement. There is an extensive rhetoric of dissatisfaction with schools. Yet, scarcely anything done in the name of improvement focuses on that dissatisfaction. Rather, improvement focuses on elements of the whole: teachers, principals, students, subjects, materials, and the like.

Lortie has pointed out that teachers have been socialized to behave independently, assuming responsibility only for their own classroom instruction.[8] In preparing for teaching, one "practice" teaches under the supervision of an experienced teacher and is exposed to little or nothing about the functioning of the school as a whole. Inquiry into problems and issues cutting across the entire school is not normal activity for teachers and principals.[9] Staff development for both focuses largely on the improvement of individual skills.[10] Collaboration with others on a faculty to determine school-wide goals, for example, is an exceedingly arduous activity[11] and appears not to be commonly attempted. Indeed, the school as an institution may well be the most inactive and ineffective part of the decision-making structure that includes classroom, individual school, district, and state.[12] One thoughtful scholar, well-known for his research into teaching and classrooms, after reading my report on the League of Cooperating Schools, told me that it would be necessary for him to give up if such an approach is the one to be followed in assuring the significant improvement of schools.

There appears to be little to support the hypothesis that the school as a unit is the key if one turns to research or commonly followed approaches to educational improvement. This leaves us with an argument based on reasoning unsupported by research findings or common practice. The argument is a rather simple, straightforward one. Administrators and teachers in colleges and universities complain that many high school graduates coming to them are ill-prepared. Many employers complain about the low reading and writing ability of persons applying for jobs. Large numbers of youth attend sporadically even while enrolled, suggesting boredom and apathy. Teachers complain about lack of student interest and about themselves as being "burned out." Some report fear for their safety in school buildings and on the playgrounds. A substantial percentage say that they would leave because of their frustration, especially if they could find a job paying more than what they perceive to be inadequate salaries for teachers. There appear to be many symptoms of schools not providing the quality of education we would like to see or adequate satisfaction for those associated with them.[13]

If *schools* are perceived by major segments of our society as not being sufficiently effective and by those attending and working in them as less than satisfying, it follows that we should seek to remedy these conditions. One way is to do away with schools. But, if we did not have schools, we probably would have to create something similar, if only to provide the custodial care of the young most parents and other adults appear to want. Another alternative, then, is to seek to improve the schools we have.

Improving schools does not mean improving the quality only of teachers, principals, teaching, administering, curricula, and materials as though each were a separate entity. It means improving all of these together. As cited earlier, some scholars have made a quite convincing case for dealing with the school all of a piece, as a social system or a culture of interacting elements. Rutter, for example, has argued effectively, with supporting data, that the ethos of individual schools can be changed so as to reduce the incidence of student misbehavior and truancy, improve student-teacher relationships, enhance achievement, and create more satisfying places.[14] The message that poor schools can be made better, whatever the social and economic circumstances of students and their families, is becoming a source of encouragement for educators and lay citizens alike. It is a welcome change from the messages many people deciphered from the earlier studies of Coleman[15] and Jencks,[16] respectively: that inputs into schools such as teachers do not overcome the handicap of limited home background and that schools do not smooth out the inequities of birth and family circumstances.

The hypothesis that the school *is* the key unit in educational improvement cannot be defended. But the assumption that the school *can be* significant and, indeed, powerful *under certain conditions* is encouraging, provocative in its implications, and well worth accepting as a working hypothesis. The challenge becomes one of discovering these conditions and seeking to make them operative.

The question might well be raised: "If the best that can be done at present is to put forward the proposition that schooling can become more effective and satisfying when the individual school is selected as the unit of analysis, planning, and action, why all the preamble? Why not state it at the outset and go on from there instead of taking up so many precious pages in apparently unnecessary discourse?"

Why not, indeed? There are several reasons. One is to press home the point that a reasonable working hypothesis is about the best we can hope for in seeking a beginning point for educational improvement. If we wait for conclusive, hard evidence, we will never begin. Education (and, therefore, schooling) is a normative process. It begins with shoulds and oughts: children should learn to read and write; a democratic society requires educated citizens; tomorrow's citizens should have a broad understanding of the world's people. We do not set out to prove such statements, in the way one endeavors to prove that the planet earth is a slightly imperfect globe. One accepts them as evident truths—or does not. Once accepted, they provide justification for research into better ways to accomplish what should be or ought to be. One does not put aside the proposition that the entire school should be the locus for improvement simply because the skeptic cries, "Prove it," anymore than one puts aside the proposition that schools should teach children to read and write because we cannot prove its truth. Let not the innovator's spirit be dampened by the critic, grandly cloaked in scientific methodology, who asks at the outset for proof that the as yet dimly perceived innovation works.

Another reason for the preceding discourse is to caution against those who would beguile us into believing that an unverified proposition is more than that—that it is a scientific principle, now so clearly established that voices raised in opposition reveal only ignorance in the words uttered. Such frequently occurs when a new mode of thinking and acting is finding its place in the sun. Thrusting aside questions not yet answered, exponents frequently move on to "scientific deductions" which, when carefully examined, do not necessarily follow but are themselves working hypotheses—useful, perhaps, if recognized as such but dangerously misleading if not.

One such piece of deduction is highly relevant to the subject matter of this chapter and I discuss it later: the school *is* the key unit for educational improvement. Therefore, the principal is the critical element. We will have good schools when we have good principals.

How smoothly this line of reasoning takes us away from the initial proposition. The principal becomes central—not teachers, students, parents, curricula, and the sum total of elements comprising a school. Not surprisingly, principals tend to enjoy this rather recently acquired centrality, quite in contrast with their expected reactions to an earlier view which saw them and the subunits they managed as relatively impotent components of the system.[17] Speakers at the 1982 Convention of the National Association of Elementary School Principals massaged the message.[18] They might have performed a more useful service by expressing some skepticism and apprising conferees of the possible implications and consequences of taking the message seriously; for unless large numbers of current principals are prepared to acquire knowledge and skills they do not now possess, a possible consequence of the message is the dismissal of principals in schools not judged satisfactory. Some principals might prefer, then, not to be center-stage. The idea of the school being the key unit for educational improvement does not necessarily put them there. But it is one possible consequence.

A practical, in part political, argument for focusing on the school as the key unit for educational improvement—in contrast to the district or system as a whole, for example—is the potential for securing much needed community support. Polls over the last several years suggest greater satisfaction with the local school than with schooling generally. Parents surveyed in "A Study of Schooling" gave a higher grade to their own schools than parents polled in other surveys gave to schools generally.[19] Such findings suggest the greater appeal of the individual school as the unit around which to rally support. Other data from the same study imply a desire on the part of those connected with schools to shift decision-making power from more remote sources to those close at hand. Principals, teachers, and parents agreed on taking power to make decisions for their school from the superintendent and board and giving more to the principal, teachers, and school-based parent groups.[20]

In summary, then, the idea that the school as a totality is a promising place—perhaps the most promising—to effect improvement is a useful heuristic. It is useful in at least four ways. First, as just stated, it appears that the individual school is a potentially good rallying point for mustering community support and simultaneously increasing satisfaction. Second, with the school as the unit kept uppermost conceptually and operationally, the danger of concentrating exclusively on and unrealistically expecting too much of just a part of schooling is minimized. Third, chances are enhanced for identifying factors impinging on the well-being of those who work in schools and, as a consequence, improving the workplace. Fourth and most tentative, chances are enhanced not only for increasing the personal satisfaction of those connected with schools but also for making schools increasingly satisfactory and effective educational settings. To the last three of these uses of the heuristic I now turn.

In much of what follows, I draw from "A Study of Schooling," already referenced. My colleagues and I studied in depth thirty-eight schools in seven states. These were examined in triples—that is, an elementary school sending students to a junior high school which, in turn, advanced students to a senior high school—except in the instance of one small junior high school and one small senior high school operating essentially as a single secondary school. We chose schools differing with respect to several general features: size, economic status, ethnicity, and whether urban, suburban, or rural. Data collection teams of more than twenty persons each spent approximately a month studying the sets of three schools and gaining information from the surrounding community. We observed and recorded activities and behavior in over 1000 classrooms and questioned all principals, 1350 teachers, 17,163 students, 8624 parents, and the districts' superintendents and board members.[21] Technical reports on methodology and other aspects of "A Study of Schooling" are available through the ERIC Clearinghouse for Teacher Education.

The relevance of the study to the theme of this yearbook and particularly this chapter is that we studied schools comprehensively, examining *contextual* variables common to schools that determine the environment of the workplace within which teachers and students live and work. We identified and provided "thick" descriptions of sixteen commonplaces of schools: teaching practices, content or subject matter, instructional materials, physical environment, activities, human resources, evaluation, time, organization, communications, decision making, leadership, goals, issues and problems, implicit (or "hidden") curriculum, and controls or restraints. To these we added demographic and impressionistic data of various kinds.

The rather heavy dependence on the findings in what follows stems not just from the author's familiarity with them but also from the fact that, beyond single case studies, few studies of schools as entities exist. I have referred to Rutter's study of twelve inner-London secondary schools; several studies of schools in the United States currently are underway.[22] Presumably, some of these will focus on total school contexts. At present, however, the relevant literature is thin.

Maintaining the Total School Focus

For purposes of discourse, I have invited the reader to join me in putting forward the working hypothesis that the individual school is the key unit on which to focus in effecting improvement within the formal educational system. The implication is that better education will result from working on schools to make them more satisfying and satisfactory. We are to focus on total schools or, if on pieces, all the pieces and the relationships among them.

If this be the purpose, we quickly see how far short current conceptions and practices fall. The concept "staff development" conveys at best half a loaf: members of a school's staff are to develop or be developed. Activities stem from the concept: teachers engage in workshops, attend lectures and seminars, and take classes designed to improve their skills and understandings, particularly of teaching and closely related matters. More often than not, they leave the school site; rarely do they work on these individually focused activities as a total faculty or in teams. Teaching is, after all, a highly isolated, individualistic enterprise.

But teaching is not all of a school. In addition to this personal element, there are "a sociological element represented by the central concept of *role expectation*, and an anthropological element represented by the central concept of *cultural value*, all embedded in a particular *environment*. Behavior in the school as a social system [is] seen as emerging from the interaction of these personal, institutional, cultural, and environmental forces."[23] Failure of a staff to address, for example, unquestioned expectations for teachers embedded in the structure of a school can effectively inhibit a teacher's use of techniques acquired in a staff development workshop. Lloyd found that the teachers in two schools, exposed as total staffs to two different but presumably equally exemplary, intensive in-service programs focused on pedagogy, could produce the desired techniques on request but rarely used them in their classrooms. She concluded that elements firmly embedded in the schools' cultures and, indeed, in the conventional wisdom of teaching itself reinforced old practices and discouraged the ones intended to replace them.[24]

Data from "A Study of Schooling" support my conclusion that staff development activities tend to focus on individual teacher development. Rarely did the teachers queried report working together on instructional improvement as a total staff commitment. The impression I gained was of what I already have described: teachers attending activities focused on teaching materials and behavior, usually designed to improve what they customarily did, and with few exceptions away from rather than in their own places of work.

Such in-service practices are a natural extension of teachers' preservice preparation. Teacher education programs, virtually since their inception, have been dominated by psychological considerations emphasizing human development, learning, and teaching methods; they have slighted sociological, anthropological, and cultural phenomena, and especially the actual functioning of the school as a social system within a larger cultural context. But even when contextual factors have received attention, as in some courses in urban education, the practice teaching experience is almost exclusively just that—practice teaching in a classroom under the supervision of a teacher who, in turn, is little involved with addressing school-wide practices. The neophyte teacher is not socialized into a staff earnestly engaged in addressing the problems of absenteeism, personal safety, student misbehavior, drugs and alcohol, parental dissatisfaction, and the like with which so many schools, especially at the secondary level, are beset—and which interfere with the teaching effort. The socialization process fails to occur because such staff processes rarely are underway and, if they were, in all probability the practice teacher would be involved only with classroom practices in any case. The future teacher is not prepared, then, with the expectation that he or she will take an active role in school-wide educational improvement processes.

Few districts support site-based staff development organized around instructional or other problems identified as significant by a faculty group. Indeed, rewards in the form of credits for salary increases and the like stem almost exclusively from participation in institute days, workshops, and college classes, as previously described. A school faculty deciding to take time to address school-wide affairs finds itself caught up in two sets of demands: the self-imposed tasks and district-wide requirements for securing in-service credits. Since only the latter is tangibly rewarded, the former usually receives short shrift, even if attempted.

If the total school is to be in more than rhetoric the focus of educational improvement, several interlocking shifts in conventional practice, all difficult, must occur almost simultaneously. First, there must be genuine decentralization of authority and responsibility for decision making, including budgetary planning, to the individual school—something many superintendents and boards are reluctant to do. The accompanying requirement is that those connected with the local school develop, under the principal's leadership, three-to-five year plans which are updated and reviewed annually.

Second, the reward structure for in-service education, in the form of both time and salary credits, must shift from the individualistic activities now prevalent, to site-based attack on school problems, the quality of the workplace, and the needs of individual teachers. It must not be assumed, however, that the principal and teachers are now ready to use this opportunity wisely. Indeed, both require considerable help in developing the necessary skills involved in problem identification, dialogue, decision making, and action.[25] The necessary support must be extraordinarily nonthreatening and sensitive.[26] Only a few persons in universities, district offices, or regional service centers currently possess the requisites.

Third, the preservice teacher education programs of colleges and universities must be rearranged to align with these shifts in district practices. Indeed, some of the initiative for such shifts might come from new kinds of collaboration between universities and neighboring schools. The former change their policy regarding placement of students in single classes and with individual supervisors; instead, students become junior faculty members in schools. University professors become allies in a school improvement process involving the entire staff of each school selected and district personnel. Teacher preparation, in-service education, and school improvement become one. The whole becomes a collaborative, pilot project into which other schools in the district are drawn and which does not necessarily include the preservice teacher education component for all of them.

Given the fact that the total-school focus in staff development, educational improvement, and teacher education runs counter to much conventional wisdom and practice, experimental ventures of the kind proposed above may be the necessary preliminary to and stimulant of more general practice. Given the attractive simplicity, however, of such notions as "it all depends on the teacher" or "the secret to good schools is the principal," it is unrealistic to assume that widespread adoption of the school-wide approach is imminent.

Enhancing Life in the Workplace

Ironically, concern for the quality of working life has come belatedly and feebly to the institution of schooling. I say "ironically" because education is supposed to be a human-centered enterprise. And yet, it is to the industrialized part of our society—the part still eliciting cold, hard, connotations of machinery, assembly lines, and human exploitation—that most attention regarding the humanization of work and the workplace has turned. Undoubtedly, the initial need was great and disturbingly visible. Unions, recently backed by social science research, have been skillful in demonstrating to employers a relationship between the quality of the workplace and productivity. Schooling, however, does not take place in a "for profit" environment. There have not been corresponding motivation and dollars to inquire into the dimensions of the school as workplace; the criteria of productivity are not clear and agreed upon; and such research as has been conducted is inconclusive.

It is the more recent concern with the quality of working life that sharpens the discrepancy between the attention we give to teachers and students in schools and workers elsewhere. Social scientists address dysfunctions of industrial society quite apart from issues of productivity in concerning themselves not only with the dignity and healthy self-development of individual workers but also with the use of humanistic models of work to help bring about a democratic society. They do not attempt to prove the validity of this thinking. Rather, they begin with principles such as security, equity, individuation, and workplace democracy, and suggest that "legislation may be needed to reward firms that humanize work and prescribe and limit institutional practices which are unhealthy for workers and society."[27]

Suppose we were to apply such thinking to schools. Why, it would effect nothing short of a revolution!

In spite of considerable criticism and some unravelling, the dominant model for thinking about schools, guiding research, and conducting practice parallels the now antiquated factory model of productivity.[28] The criteria applied to classroom practices and teacher accountability pertain to output as measured by achievement tests, and say nothing about the health of students and teachers or, for that matter, additional possible outcomes such as compassion, sociability, work habits, creativity, and happiness. To suggest that practices should be humane in their own right, that school and classroom life should be free of unhealthy conditions and practices—that ends do not automatically justify means—is to be countervailing, indeed. And yet, again attesting to the irony, even the goals on which the several states are largely agreed clearly state our commitment, at least ideologically, to a broad array of humanistic values. Parents sampled in "A Study of Schooling" were supportive of such goals and were concerned about their children being known, cared for, and given individual attention at school.[29] Given our continuing love affair with ends-means relationships, surely we might be expected as a people to evaluate what our schools do on criteria extending well beyond a narrow range of academic considerations.[30]

Surely, too, if we can accept the concept of quality in industrial working life as a good in itself, we can accept, equally, the goodness of quality in life in schools. No proof is necessary. What, then, are some of the implications of this acceptance?

First, we must get over and beyond some stereotypic ways of thinking. Major among these ways is the concept of the school as instrument: "Schools are factories, taking raw materials (students) and processing them through its [sic] operations (curriculums) to satisfy demands for products and services (jobs) in society."[31] Of course, schools are instrumental: to learning, further education, jobs, and more. But they are not merely or only or perhaps even primarily instrumental. For those who work in them, they are as much life itself as wherever and whatever else they are and do.

For students, school is not a place where all else is set aside in favor of the goals society sets for schools. Data from "A Study of Schooling" show friends, games and sports, and student attitudes looming far above classes and teachers as the best things about the secondary schools attended. Athletes and good-looking students won the popularity choices hands down over smart students. Not curricular or instructional shortcomings but drugs, alcohol, and student misbehavior ranked high as school problems. Social, emotional, and personal concerns of the age period took precedence over academic matters in the preoccupations of the adolescents studied.

For teachers, school is the place of one's work, where the individual frustrations and satisfactions have the same significance as they do for workers elsewhere. The majority of teachers in our sample entered teaching because they saw teaching as a good service profession or wanted to teach something or someone. They would leave because of circumstances blocking the fulfillment of their perceived teaching role: disinterested students, insensitive administrators, tensions with colleagues, inadequate facilities and instructional resources, and a sense of impotence or lack of involvement in decisions affecting them and their work. It is difficult to believe that these circumstances, together with the preoccupations of their students, have nothing to do with their performance of the teaching role. Of first importance, it is difficult to believe that these circumstances have no bearing on their health and self-fulfillment in and out of school.

It is high time, then, that we paid attention to the quality of the school workplace, the conditions and practices that make it unhealthy, and how to create and maintain the healthiest ecosystem possible. The principles involved probably are in harmony with academic achievement but they are not necessarily the same and they are more encompassing. I illustrate some of these with two examples, one pertaining to students and the other to teachers.

The example of students illustrates the principle of equity in the humanization of work. Presumably, students in schools should have equal opportunity to learn, which means, in turn, that they have equal access to knowledge and the means of acquiring it. In "A Study of Schooling," we analyzed many tracked classes, especially in mathematics and English, out of the 362 junior high and 525 senior high classes observed in detail—that is, classes to which students had been assigned because of their high, average, or low attainment. We found marked differences among tracks in regard to curricular content offered, instructional practices, students' attitudes, and the ambience of the classrooms. We found, further, that poor children, disproportionately representative of minorities, were overenrolled in the low-track classes in proportion to their representation in the schools' populations as a whole.[32]

The content of the high-track classes, in which a disproportionately large percentage of white, affluent children were enrolled, emphasized what might be called high-status knowledge of a kind preparatory to further education and schooling. Low-track classes favored utilitarian knowledge of a kind likely to have application to daily tasks and in more routine kinds of work. Teachers in high-track classes, significantly more than teachers in low-track classes, varied their pedagogical practices, were clear in giving directions and setting expectations, gave feedback with accompanying guidance, and were enthusiastic—characteristics associated in the literature with improved learning. Teachers in high-track classes, more than teachers in low-track classes, expected the higher forms of cognition, independent thinking, and more student participation in class processes. Teachers in low-track classes were more likely to set expectations of passivity and the following of rules. Students in high-track classes reported the highest levels of educational aspirations and possessed more positive academic self-concepts. Although students in low-track classes graded their schools about the same as did those in high-track classes and liked their subjects about as well, they had more negative attitudes about themselves, viewing themselves as needing to change, as not as well liked as most people, and as sometimes thinking of themselves as no good at all.

We studied some mixed or heterogeneous classes. Contrary to the conventional wisdom, which maintains that practices in such classes drop to a lowest common denominator, practices in virtually all of the above areas resembled those in the middle and high tracks more than they did practices in the lowest. Must tracking be abolished in order to obtain equity regarding access to knowledge and learning inside of schools?

In the past, tracking has been dealt with in research and practice almost exclusively as it appears to relate to academic achievement. The effects appear to be particularly detrimental to the achievement of the slower learners.[33] When we look at tracking in the context of the school and classroom environment, its invidiousness appears to be quite disharmonious with the principles of equity and personal worth associated with a workplace good for humans.

It often is said that schools are for students. Yet, another cliché, used in referring to school quality and stated earlier, is "It all depends on the teacher." And, more recently, we have the third cliché, "It all depends on the principal." Obviously, schools are for all those associated with them as well as for society. It is difficult to conceive of good schools being unsatisfying for principals, teachers, and students or any one of these groups. The relationships among them are such as to be affected by the well-being or lack of it in any one group. Consequently, maintaining the physical and psychological health of these workers through the removal or alleviation of stressful conditions is of great importance.[34]

Data from "A Study of Schooling" point to the principal and the principal-teacher relationship as key factors in teacher satisfaction. It is important, apparently, for teachers not only to have principals they regard as competent, independent professionals but also for their principals to possess and use professional autonomy. The principals in the schools of our sample perceived to be most satisfying not only by teachers but also by students and parents felt themselves to be significantly more in control of their jobs, as having more control over their use of time, and as having more influence over decisions about their schools than did principals of schools perceived to be less satisfying. Without exception, the principals of the "more satisfying" schools saw the amount of influence they had as congruent with the amount of influence they thought principals *should* have.[35]

There were interesting differences in principals' and teachers' perceptions of each other in the more as compared with the less satisfying schools. All principals of the latter saw "poor teaching or teachers" as a problem; none in the former saw this as a major problem. Fifty-seven percent of the principals of the less satisfying schools, compared with 20 percent at the more satisfying schools, saw staff relations as a problem at their schools.

Teachers in the less satisfying schools perceived their environment to be less than ideal. They tended to view the principal as neither competent nor supportive. They agreed, significantly more than teachers in the more satisfying schools, that there were problems in staff relations and in effecting school-wide decisions. They perceived their own role in school decisions to be low, just as they viewed the principal not to have a strong hand. Many were less than satisfied with their amount of autonomy in making classroom decisions and with the teaching job being done by peers. Much more often than teachers in the more satisfying schools, these teachers perceived themselves as not treated as professionals by their principals.

In addition to having more positive views of their workplace, teachers in the most satisfying schools tended to score higher on indices of professionalism. Also, they perceived themselves to be spending more time on instruction and less on routines and controlling behavior in the classroom. As I have said, they worked in schools to which they, their students, and the parents gave the highest ratings on several indices of satisfaction.

These findings imply the need for great caution regarding the principal's role and the principal-teacher relationship in the improvement of teaching. The state of California, for example, has created a model for evaluating principals and teachers which derives its rationality and justification somewhat as follows. There is now a scientific basis for teaching; that is, there are highly transferable principles which, in turn, translate into definable, measurable competencies for teachers in all situations. The improvement of schooling depends on teachers acquiring these proficiencies, not others. ("It all depends on the teacher," remember.) To assure that teachers will acquire and use these competencies, they are to be taught to principals who, in turn, are to be responsible for both teachers' acquisition of them and the evaluation of their teachers' performance.

I shall not enter here into all the questionable assumptions underlying this egregiously deceptive form of rationality nor into the dubious relationships implied by the linkages. Let us look at the probable consequences to the workplace of implementing what I hope will collapse of its own weight.

The proposition that the individual school could become the key unit for educational improvement puts considerable responsibility for leadership on the principal: for planning, staff relations, curriculum development, instructional improvement, and the like. We can take seriously the proposition that the principal is to become the model of instruction only if he or she spends all or most of the time at it. Few principals of average-size schools teach or intend to teach. Principals of small schools who both teach and administer lead hectic lives, precluding much attention to the teaching of others. Some principals once were superior teachers. But it is virtually an insult to teachers who teach full time to propose that their principals, who teach not at all and at the secondary level at least have limited knowledge in some subjects, are to become the exemplars of teaching, no matter what in-service education they receive for this purpose.

It appears that mutual trust between principal and teachers, considerable autonomy in the classroom for teachers, support for teachers by the principal, and respect for each other as professionals are important elements in the healthy school workplace. I cannot imagine developments likely to be more destructive to this health than the injection of the expectation or requirement that the principal is to be both model and judge of teaching.

If attention is now to shift to the school, as current rhetoric suggests, the quality of life for those in schools becomes of prime importance. All practices must be examined critically from the perspective of their negative or positive contributions to the workplace as a habitat for all who live there. It seems reasonable to assume, from the array of studies now available, that the quality of whatever the workplace is expected to produce will then improve accordingly.

More and Less Satisfying Schools

I have argued, more implicitly than explicitly, that the satisfaction of those who work in schools is a good indicator of the quality of working life. However, researchers in particular regard satisfaction as a "soft" index of the educational quality of schools. Of course teachers are more satisfied if they have the autonomy in the classroom they desire, but that simply gives them freedom to do as they please. It does not assure better teaching, says the skeptic. I agree.

But let us both harden up the concept of satisfaction and deal with more of the complexity of schools, not just a segmented piece. This we attempted to do in "A Study of Schooling." First, we developed a composite index of satisfaction derived from several related but different chunks of data: the grade (A, B, C, D, F) given each school by teachers, students, and parents; the number and seriousness of school-wide problems perceived by these three groups; and the congruence between goals desired by all three and goals perceived to be emphasized in their schools. Satisfaction determined from such information goes far beyond direct questioning into how pleased individuals are with their experiences in or with the school.

We then arranged the schools in rank order by groups—elementary, junior high, and senior high—according to their rating on the satisfaction index. Those in the first quartiles were classified as the "more satisfying schools," those in the fourth quartile as "less satisfying." Subsequently, we similarly arranged the schools on several sets of characteristics compiled from varying kinds of data including demographics, information derived from classroom observations, and the perceptions of principals, teachers, students, and parents, as appropriate. We were able to array the schools qualitatively for several of these categories and, again, to select out for comparative analysis those in the first and fourth quartiles.

The first ordering of schools—that is, for satisfaction—turned out to be an extraordinarily accurate predictor of nearly all the others. Those in the first and fourth quartiles initially reappeared there at a high level of consistency. In effect, the characteristics represented in the comparisons of schools become correlates of satisfaction as defined and measured.

The first of these we labeled "school-related issues": curriculum relevance, academic interest or apathy, quality of education provided (perceptions of students only), access to counselors (secondary students only), and other components. The ordering of schools on these issues came out nearly the same as for the one on satisfaction. Taken together, these two sets of indicators proved to be almost perfect predictors of those schools placing in the first and fourth quartiles on the other characteristics examined. One generalization which emerges is that the overall climate of the more satisfying schools was more academic in its orientation than was the climate of the less satisfying schools.

The positive school-wide views of the students in the more satisfying schools carried over into the classrooms. Students tended to view their teachers as trying to make the class enjoyable, as listening to them, and as not ridiculing them or hurting their feelings. They generally knew what was expected of them, saw themselves as getting corrective feedback, and understood the words used by their teachers. Further, they tended to see their teachers as fair, as not having favorites, and perceived their fellow students as helpful. Students in the less satisfying schools were significantly more negative in their perceptions of these matters.

I already have described some of the factors correlating with teachers' and principals' satisfactions in the schools classified as more or less satisfying. Differences between the parent groups are interesting, too, those in the more satisfying schools perceiving themselves to be quite well informed about school programs and activities and as having easy access to teachers. Those in the less satisfying schools perceived themselves as not having ready access either to teachers or information. Many had not spoken with their children's teachers during the year. Parents connected with more satisfying schools perceived there to be an appropriate balance of power between the teachers and the principal. Many in the less satisfying schools often had an impression of nobody in charge, of a school needing to come to grips with its problems.

One set of presumably important characteristics, however, was not at all predicted by the satisfaction indicators: pedagogical techniques. Teachers in the more satisfying schools used with about equal frequency the array of procedures found in the less satisfying schools: lecturing, questioning, assigning textbook and workbook activities, monitoring seatwork, and so forth. A very small number of procedures, more in the primary than in the higher grades, accounted for an extraordinarily large percentage of the pedagogical techniques we observed in more than 1000 classrooms.[36] Given this overall and consistent lack of variability, one could not anticipate school-to-school differences of sufficient magnitude to permit meaningful ranking of schools. Some teachers differed in using many differing ways of teaching, but these were scattered across schools, not gathered so as to constitute most of the faculty in some schools.

Returning to an earlier observation, where we did find between-school differences regarding classroom characteristics was in the climate: interaction between teachers and students and among students, teacher attention and feedback to students, and some teaching attributes such as clarity of instructions and enthusiasm. Those things we tend to associate with support and caring in the learning process were perceived by students more frequently in the more satisfying than in the less satisfying schools.

Another analysis of our data resulted in the differentiation of eighteen schools on indices of self-renewal: continuous evaluation of programs, examination of alternative procedures, willingness of faculties to try new ideas.[37] The nine more renewing and the nine less renewing schools virtually overlapped the ordering of the more and less satisfying schools, respectively. Teachers in the schools identified as more renewing perceived their schools to be solving their problems, to provide appropriate conditions for them to do their job, and to have staffs capable of doing what needed to be done. In effect, the more renewing schools were perceived more generally by their teachers as taking care of their business. Included in their views of a school capable of doing its business was the perception that the principal was "open" and supportive in his or her relations with the staff.

The implications of the foregoing for staff development are enormous, in my judgment. And the challenge to the staff will be greater in some schools than in others. The demographic datum correlating most consistently with satisfaction and the accompanying characteristics was size. Generally, the more satisfying schools were the relatively small ones in our sample. Although there was a moderate correlation of satisfaction with socioeconomic status, it is encouraging that some schools populated heavily by children of low-income and low-education parents came out very well.

Summary and Implications

I have endeavored to keep before us the proposition that the individual school is the key unit for educational improvement, in the sense that it is a promising place, probably the most promising place, to focus our efforts. Early on, I discarded the idea that it generally functions effectively toward this end and substituted the idea that it could. For schools to become active agents in the improvement process, presumably staff development activities must be directed toward this end.

I have viewed improvement from two perspectives: first, that of making the school a humane workplace—a good, satisfying place for the humans inhabiting it; second, that of making the school a productive workplace—engaged in the teaching and learning we associate with quality education. I have argued for the former in its own right and suggested but by no means attempted to "prove" that a workplace good for humans is necessarily and simultaneously the most productive workplace possible. This would depend largely on what one expected this workplace to produce. I have implied, however, that a good workplace is likely to be also a good educational setting by virtue of the characteristics shared by both, as I have defined them.

I have presented data on a small, representative sample of elementary and secondary schools that reveal rather marked differences in the characteristics of those schools perceived by the persons associated with them to be more or less satisfying. These differences pertained primarily to the relationships among those associated with the school. Principals in the top quartile of schools on the satisfaction criteria, compared to those in the bottom, were more supportive of teachers; teachers were more supportive of students; and parents felt closer to teachers and their schools. Academic apathy was less; interest in learning appeared greater; school-wide problems were less intense, interfering less with learning and teaching. The ambience of the school as a whole appeared more supportive of the classroom effort to teach and to learn. Qualities generally associated with good teaching were more frequently perceived in the classrooms of the more satisfying schools; students were less likely to view their school as not providing them with a good education.

The schools most representative of these characteristics appeared to be taking care of business: keeping problems under control, maintaining an ethos supportive of learning, and the like. Schools at the other end of the scale, especially senior high schools, often appeared to be scarcely staying afloat; considerable time and energy of administrators and teachers were spent in coping with behavior problems. There were few signs of ongoing self-renewal.

Yet, there were no significant differences between more and less satisfying schools or more and less self-renewing schools in regard to the pedagogical techniques in use. The same lack of variety, the same monotony of lecturing, quizzing, and monitoring seatwork, especially at the secondary level, pervaded most classrooms, regardless of the presence or absence of the other characteristics just described. Why?

I put forward an interrelated set of possible explanations. The major one of these is that teaching has not been legitimated as an institutional concern. It is still a highly individualistic, isolated endeavor. The teacher closes the door and does what he or she pleases. Teachers do not wish to give up this autonomy and, indeed, we must hesitate before concluding that they should. Note the perceptions of greater autonomy and of being treated as professionals by the principal on the part of teachers in the more satisfying schools.

Why did not these teachers use this autonomy, then, to become more creative in their pedagogy? Why were not their classes places where students engaged in more problem solving, participated more in self-directed learnings, used a greater variety of instructional activities, interacted more in small groups—all those activities we associate with the higher cognitive processes implied by our educational goals? One explanation is that such activities are not easily carried out in the classroom. As Benham has insightfully pointed out, such procedures require that teachers transcend the circumstances (such as small spaces for relatively large groups) of their classrooms in conducting them.[38] Our data show the concern of teachers with control, especially at the junior and senior high levels, and their unwillingness to endanger that control through, for example, the encouragement of small-group endeavors. It is easier and potentially less threatening simply to slip into the more controlling, directive techniques characterizing most classrooms.

And this brings me to a related explanation for the conformity to a few standard practices. These are what teachers experienced throughout sixteen or more years as students in schools and colleges. They may have read and talked about alternatives in a teacher preparation course or two, but their professors probably used lecturing as the dominant procedure even while introducing them to John Dewey's processes of inquiry. Then, the most compelling part of their teacher education program was student teaching—with a supervising teacher using the time-worn pedagogical processes. The professional education of teachers simply is too thin and too limited to transcend the conventional wisdom regarding what teaching is. Teachers teach as they were taught.

As I have noted, staff development as conducted is focused predominantly on improving these same skills, teacher by teacher, largely away from the context of school and classroom. Even if a teacher were fortunate enough to engage in countervailing practices, the setting for using them is not likely to be receptive and reinforcing, as Lloyd found in her study reported earlier. Countervailing practices are demanding and difficult virtually by definition; for implementation they require institutional support and legitimization. This will not occur unless school staffs are willing to take their teaching out of the closet of the classroom, admit to the need to improve, and make it, along with the rest of the daily program, the focus of school-wide, on-site staff development.

The characteristics listed earlier, on which schools in our sample differed quite markedly, are not cloaked in the mystique of teacher autonomy and professionalism. Trust between principals and teachers, good staff relations, teacher support and encouragement of students' learning (this was part of the belief structure of most of the teachers in our sample), and good community relations are all part of the lexicon of good schooling. The words and phrases were taken more seriously in some of our schools than in others. Some of the schools were more disadvantaged or favored by circumstances than were others. For example, it is not impossible for large schools to be satisfying; our data suggest that it simply is more difficult to make them so. At any rate, some of our schools were doing a better job of getting their act together. But, apparently, for all of the reasons cited, they did not include on their agenda the central task of studying and improving, school-wide, the nature and quality of teaching. This was left, as it has been traditionally, to individual initiative and the dubious but compelling motivation of district-wide admonitions and incentives.

Let me conclude with a word of caution to those school staffs about to embark on a school-wide agenda of instructional improvement. In my judgment, the initiation of such efforts in any of the less satisfying schools in our sample would have resulted in unmitigated disaster. These schools almost uniformly were experiencing severe problems of many kinds: lack of authority or inability to exercise authority on the part of the principal, mutual distrust between principal and teachers, low faculty morale, student misbehavior and academic apathy, poor home-school relations, and more. These conditions are deeply embedded in the daily life of unsatisfying schools. They are highly amenable, our data suggest, to collaborative effort by those who share and relate to the school workplace. These school-wide problems must be addressed first if the workplace is to be capable of addressing the less amenable, less obvious, less open subject of pedagogy. Teachers' pedagogical habits are extraordinarily resistant to change, protected as they are by the mystique of professionalism and academic freedom and hidden behind classroom doors. Direct attack on this sensitive area of assumed teacher autonomy could bring down a school in which the problem-solving capability of the staff is at a low level. Why tackle the most difficult first?

The most satisfying schools in our sample appeared to have developed some capability to cope with problems besetting all schools to some degree. Most probably need to acquire greater self-awareness of the processes through which such capability was acquired and to refine them. And they should be challenged into legitimating teaching as a right and proper agenda item for school-wide study and action. Collaboration with colleges and universities, with district support, in programs combining preservice, in-service, and school improvement activities, as suggested earlier, is a promising way to go.

For all schools, the priority item always to be on the agenda is the quality of life in the workplace—its assessment and subsequent continuing improvement. Creating a satisfying place of work for the individuals who inhabit schools is good in its own right but it appears also to be necessary to maintaining a productive educational environment.

FOOTNOTES

1. Ernest R. House, *The Politics of Educational Innovation* (Berkeley, Calif.: McCutchan Publishing Corp., 1974).

2. Arthur E. Wise, *Legislated Learning* (Berkeley, Calif.: University of California Press, 1979).

3. Seymour B. Sarason, *The Culture of the School and the Problem of Change*, 2d ed. (Boston: Allyn and Bacon, 1982).

4. See, for example, Paul Berman and Milbrey McLaughlin, *Federal Programs Supporting Educational Change, vol. 1: A Model for Educational Change* (Santa Monica, Calif.: Rand Corp., 1974).

5. For an analysis of approaches to educational change, see Neal Gross, Joseph B. Giacquinta, and Marilyn Bernstein, *Implementing Organizational Innovations: A Sociological Analysis of Planned Educational Change* (New York: Basic Books, 1971).

6. John I. Goodlad, "The Individual School and Its Principal: Key Setting and Key Person in Educational Change," *Educational Leadership* 13 (October 1955): 2-6.

7. John I. Goodlad, *The Dynamics of Educational Change* (New York: McGraw-Hill, 1975).

8. Dan C. Lortie, *School Teacher: A Sociological Study* (Chicago: University of Chicago Press, 1975).

9. William J. Tikunoff and Beatrice A. Ward, "Inquiry Is an Unnatural Schooling Activity" (Paper presented at the annual meeting of the American Educational Research Association, Los Angeles, 1981).

10. John I. Goodlad, *A Place Called School* (New York: McGraw-Hill, 1983).

11. Robert M. McClure, "Instructional Decisions in Curriculum," in John I. Goodlad and Associates, *Curriculum Inquiry: The Study of Curriculum Practice* (New York: McGraw-Hill, 1979), pp. 129-50.

12. Gary A. Griffin, "Levels of Curriculum Decision Making," in Goodlad and Associates, *Curriculum Inquiry*, pp. 77-99.

13. For supporting data on these generalizations, see Goodlad, *A Place Called School*.

14. Michael Rutter, Barbara Maughan, Peter Mortimore, Janet Ouston, with Alan Smith, *Fifteen Thousand Hours: Secondary Schools and Their Effects on Children* (Cambridge, Mass.: Harvard University Press, 1979).

15. James S. Coleman, *Equality of Educational Opportunity* (Washington, D.C.: U.S. Government Printing Office, 1966).

16. Christopher Jencks et al., *Inequality* (New York: Harper and Row, 1973).

17. Daniel E. Griffiths, "Administrative Theory and Change in Organizations," in *Innovation in Education*, ed. Matthew B. Miles (New York: Teachers College Press, 1964), p. 435.

18. The theme of the program was "The Principal: Architect for Achievement."

19. See Goodlad, *A Place Called School*, chap. 2.

20. Ibid., chap. 9.

21. For further information regarding the sample, purposes, and general design of the study, see John I Goodlad, Kenneth A. Sirotnick, and Bette C. Overman, "An Overview of 'A Study of Schooling'," *Phi Delta Kappan* 61 (November 1979): 174-78.

22. Educational Development Center, *American Schools: Today and Tomorrow: A Summary of Eighteen Key Research Projects* (Newton, Mass.: The Center, 1981).

23. Jacob W. Getzels, "Introduction," in Richard C. Williams, Charles C. Wall, W. Michael Martin, and Arthur Berchin, *Effecting Organizational Renewal in Schools* (New York: McGraw-Hill, 1974), pp. vi-vii.

24. Dorothy M. Lloyd, "The Effects of a Staff Development In-Service Program on Teacher Performance and Student Achievement" (Doct. diss., University of California, Los Angeles, 1973).

25. Mary M. Bentzen and Associates, *Changing Schools: The Magic Feather Principle* (New York: McGraw-Hill, 1974).

26. Kenneth R. Howey, *Dimensions of Professional Development in Collaborative Inquiry: Perceptions of a Total School Faculty* (San Francisco: Far West Laboratory for Educational Research and Development, n.d.), p. 47.

27. Neal Q. Herrick and Michael Maccoby, "Humanizing Work: A Priority Goal of the 1970s," in *The Quality of Working Life*, vol. 1, ed. Louis E. Davis and Albert B. Cherns (New York: Free Press, 1975), p. 63.

28. What Callahan wrote about his model two decades ago remains timely and relevant. See Raymond E. Callahan, *Education and the Cult of Efficiency* (Chicago: University of Chicago Press, 1962).

29. Bette C. Overman, *Functions of Schooling: Perceptions and Preferences of Teachers, Parents, and Students,* Technical Report no. 10, A Study of Schooling (Los Angeles: Laboratory in School and Community Education, Graduate School of Education, University of California, 1980).

30. John I. Goodlad, *What Schools Are For* (Bloomington, Ind.: Phi Delta Kappa Educational Foundation, 1979).

31. Bruce Gunn, "The System Is the Answer," *Florida School Administrator* 2 (April 1979): 31.

32. Jeannie Oakes, *A Question of Access: Tracking and Curriculum Differentiation in a National Sample of English and Mathematics Classes,* Technical Report no. 24, A Study of Schooling (Los Angeles: Laboratory in School and Community Education, Graduate School of Education, University of California, 1981).

33. Warren Findley and Miriam Bryan, *Ability Grouping—1970* (Athens, Ga.: College of Education, University of Georgia, 1970). ED 048 382.

34. Jerome M. Rosow, ed., *The Worker and the Job* (Englewood Cliffs, N.J.: Prentice-Hall, 1974).

35. For elaboration of these and other findings on the principal-teacher relationship, see Monica B. Morris, *The Public School as Key Element in Teacher Satisfaction,* Technical Report no. 32, A Study of Schooling (Los Angeles: Laboratory in School and Community Education, Graduate School of Education, University of California, 1981).

36. Kenneth A. Sirotnik, *What You See Is What You Get: A Summary of Observations in over 1000 Elementary and Secondary Classrooms,* Technical Report no. 29, A Study of Schooling (Los Angeles: Laboratory in School and Community Education, Graduate School of Education, University of California, 1982).

37. Paul E. Heckman, *Exploring the Concept of Self-Renewal: Contextual Differences and Similarities between More and Less Renewing Schools,* Technical Report no. 33, A Study of Schooling (Los Angeles: Laboratory in School and Community Education, Graduate School of Education, University of California, 1982).

38. Barbara J. Benham, "Thoughts on the Failure of Curriculum Reform," *Educational Leadership* 35 (December 1977): 205-8.

CHAPTER IV

The Organizational Context of School Systems and the Functions of Staff Development

PHILLIP C. SCHLECHTY AND BETTY LOU WHITFORD

On a day-to-day basis it is sometimes difficult for teachers, building administrators, and those who study life within schools to see that events occurring outside the context of school buildings have any relevance for them or the problems they confront. Indeed, among teachers and building administrators, there is a tendency to disparage those who occupy positions outside the school as "useless bureaucrats" who use up valued resources that would be better spent for instructional purposes. Furthermore, there is a tendency among practitioners to view whatever impact these outsiders have as largely negative—interrupting routine operations in schools for needless meetings, "snoopervising," and so on.

If, however, one takes a larger view of the problems of schools and classrooms and if one thinks of careers as well as jobs, biographies as well as personalities, and trends as well as events, the meaning of what happens in classrooms and corridors cannot be properly understood without reference to the system-level context in which schools and classrooms exist. For example, in some schools it would be difficult to understand the relationship between younger teachers and older teachers without taking into account how school system policy relating to reductions in force is shaping those relationships. Furthermore, one cannot properly understand school system policy relating to reductions in force without understanding how teacher organizations

---

The authors are indebted to Dr. Anne Joslin for her thoughtful comments on various drafts of this chapter.

function in the school system, how the demography of the community served by the system is changing, and how persons are recruited to teach in the school system in the first place.

The purpose of this chapter is to illuminate some of those system-level events and larger social structures that appear to have critical effects on the way staff development and other forms of continuing education are conducted in schools.

Definitions

There is considerable confusion surrounding the meaning of terms such as staff development, continuing education, professional development, and personal development. Given this confusion, it is essential to indicate how these terms will be used here.

Continuing education refers to any systematic course of study or set of experiences intended to achieve increased awareness of and improved skill in the use of, or a deepened appreciation for, those aspects of culture (including technical culture) and environment (including work environment) about which a participant is interested or concerned. (The term "systematic" is used rather than "formal" in order to avoid limiting the meaning to courses and programs offered or prescribed by institutions.)

Self-initiated continuing education refers to any form of continuing education that an individual undertakes voluntarily and without support or inducement from an employer and over which the employer does not have authority.

Job-oriented continuing education refers to any form of continuing education sponsored or supported by the school system as an employer, or honored by that employer in terms of pay, status, or other rewards. Job-oriented continuing education affects persons as well as employers. Thus, individuals may participate in job-oriented continuing education voluntarily, that is, as if it were self-initiated. However, it seems important to distinguish between those forms of continuing education undertaken because of the conditions of one's employment or membership in an occupational group as opposed to those forms undertaken because of idiosyncratic interests or strictly personal goals. The focus of this chapter will be on *job-oriented continuing education activity*.

Goals and Legitimacy

In organizations, goals serve at least three functions: as a source of legitimacy, as a source of direction, and as a basis for evaluation.[1] First, as a source of legitimacy, goals serve to justify and symbolize the rightfulness of the actions of an organization. For example, business organizations can justify layoffs in a time of recession by referring to the fact that continued employment of unneeded personnel would be harmful to the organization's pursuit of the profit goal. This justification is generally accepted in our society even though such layoffs may create considerable suffering for individuals. At the same time, there have been times in the history of American society when government actions intended to create work for the unemployed (for example, the WPA) have been justified on the basis that one of the legitimizing goals of government is to promote the general welfare.

A second function of goals is to provide a source of direction for action; that is, goals indicate what actions should be taken and how those actions should be carried out. For example, when a business organization is confronted with a decline in worker morale, decisions about whether this condition requires some organizational action will be shaped largely by judgments regarding whether improved morale will increase productivity and whether a continued decline in morale will lead to disruptions in the organization (for example, strikes). Fraternal organizations, on the other hand, have as one of their primary goals the promotion of comradery among members. Thus, evidence of a decline in morale among members is, prima facie, a problem that calls for organizational action.

A third function of goals is to serve as a basis for evaluation and to suggest criteria by which the effects and effectiveness of various actions should be assessed. Business people, for example, frequently use the term "the bottom line" to refer to the fact that the ultimate success of the actions they take is properly evaluated in terms of profit and loss. Members of a fraternity or sorority, on the other hand, might more appropriately evaluate the success of the actions of their organizations in terms of attracting new members who have the characteristics the organization values and maintaining support from loyal alumni.

In schools, the primary legitimizing goals have to do with the education of children. Logically, then, the goals that should provide direction for the organization are goals that have to do with the education of children; and, the effects and effectiveness of actions sponsored by the organizations should be assessed in terms of the efficacy of the action in achieving these same goals.

In spite of the claims of rationalists, schools and other organizations do not operate on the basis of deductive logic, but rather on the basis of a *sociologic*.[2] Sociologic takes into account nonrational elements as well as those that are rational. For example, sociologic takes into account negotiations among competing interests and competing goals and the compromises that necessarily take place between the efficient pursuit of primary goals and the expectations embedded in the larger environment.[3] These nonrational (which is not to say incomprehensible) forces most clearly come into play when an organization takes on goals and functions that are, or appear to be, in competition with the goals which serve as a primary basis for legitimizing the organization. For example, Perrow provides an interesting account of the conflict and tension caused in an industrial setting when the organization took on responsibility for managing a Job Corps program.[4] A part of the justification for the Job Corps was to upgrade the skills and abilities of unskilled workers *on the job*. At the same time, production supervisors were expected to uphold production quotas developed on the assumption that skilled workers would be assigned to jobs. This condition, of course, resulted in considerable tension.

The condition of job-oriented continuing education in schools is roughly analogous to the condition described by Perrow in his discussion of the Job Corps program. The goals used to legitimize actions in schools are primarily goals associated with the education of children. All other goals are, or are perceived to be, subordinate to these child-oriented goals. Job-oriented continuing education, on the other hand, centers on the education of adults. The goals that provide direction for these activities are goals associated with perceptions of the proper education of adults. Frequently, those actions that are necessary, or are perceived to be necessary, to pursue properly goals associated with the education of adults may interfere with, or appear to interfere with, the goals associated with the education of children.

For example, providing teachers with released time to attend in-service activities removes teachers from classrooms. Many teachers and administrators view the uninterrupted presence of the teacher in the classroom as critical to the continuing growth of children. Thus, any job-oriented continuing education activity that systematically removes teachers from the classroom is likely to be resisted by some teachers and administrators as distracting from the primary mission of the schools.[5] While organized teachers and many staff development specialists argue that staff development should occur on school time, it is difficult to dismiss the fact that, as schools are now organized, honoring this expectation can create the perception that schools are not attending to the business they have been legitimized to conduct, that is, the business of educating children. Furthermore, many teachers who have received released time are as outspoken in their criticisms of its disruptive nature as are those who do not receive released time.[6]

The important point here is that the goals used to *legitimize* actions in schools (goals associated here with the education of children) are often in competition with the goals that give *direction* to job-oriented continuing education activities. In addition, school systems are organized in such a way that it is presently impossible to legitimize continuing education in any terms other than those suggested by the child-oriented goals of the school. Thus, it is essential that job-oriented continuing education activities seek legitimacy in terms of child-oriented goals. Furthermore, programs of continuing education sponsored by schools that are not clearly linked to improved performance of children are always of questionable legitimacy. Those programs that are perceived to be disruptive to the efficient pursuit of these goals (for example, programs that provide too much released time or programs that require teachers to give "too much" time to their own education) are likely to be viewed as nonlegitimate. In sum, the inability of schools, as they are presently organized, to legitimize job-oriented continuing education as a worthy pursuit in its own right creates dynamic and complex patterns of competition and conflict between the requirements of high-quality continuing education for teachers and high-quality educational services for children.

Perhaps more critical is the fact that the failure of continuing education to be directly linked to any legitimizing goals other than those associated with the education of children makes the resources officially committed by the system to support continuing education highly problematic and subject to continual negotiation. For example, those persons most likely to be called on to assume nonroutine assignments or to take on assignments with a seasonal character (for example, class scheduling, grant writing, and preparation of reports to federal and state agencies) are most likely to be drawn from the ranks of those whose official job assignments are primarily to support job-oriented continuing education.[7]

The dubious legitimacy of continuing education creates a strong drive in schools to delegate responsibility for long-term and systematic continuing education programs to those institutions where the education of adults is legitimate, that is, institutions of higher education. For example, in one school system an initiative was taken by the school board to establish an incentive program intended to encourage teachers to undertake individualized programs of study aimed at improving their performance in the classroom.[8] Initially, this program was based upon a diagnostic-prescriptive model in which the teacher, the building principal, and specialists in staff development cooperated in the identification of continuing education needs and collectively agreed to a course of study intended to respond to those needs. In the initial design, it was assumed that this course of study would include some college courses, some locally developed workshops, and some independent study. Also, in the initial design, the program was not directly tied to the pursuit of certification or to certificate renewal.

Given the technical and logistical requirements of such a program, it was clear from the outset that the adequate management of this enterprise would require commitment of considerable system resources, and require that continuing education be accepted as a legitimate goal of the school. However, such a legitimizing structure did not develop. Rather, over a three-year period the goals of the program were changed to the point that the purpose was to provide incentives for persons to pursue regular graduate programs leading to advanced certification. Furthermore, the way these programs were structured depended exclusively on decisions made by institutions of higher education. The school system had no official way to influence this structure. Thus, what started out as an effort on the part of the school system to develop a continuing education program intended to respond simultaneously to system and personal needs evolved into an incentive program encouraging teachers to pursue graduate courses at universities. In large measure, the reason for this shift in goals and direction had to do with the lack of a clear basis for legitimizing continuing education in the school system.

There is little empirical evidence to support assertions that participating in continuing education activities clearly results in an improved capacity to pursue the legitimizing goals of schools, that is, goals associated with the education of children.[9] In addition, many practitioners have a general disdain for the present quality of job-oriented continuing education.[10] Thus, it is not surprising that when decisions must be made regarding whether to support continuing education that is perceived to be disruptive to routines associated with the education of children, those decisions are typically unfavorable to the continuing education enterprise. Similarly, it is not surprising that when budget cuts must be made, one of the first areas to be affected is continuing education.

Those organizations that do have legitimate authority in the area of continuing education (for example, institutions of higher education) are typically located outside the authority structure of school systems. In addition, those in schools have little ability to affect directly these outside organizations. Thus, it is not surprising that the legitimized continuing education programs that are developed tend to serve the peculiar interests of institutions of higher education as frequently as they do the job-oriented interests of practitioners.[11]

Until these issues are directly addressed, there seems to be little prospect that the quality of job-oriented continuing education in schools will be substantially improved. Furthermore, given the dubious legitimacy of continuing education, economic retrenchment may reduce the quantitative emphasis as well. For example, one of the more pronounced effects of recent federal budget reductions has been to reduce the amount of money available for staff development activity in school systems.

It is, of course, possible to conceive of alternatives to the present circumstances. For example, it may be that public schools and universities could join together to form a new type of organization which unifies the delivery of quality services to children, the conduct of research and development activity, and the professional preparation of teachers, and in which each of these functions is viewed as legitimate in its own right. Hospitals engaged in both teaching and research have managed such arrangements. Unfortunately, where efforts have been made to develop such models in education (for example, laboratory schools and some normal schools) difficulties have been encountered precisely because one of the functions came to dominate the others. For example, university laboratory schools frequently are centers for child study and relegate the education of teachers to a peripheral position. Normal schools tended to emphasize "the practical" and thus usually overlooked, or looked past, research. When public schools become involved in teacher education (for example, the Teacher Corps), there is a strong tendency to use resources committed to teacher education for purposes of program maintenance.[12] It is clear, therefore, that if staff development is to be integrated into the everyday world of schools and the life of teachers, new organizational arrangements will need to be created.[13]

Rewards and Incentives

If one is to understand how job-oriented continuing education operates in schools, one must understand how such activities are associated with the reward structure of the school. There are several conditions that seem to be typical.

First, in most schools, rewards that can be purposefully distributed on a differential basis (for example, merit pay increases, promotions, opportunities for travel) are scarce. The way schools are organized [14] and the way the teaching occupation is structured[15] make rewards generally scarce, and those rewards that do exist are likely to be distributed equally among categories of employees (for example, salary increments based on experience).

Second, to the extent that schools do differentiate among employees in terms of rewards, especially monetary rewards, this differentiation is more likely to be based on participation in continuing education than on any other condition. Indeed, the idea of differentiating among employees for pay purposes on any basis other than participation in continuing education (and experience) is ideologically repugnant to many teachers.

Third, opportunities for status rewards are also closely linked with participation in continuing education. For example, if one aspires to move from the ranks of teachers to the ranks of administrators, one must pursue a course of graduate study.

Continuing education is related to the reward structure of schools in other ways as well. For example, due to federal funding policies and lobbying efforts by teacher organizations, there is a growing feeling among teachers that any continuing education activity they undertake other than that which occurs on school time should be rewarded with direct payment in the form of salary supplements or stipends. Colleges and universities have frequently used the right to participate in continuing education as a means of inducing teachers to do work they (the institutions of higher education) need to have done. For example, many colleges provide teachers with tuition remission in exchange for supervising student teachers. In addition to the personal satisfaction one might gain from participation in college courses and the opportunity for self-improvement that these courses may provide, the fact that such courses can produce increases in salary is also an important consideration.

In addition, more subtle forms of reward seem to get attached to participation in continuing education activity. For example, much of the activity sponsored by teacher centers seems to be associated with the psychic rewards gained through instructing other adults and the honor one gains for being acknowledged by one's peers as being successful in the enterprise. The visibility one gains from participating in (or better yet, taking a leadership role in) systemwide in-service activities can also be highly valued by classroom teachers who desire to move up in the system, for such visibility is often a prerequisite to upward mobility such as promotion or transfer to a preferred school.

In sum, the way schools are organized creates a condition in which participation in continuing education is a powerful force in determining the degree to which one will gain access to those few differential rewards that are available in the system. Since such rewards are scarce in schools, this relationship is an important one.

In addition, it is important to understand that the way continuing education is embedded in the reward structure of schools makes it difficult for building-level staff to exercise control over how these rewards will be distributed or to whom they will be extended. The financial resources of schools are seldom controlled at the building level. Furthermore, even when building administrators and staff are granted some autonomy with regard to budgets, this autonomy is usually limited by proscriptive guidelines that border on being prescriptive. The fact that school buildings frequently appear to operate as relatively autonomous units sometimes serves to distract attention from the fact that most material rewards and many symbolic rewards available to support continuing education are controlled by or located in organizational units that transcend the confines of the local building unit and sometimes the school system. For example, few building principals or faculties are in a position to determine the content of college courses or the performance one must engage in to complete these courses. Making these determinations is a jealously guarded prerogative of institutions of higher education.

Similarly, the offering of stipends, tuition remission, and released time are all typically controlled at levels beyond the building level. Sometimes these controls are located at or below the level of the school board, such as the superintendent or someone to whom the superintendent delegates authority, and sometimes the controls are located outside the school system in institutions of higher education, state education agencies, federal agencies, or private foundations. Frequently, these controls are lodged in offices concerned more with budgets and auditing procedures than with programmatic considerations. Unfortunately, those in positions to conduct audits and those who must respond to audits find it inconvenient to give others discretionary authority. Rather, their tendency is to promulgate guidelines that provide protection against the worst possible case. Such accounting procedures generally emanate from the system level or outside the system, thus limiting the discretionary authority of those at the building level to reward participation in continuing education.[16]

The result of this condition is that those building-level units that are most likely to gain access to the rewards associated with job-oriented continuing education and at the same time maintain control over the shape of the activities in which they will participate are those buildings that have "system-wise" administrators and teachers. For example, Schlechty et al. observed that school buildings and intermediate administrative units that had as their chief administrator persons with prior experience in central office administrative roles or who served on systemwide committees seemed to have had available to them more discretionary resources to support continuing education activity than those without such experiences.[17] It is, of course, possible that this differential was based upon favoritism and associated with informal influence networks. The data do not make it possible to rule out this latter hypothesis definitively. However, there is some evidence in this instance to indicate that access to systemwide resources to support staff development (for example, opportunities to participate in high-demand systemwide workshops with limited enrollment) was attributable to the fact that building-level administrators and staff development specialists who had had prior experience at the central office knew better where to seek information and acted on that information with more dispatch than did administrators and staff development specialists who had not had systemwide experience. There was no evidence that system-level personnel initiated action toward those who received more favorable responses any more than they did toward those who received less favorable responses. Furthermore, the data make it abundantly clear that persons who participated in systemwide staff development activities were more likely to participate in other activities, at least in part because participation made them more aware of other opportunities, while those who did not participate were less aware. It is this quality of "being aware" of what resources are available and how they can be used that is referred to here as being "system-wise."

There are, in addition, a number of other important consequences that flow from the way staff development and continuing education are embedded in the reward structure. First, given the scarcity of differential rewards available in schools, and given that participation in continuing education is (a) one of the clearest ways to access these rewards, and (b) one of the few legitimate means by which rewards can be distributed on an unequal basis, policy and procedures for continuing education become subject to a variety of pressures and interests that are only tangentially concerned with instructional improvement and professional growth. For example, there can be little doubt that linking pursuit of graduate degrees to differential salary increments encourages some teachers and administrators to pursue degrees for no other reason than to advance on the salary scale or gain a promotion. That the pursuit of such study could, should, or might lead to professional growth and improved instruction is not denied. However, one would be naive to assume that present conditions do not encourage a great deal of ritualism, whereby teachers and administrators "tolerate" a wide range of irrelevant (from their perspective, at least) courses in order to achieve their primary goal, a promotion or salary increment.

Furthermore, in a time when college enrollments are declining (especially in education) and the worth of salary increments is diminishing, there is strong pressure on teachers, administrators, and higher education personnel to engage in an unspoken conspiracy to assure easy access to what few rewards there are in exchange for job-saving enrollments in college programs. The fear that such a "conspiracy" is already under way is certainly widespread among educators and some school boards.[18]

A second consequence of the way job-oriented continuing education is embedded in the reward structure of schools is that there is considerable pressure to use the rewards attached to participation to support many activities other than or in addition to those for which the rewards are intended. For example, the authors are aware of at least four states in which school system personnel commonly negotiate credit (renewal credit and sometimes college credit) for faculty who take active roles in the preparation of regional accreditation studies. One need not deny the potential value of regional accreditation studies as staff development to inquire as to why the rewards one receives for giving time above and beyond the routine job requirements are those rewards associated with continuing education (for example, renewal credit). Is it because there is a logical connection between what must be done and the continuing growth of teachers, or is it because in a system of scarce rewards, one uses the available rewards to do what one must?

There are, in addition, more blatant illustrations of how the reward structure is co-opted to support programmatic concerns other than, and sometimes in competition with, the development of systematic continuing education programs. For example, as McDonald notes, colleges and universities have a vested interest in maintaining the link between the pursuit of graduate degrees and salary increments, precisely because this linkage serves to maintain college enrollments.[19] Similarly, building principals sometimes use stipend-producing workshops, travel to conferences, and released time as a means of rewarding teachers for past performance rather than as a means of assuring continuing growth. Thus, in effect, participation in continuing education, especially if that participation involves stipends, tuition remission, or graduate credit leading to salary increments, functions—or can function—as a proxy for merit pay.

A third consequence of the relationship of continuing education to the reward structure in schools is that the nature of this relationship can serve to enhance latent sources of conflict in school, activate (for good or ill) competitive actions between and among school buildings, departments, and administrative units, and foster feelings of relative deprivation among groups that are structurally denied access to the rewards that are available. In the study conducted by Schlechty et al., there are numerous illustrations of the ways staff development policies and actions enhance latent role conflict.[20]

For example, state and federal programs intended to address equity issues in the school system studied were typically focused more at the elementary school level than at the secondary level. In addition, these programs typically placed considerable emphasis on the provision of rewards for participation in continuing education activities, including stipends, tuition remission, graduate credit, and advanced degrees. The fact that secondary teachers were largely precluded from participation became a source of resentment. This condition also served to reinforce among secondary teachers a preexisting view that "whatever staff development is, it has more to do with elementary teachers than secondary teachers."[21] Thus, the structure of the reward system, which is often shaped by system goals and priorities and goals derived from sources outside the system, can drive an even deeper wedge between groups in schools (in this case between elementary and secondary teachers) and create negative as well as positive affect toward the job-oriented continuing education enterprise.

With regard to the tendency of the linkage between system rewards and continuing education to enhance competition between buildings or between departments or intermediate school districts, one needs to take into account the fact that control over these rewards is typically located outside these units. Thus, decisions about the distribution of the rewards are decisions regarding which units will or will not enjoy a relatively advantageous position vis-à-vis the reward structure. For example, if a school building is designated as a pilot center for one or another project and a part of the project involves systematic continuing education leading to advanced degrees, other faculties and administrators are likely to be resentful of those in the preferred building. Furthermore, this resentment is likely to become sufficiently strong to exert pressure on the central administration to distribute resources among buildings in an equalizing fashion. Given the absolute scarcity of such resources and rewards, the effect may be to dilute the impact of the rewards available to the point that there is little effect in any building.

With regard to fostering feelings of relative deprivation, the following is an example. Schlechty et al. observed that the colleges and universities serving the school system seemed to find it easier to operate site-based programs and courses for specialists (for example, reading specialists, special educators, and school administrators) than programs and courses that required cooperation from liberal arts faculties. The consequence was that persons who were pursuing degrees in reading, special education, and administration were more frequently able to access appropriate courses on the school site, whereas those who were pursuing programs in secondary English, mathematics, science, and so on were required to commute to campuses. Furthermore, the liberal arts faculties on university campuses seemed much less inclined to adjust their teaching schedules to accommodate these commuter students than did those in education departments.[22]

One of the results of this condition was that some teachers perceived that school-sponsored and school-supported continuing education, especially that which led to degrees and salary increments, was reserved for special and select categories of persons. In addition, the fact that most of the programs delivered to the school were taught by professors of education and seldom by liberal arts professors reinforced, especially among older secondary teachers, the stigma that sometimes attaches to extension programs regarding "inferior quality."[23] Unpleasant though it may be for educators, it is a fact that many teachers view education courses with disdain, and degrees that rely primarily on education courses are seen by many as "inferior."

This discussion of the relationship between the reward structure of schools and the operation of job-oriented continuing education has made this basic point: given the way continuing education is related to the reward structure of schools, job-oriented continuing education is called on to serve many functions in addition to providing for the systematic improvement of instruction. It is the failure to distinguish between and among these functions that accounts for much of the confusion regarding what continuing education, staff development, and professional development are or should be. This failure to distinguish among the functions also leads to considerable confusion about who should control what and at whose expense. The purpose of the following sections is to provide some suggestions regarding the ways the functions of job-oriented continuing education can be conceived.

The Functions of Continuing Education

Like other organizations, schools are concerned with both stability and change. If schools are to pursue effectively the goals for which they have been established, they must maintain sufficient stability to assure that most of the energy expended is directed toward those goals. On the other hand, if schools are to be effective, they must have the capacity to adapt to new conditions and the capacity to insure that those who work in schools perform at an optimal or nearly optimal level.

The literature in education, especially the literature in teacher education and staff development, is much more attuned to issues of change than issues related to maintaining stability. Indeed, many practitioners and researchers find the ability of schools to resist change one of the most perplexing and interesting problems they confront.[24] Furthermore, the literature in teacher education and staff development is much more concerned with linking continuing education to change in schools than with linking continuing education to stability.

In the educational literature, there are useful examples of how change has been effectively introduced in schools and how continuing education has been used to support these change efforts. Yet one cannot read that literature without gaining the impression that for the most part, efforts to change schools have been relatively ineffective, and job-oriented continuing education has not been proven to be an effective means of bringing about change in schools. In spite of these apparent failures, however, educators continue to value continuing education for teachers, and some of the most volatile issues in schools have to do with who should have the right to control job-oriented continuing education. Given the apparent deficiencies of continuing education, the general disdain practitioners have for much that goes on in the name of continuing education, and the inability to demonstrate clearly that continuing education in fact achieves what is claimed for it, one cannot help but wonder why anyone cares enough about the control of continuing education to fight over it. The fact is, however, educators do fight over the control of continuing education. This suggests that job-oriented continuing education is perceived to serve some vital functions, though the functions it serves may not be the functions that are claimed for it.

Consider the functions that most staff developers and practitioners claim continuing education could and should serve. Two such functions are easily identifiable. First, continuing education could serve to support the introduction of new programs, new technologies, and new procedures in schools. It is convenient to label this function the *establishing function.* Second, continuing education could serve to enhance the performance capacities, refine existing skills, and expand existing knowledge regarding new developments in the field. This function will be referred to as the *enhancement function.*

In the preceding discussion on rewards and incentives, it was suggested that continuing education also serves a third function. That function will be labeled here as the *maintenance function.* Maintenance function refers to those conditions that must be fulfilled to assure compliance with preferred administrative routines, to support organizationally preferred modes of operating, and to protect those engaging in these activities from unwanted outside influence.

If one considers the dubious legitimacy of continuing education in schools and the way job-oriented continuing education is related to the reward structure, one can gain a fuller appreciation of the reasons why continuing education so often serves the maintenance function exceedingly well while it infrequently serves the establishing or enhancement functions in satisfactory ways. If one considers the way schools are related to their larger environment and the pressure that environment places on schools to change, one can more fully understand why it is perceived by many to be important to attach job-oriented continuing education publicly to enhancement and establishing activities and eschew identification with maintenance. Finally, if one considers the pressure that the emphasis on change places on school maintenance systems, and if one understands that the few flexible resources schools have are disproportionately given over to continuing education, one can understand more fully why school personnel so often fight over the control of continuing education. Put directly, keeping things from getting worse while undergoing the dislocations produced by change requires more maintenance effort than is required when a situation is stable. Thus, as pressures for change increase, pressures on the existing maintenance system increase as well. Since the amount of resources that school systems have for maintenance purposes is limited to begin with, there is strong pressure to co-opt flexible staff development resources, ostensibly committed to change, for the purpose of maintaining the system rather than changing it. The purpose of the remainder of this section is to provide illustrations in support of the assertions made above.

As indicated in the earlier discussion of rewards, the way job-oriented continuing education is related to the differential reward system of schools places strong pressure on line administrators, such as building principals, to attempt to co-opt that reward structure to provide incentives for teachers and others to do necessary maintenance activity outside of regular working hours. For example, the preparation of regional accreditation reports is a necessary maintenance activity, for schools that lose accreditation have, by definition, had the stability of their structure challenged. Few school systems have the resources within their operational budgets to compensate persons adequately for the additional hours such reports require. Thus, there is considerable pressure on administrators to turn to the reward structure that is linked to continuing education (for example, renewal credit) and to those flexible, though limited, financial resources available to the staff development enterprise for support. Furthermore, since many of these maintenance activities have prima facie legitimacy in the system, whereas continuing education in schools is less fully legitimitized, it is difficult for those who control these rewards and resources to resist the co-optive efforts. It is especially difficult to resist co-optation when one is employed by the same system and influenced by the same legitimizing structures.

It is the case that school systems do sponsor and support many activities that are explicitly aimed toward the establishing function. However, the more sweeping and comprehensive the change being introduced becomes, the more claims it will make on those resources that are needed to maintain the system. Thus, there is strong pressure on schools to seek external funding to support establishing activities and to conserve local resources in order to maintain the stability of the system. But here enters another problem. Given the crisis orientation of schools and the multiple pressures brought upon schools to change in this or that direction, the demands on the system for resources to maintain itself frequently outstrip, or are perceived to outstrip, the supply of those resources. Thus, there is strong pressure on school personnel to use external resources procured to support activity aimed at the establishing function for purposes of organizational maintenance. For example, Corwin found that when the fiscal authority of the change projects he studied was located in the school, less change occurred than when the fiscal authority was located in outside organizations.[25] At least a part of the explanation for this condition must lie in the fact that when the fiscal authority is within the school system, it is easier for insiders to co-opt the resources for maintenance purposes.

One need only read newspapers or watch television news to know that there is tremendous pressure on schools to change and improve. Indeed, many public educators are convinced that if schools do not change and improve, the future of public education is threatened. Improvement and change require considerable organizational resources and the expenditure of additional time. Change also requires that high priority be given to those research and development activities that are necessary to produce the information and technologies upon which change is based. Change also requires detailed planning. At the same time, a system undergoing change must make provision to maintain itself in such a way that present performance levels do not erode.

For those who are knowledgeable about the operation of the typical school system, it should not be necessary to document the fact that long-term planning and research and development activity are not high priority items. Rather, the style is to "do something even if it's wrong" and that which is more frequently done is staff development. If drug abuse is perceived as a major issue, there is strong pressure to run workshops for teachers that focus on drug education. If native Americans bring pressure to bear to assure that their children are treated equitably, the most likely response will be to run a workshop for teachers on "Indian education." Conceivably, such workshops could bring about change, but if they were to do so, they would require considerable follow-up and the type of support necessary to *establish* new programs, procedures, and technologies. However, programs that support the establishing function are likely to be even more draining on existing resources than are programs that support the maintenance function.

Given the fact that the demand for change is seldom coupled with additional resources to support the change, there is strong pressure to use those limited resources that are available for in-service activities that are primarily oriented toward maintenance. For example, running workshops on "drug education" for all the teachers in the school system can be used to convince concerned parents that something is being done to deal with the drug problem.

The fact that the way job-oriented continuing education is presently organized and controlled clearly serves some interests and threatens others is now reasonably well documented.[26] It is also clear that for many, the issue of quality in continuing education is an issue of governance as well as substance.[27] For example, the teacher center movement in America has sometimes been as much concerned with assuring that organized teachers would have a dominant voice in running those centers as with the substantive component of the offerings of the centers. The assumption, of course, is that as recipients of the services of teacher centers, teachers are in a better position to identify their own needs than are others.

Furthermore, it is the case that in recent years established patterns of control have been somewhat modified in some situations. For example, accrediting agencies, like the National Council for the Accreditation of Teacher Education, are considerably more attentive to the way teacher education institutions are governed and to evidence of practitioner involvement in the governance than was once the case. In some school units, teacher organizations have effectively bargained for the right to control in-service offerings in the school system. Teacher centers, too, have served to give increased legitimacy to teacher participation in policy decisions regarding continuing education.

In spite of these facts, it remains the case that institutions of higher education retain final authority over the most clearly legitimized forms of continuing education, that is, those forms that carry with them the promise of college credit. Furthermore, as Moore and Hyde observed, school systems expend a considerable amount of their staff development budgets to reward persons for participating in such activities.[28] Indeed, as was observed earlier, participating in college degree programs is the only assured and legitimized means by which teachers can gain access to the differential reward structure of schools.

This creates a condition that encourages teachers and administrators to show strong preferences for continuing education activities that carry graduate credit. Furthermore, this condition encourages teachers, administrators, and college personnel to bargain among themselves in order to assure that college credit is offered under conditions that are most advantageous to each party and least threatening to the maintenance needs of all. Thus, administrators encourage teacher educators to offer programs that are practical, and practicality frequently translates into nothing more or less than teaching teachers how to comply with the peculiar requirements of the local school system. Teachers, on the other hand, demand that courses be relevant to their needs. One need not disparage teachers' motives to suggest that, in a system of scarce rewards where one of the most pressing problems is finding enough time to do the routine work one is assigned, it is likely that some teachers pursue courses of action intended to produce maximum reward with minimum effort. That many fear that this drive is stronger than some care to admit is easily documented.[29]

It should be observed that school systems, as employers, are under strong pressures to support the demands of some teachers for courses delivered to the school site on terms that are convenient and on terms that do not place demands on them that interfere with their "real" work. From the point of view of the school system as employer, providing support for these claims is one of the ways that differential rewards can be provided to valued employees. At the same time, it is also a way to demonstrate to the community that the school system is doing something about teacher competence. Also, as was observed earlier in this chapter, declining enrollments and the need to maintain existing systems of control serve to encourage colleges and universities to cooperate with school systems in this regard. The nature of this cooperation involves compliance by colleges and universities with the demands of reward-starved school systems and reward-starved teachers in exchange for the continuing acceptance of the right of the colleges to be the exclusive source of "real credit" and for the course enrollments required to keep the system going.

What is being suggested here is that the way schools are organized and the way continuing education is embedded in that organization make it difficult, if not impossible, for continuing education to serve either the establishing or enhancement functions in any systematic way. The only function that continuing education can serve in a systematic way is the maintenance function. Indeed, persons who are responsible for continuing education are unable to resist demands that their activities support the maintenance function even when the activity is legitimized in terms of the pursuit of enhancement goals or goals related to establishing new programs and new technologies.

Implications

Assuming that the analysis presented here is valid, one of the clearest implications is that it may be necessary for those who have job-oriented continuing education responsibilities to rethink their present ideological commitments and reconsider the high value they place on change and enhancement and the relatively low value they place on maintenance. Pursuit of maintenance goals is among the most organizationally legitimate activities one can engage in. Furthermore, pursuit of maintenance goals is not necessarily linked to a defense of the status quo. Indeed, maintaining the health of the organization is a prerequisite to change, since an organization that cannot keep things from getting worse is in no position to make them better. The ability to argue this case effectively is one of the more critical abilities to be demonstrated by those who occupy positions that give them responsibility for staff development in schools. Perhaps it is because of the failure to argue this case effectively that many school systems are now confronted with low teacher morale, a breakdown in communication between teachers and administrators, a breakdown in communication between schools and communities, and a general feeling of distress regarding the future of public education in America.

A second implication has to do with the proper evaluation of the effects and effectiveness of job-oriented continuing education. Assuming that the distinctions that have been made between the various functions of continuing education are important, evaluation designs should take these functions into account. Furthermore, in developing evaluation designs for continuing education programs, evaluators might do well to consider both the manifest and latent functions of the programs.[30] In examining the manifest functions, one would seek to determine the intentions of the program through an examination of the goals that are officially used to legitimize it. To examine the latent functions, one might turn attention to the goals that provide direction and the operational criteria participants in the program and staff developers use to evaluate the worth of the program.

In a similar vein, the functions that continuing education is intended to serve and the functions the activity in fact serves should provide direction to the kinds of criteria appropriate to an evaluation. If one is interested in assessing the effectiveness of a program in serving maintenance functions, one is more interested in criteria concerned with stability than with change. Thus, one is oriented toward seeking the absence of an undesired phenomenon rather than the increasing presence of a desired phenomenon. For example, and only partially facetiously, it is reasonable to assume that teachers who have "burned out" were, at some time in their biographies, "on fire." To understand the effectiveness of a program intended to prevent teacher burn-out, therefore, it would be reasonable to assess beginning and relatively inexperienced teachers in the system as well as more experienced teachers in order to gain an approximation of just how much heat was there in the first place. It might also be useful to compare the rate and frequency of teacher burn-out among partici- pants in the program being evaluated with comparable nonparticipants, for it may be the case that the conditions of employment in any job are such (and human nature is such) that some built-in proportion of the population initially recruited becomes disaffected and bored. Develop- ing programs that entice the disaffected and bored to stay with the job may be dysfunctional, both for the organization and for the individ- uals.

In sum, it is being suggested that the criteria appropriate to assessing maintenance-oriented continuing education should be norm referenced and should deal with the rate and frequency of the occurrence of an undesired event or problematic situation. The unfortunate fact is, however, that schools seldom publicly attend to issues of maintenance until the condition has deteriorated so far below the norm that any but the most insensitive recognize the pathology. For example, it is not typical for school systems to engage in staff development activity intended to maintain harmonious relationships among minority and majority faculty until cleavages along racial or ethnic lines produce organizational crises. The development of such crises should, in itself, be evidence that staff development has not served the maintenance function well. Indeed, it may be that the failure to understand how important the maintenance function is, the failure to understand how significant staff development is in serving that function, and the failure to accept maintenance as a legitimate staff development function all contribute to the crisis conditions to which staff development is frequently called upon to respond. This same condition may help to account for the fact, so often noted by critics, that staff development is often more concerned with remediation than with improvement.

If the maintenance function is concerned with stability, then both the enhancement and establishing functions are concerned with change. However, the target of the change is substantially different for each of these latter two functions. Enhancement centers attention on the individual's performance capacities. Criteria related to assessing personal and professional effectiveness are therefore the appropriate criteria for assessing the effects of enhancement-type activities. Establishing-oriented activities are, however, aimed at systems as well as individuals. It is certainly the case that the capacity of individuals to perform in ways indicated as desirable by the new technologies, procedures, or programs being introduced is a critical area of concern. Therefore, like enhancement activities, establishing activities are properly evaluated in terms of performance criteria. However, the use of performance criteria alone is not adequate. First, establishing new technologies, procedures, and programs necessarily requires that the structure of organizational arrangements and existing patterns of relationships be altered in ways that accommodate the innovation. Failure to take these contextual factors into account often leads to failure to implement change successfully.[31] Similarly, failure to take these contextual factors into account also flaws evaluation designs aimed at determining the effects and effectiveness of establishing-type programs. In addition, establishing-type programs are predicated on the assumption that if appropriate performance can be assured, and if the desired organizational changes occur, then the introduction of the new technologies, procedures, or programs will have a salutary effect on the ability of the organization to achieve one or more of its goals. Thus, a proper evaluation of an establishing-type program necessarily must attend to measures designed to assess the extent to which the introduction of the new technologies improved the capacity of the organization to pursue one or more of its goals. For example, if the purpose of introducing a reading skills management system is to improve student achievement in reading, then it is essential that the evaluation design attend to evidence regarding reading achievement.

In practice, evaluators frequently do not distinguish between programs that are enhancement-type activities and those that are establishing types. The results of this confusion are often detrimental. For example, enhancement-type programs are intended to improve the capacities of adults to perform in some predetermined way. A proper evaluation of the effectiveness of such a program must attend to the degree to which these predetermined performances are forthcoming. However, to attempt to evaluate the effects of an enhancement-type activity by assessing the effects of desired performance on others (for example, measuring the effectiveness of an in-school workshop by seeking evidence that students achieve more) is to confuse enhancement with establishment. It is quite possible that a training program could be very effective in causing teachers to behave in ways the program intended without the behaviors themselves having salutary effects on children. Indeed, it is conceivable that enhancement-type programs could have negative effects on children precisely because the knowledge transmitted and the skills developed were somehow flawed in their conception. For example, primitive tribes have very effective apprenticeship programs for aspiring witchdoctors. The ability of master witchdoctors to pass on intricate rituals and involved procedures with considerable fidelity and success is quite amazing. In some tribes, the more involved procedures have to do with intricate dance steps designed to bring rain. There can be little question that these dance steps are passed down very effectively from generation to generation. There is considerably more question, however, whether mastery of the dance steps makes one more effective in producing rain.

The point here is that it is conceptually possible to distinguish among criteria appropriate to assessing the effectiveness of a program in maintaining stability, criteria appropriate to measuring changes in the capacity of individuals to perform in desired ways, and criteria appropriate to assessing changes in the structure of organizations and the structure of relationships within organizations. It is also possible to identify criteria appropriate to assessing the relative effectiveness and efficiency with which organizations pursue goals. It is important to understand, however, that no one set of criteria is appropriate to evaluate the effects of all forms of continuing education. The choice of criteria and the complexity of that choice depend in large measure on the way one views the intended and unintended functions of job-oriented continuing education. The way one views job-oriented continuing education, furthermore, should be informed by both the goals that are used to legitimize the activity and the goals that give it direction.

Summary and Conclusions

The intent of this chapter has been to illuminate some of the ways in which system-level events and structures affect the operation of the continuing education of teachers and administrators. In the first section, attention was centered on issues related to goals and legitimacy. It was argued that the emphasis of schools on the education of children and the emphasis of continuing education on the education of adults create a situation in which the legitimacy of continuing education is always problematic.

In the second section, it was suggested that the way continuing education is related to the reward structure of schools encourages school systems to use continuing education for many reasons in addition to those reasons for which the programs are officially designed.

In the third section of this chapter, three functions of continuing education were distinguished: maintenance, enhancement, and establishing functions. It was suggested that the dubious legitimacy of continuing education, combined with the way continuing education is related to the reward structure, tends to encourage the use of continuing education primarily for maintenance purposes, even though the official functions of continuing education have more to do with the enhancement and establishing functions.

In the final section of this chapter, some of the implications of the analysis presented were discussed. If the analysis presented here is valid, it helps to explain why the literature so frequently makes reference to the fact that staff development in schools is piecemeal, disorganized, and lacking in consistent direction and thrust. It also helps to explain why so few efforts to introduce change in schools systematically have the desired effects,[32] especially when continuing education becomes the primary mechanism used to introduce such changes. Given the problematic legitimacy of continuing education in the context of schools and the way continuing education is related to the reward structure of schools, it is hardly surprising that most of the time, energy, and resources given over to supporting continuing education eventually come to serve maintenance functions rather than supporting change or enhancing performance. Given the pressure on schools to change (and thus the legitimacy of change efforts in schools), it is hardly surprising that staff developers are encouraged to legitimize their activity as primarily serving enhancing or establishing functions.

The most basic conclusion to be drawn from the analysis presented here is that as schools are now structured and as continuing education is now embedded in that structure, there is little likelihood that continuing education will develop the level of legitimacy required for it to be an effective force in producing desired change or enhancing the performance capacities of individuals. This is not to say that continuing education has never brought about change or that individuals are never enhanced by participation in such activity, for it has and they are. However, the history of the effective use of continuing education to introduce change and to enhance performance demonstrably contains many more examples of failure than of success. Furthermore, it is reasonable to speculate that in those situations in which there have been successes, it is likely that the continuing education effort has enjoyed a peculiar (that is, atypical) relationship to the reward structure of schools and to the power and authority system intended to coordinate action toward the primary goal of schools, the education of children.

If one accepts this conclusion, those who are concerned about improving staff development are confronted with an awesome task, for to improve the quality of the services delivered to schools through continuing education it would be necessary to restructure the reception system (that is, the schools) as well as the system of delivery. Such a change would involve reform in schools coupled with reform in teacher education. In the past, neither schools nor teacher education institutions have shown much capacity for effective change. Perhaps the reason is that one organization cannot be changed without fundamental changes in the other. For example, it may be unreasonable to expect teacher education institutions to recruit and train superior teachers if school systems are not prepared to reward those with superior talent in ways that differ from the present circumstance. On the other hand, there is likely to be little public support for more enriched rewards for teachers so long as there is evidence that graduates of too many teachers colleges come disproportionately from among the least able (academically and otherwise) of all college students.[33] Similarly, it may be unreasonable to expect many teachers to be other than calculative regarding their involvement in continuing education (for example, How much does it cost? How much inconvenience is involved? How much reading is involved?) unless they can be assured that if, in fact, their performance capacity is improved, they will be rewarded for it. On the other hand, it may be unreasonable to expect school systems to provide large enough rewards for differences in performance to make the threat of evaluation tolerable[34] until there is convincing evidence that it is possible systematically to produce teachers with demonstrably superior skills and that such teachers owe a part of their ability to perform to conditions other than "innate ability."

To address these issues, and similar ones, it will be necessary for public school systems, teacher organizations, and institutions of higher education to join together to create organizations that can legitimize job-oriented continuing education as a necessary concern of the public schools. At the same time, such organizations will need to foster the development of attitudes among teachers and administrators that support the systematic use of disciplined knowledge to guide and inform practice. Indeed, until public school practitioners come to value theory and research rather than disparage them,[35] and until more educational researchers directly link their efforts to the continuing education of teachers as well as to the routine problems of teaching, there is little chance the progressive knowledge assumed by the idea of continuing education will be sufficiently plentiful to justify large-scale continuing education.

There have been new developments in education, but it is doubtful that these developments are being produced at a rate that would sustain a high-quality continuing education program. Life-long professional learning depends on changes in the knowledge base upon which the professional proceeds as well as changes in the professional who makes use of that knowledge. Vital continuing education depends on vitality in the area of developmental research as well. Thus, it is imperative that educational researchers, teacher educators, and public school practitioners find ways of creating organizations that link research and continuing education as well as legitimizing continuing education as a singular responsibility of the organizations they create.

FOOTNOTES

1. The following discussion of goals and legitimacy owes much to a wide range of literature in the field of sociology, especially the literature in sociology of complex social organizations. Especially instructive were Charles Perrow, *Organizational Analysis: A Sociological View* (Belmont, Calif.: Wadsworth Publishing Co., 1970) and Sanford M. Dornbusch and W. Richard Scott, *Evaluation and the Exercise of Authority* (San Francisco: Jossey-Bass, 1975).

2. In sociology, there are two broad schools of thought regarding the proper study of organizations. One school of thought emphasizes the rational aspects of organizational behavior and is commonly referred to as the rational systems approach. The second approach, frequently referred to as the natural systems approach, gives more emphasis to what is referred to here as the sociologic of organizational life. In education, much of the work in school administration and in instructional design has been based upon a rational systems approach, especially the normative literature. For example, management by objectives is predicated upon the assumption that schools can or should work in ways suggested by deductive logic. Classroom instructional models that give emphasis to behavioral objectives and the assessment of learning in terms of predetermined outcomes are also based upon assumptions that parallel rational systems models in education.

Much of the rationalists' thinking underlying conceptions of management in schools derives, of course, from classical literature in American industrial management. Persons interested in the design and implementation of staff development programs would be well advised to consider management thought emanating from Japanese models. See, for example, Richard T. Pascale and Anthony G. Athos, *The Art of Japanese Management* (New York: Simon and Schuster, 1981), for these models are more clearly attuned to what we have labeled as the sociologic of organizational life.

3. The recent emphasis of educational researchers on the development of grounded theory and the growing preference for naturalistic research as opposed to experimentally designed research are informed by the same kinds of considerations that are of concern to sociologists who study organizations from a natural systems perspective. However,

many sociologists who use a natural systems approach to the study of organizations would argue that it is possible to approach such study from a predetermined theoretical framework and to seek explanations in terms of that framework as well as to approach the study from a grounded theory perspective. Our own position is that a preference for grounded theory (which we share) is no excuse for being theoretically ungrounded. Therefore, much of our discussion is informed by classic sociological theory even though many of the examples we provide were developed employing techniques with which many grounded theorists would find themselves comfortable.

4. Perrow, *Organizational Analysis.*

5. Phillip C. Schlechty, Deane Crowell, Betty L. Whitford, Anne W. Joslin, Victor S. Vance, George W. Noblit, and W. I. Burke, *The Organization and Management of Staff Development in a Large City School System: A Case Study* (Chapel Hill, N.C.: University of North Carolina at Chapel Hill, 1982). This study, funded by the National Institute of Education, was conducted with the support and cooperation of the Metrolina Education Consortium, Charlotte-Mecklenburg Schools, North Carolina, 1979-1982.

6. Ibid.

7. Ibid.

8. Ibid.

9. Frederick J. McDonald, "Criteria and Methods for Evaluating In-service Training Programs," in *Issues in In-service Education* (Syracuse: National Council of States on In-service Education, 1977): 69.

10. Rita Hodgkins et al., *Continuing Education for Teachers: A Framework for New Practices* (Washington, D.C.: National Education Association, 1980).

11. McDonald, "Criteria and Methods for Evaluating In-service Training Programs."

12. Ronald G. Corwin, *Reform and Organizational Survival: The Teacher Corps as an Instrument of Educational Change* (New York: John Wiley and Sons, 1973).

13. There are several promising suggestions in the literature regarding the forms such organizations might take. There are also some encouraging real life models that deserve serious attention. For example, see B. Othanel Smith, "Pedagogical Education: How About Reform?" *Phi Delta Kappan* 62 (October 1980): 87-91, and Phillip C. Schlechty, Julius R. George, and Betty Lou Whitford, "Reform in Teacher Education and the Professionalization of Teaching," *High School Journal* 61 (April 1978): 313-20. One existing model that is at least an effort in the direction suggested here is presently operating in Prince Georges County, Maryland. Another model is operating in Charlotte, North Carolina, and is described in *The Metrolina Education Consortium Program Planning Handbook* (Charlotte, N.C.: Charlotte-Mecklenburg Schools, 1981).

14. Phillip C. Schlechty, *Teaching and Social Behavior* (Boston: Allyn and Bacon, 1976).

15. See Robert Dreeben, *On the Nature of Teaching: Schools and the Work of Teaching* (Glenview, Ill.: Scott, Foresman and Co., 1970) and Dan C. Lortie, *Schoolteacher* (Chicago: University of Chicago Press, 1975).

16. See Schlechty et al., *The Organization and Management of Staff Development in a Large City School System*; Betty Lou Whitford, "Change and the Effects of Organizational Context: A Case Study" (Doct. Diss., University of North Carolina at Chapel Hill, 1981); and Anne W. Joslin, "The Effect of School Context on the Implementation of an Innovation: A Case Study" (Doct. Diss., University of North Carolina at Chapel Hill, 1981).

17. Schlechty et al., *The Organization and Management of Staff Development in a Large City School System.*

18. See, for example, *New York Times*, September 7, 1980, Section 12, p. 1.

19. McDonald, "Criteria and Methods for Evaluating In-service Training Programs."

20. Schlechty et al., *The Organization and Management of Staff Development in a Large City School System.*

21. Ibid.

22. Ibid.

23. Ibid.

24. See, for example, Seymour B. Sarason, *The Culture of the School and the Problem of Change* (Boston: Allyn and Bacon, 1971), and Robert E. Herriott and Neal Gross, eds., *The Dynamics of Planned Educational Change* (Berkeley: McCutchan Publishing Corp., 1979).

25. Corwin, *Reform and Organizational Survival.*

26. See Dreeben, *On the Nature of Teaching*; Schlechty et al., "Reform in Teacher Education and the Professionalization of Teaching"; David L. Clark and Gerald W. Marker, "The Institutionalization of Teacher Education," in *Teacher Education*, Seventy-fourth Yearbook of the National Society for the Study of Education, Part 2, ed. Kevin Ryan (Chicago: University of Chicago Press, 1975), pp. 53-86; and McDonald, "Criteria and Methods for Evaluating In-service Training Programs."

27. Hodgkins et al., *Continuing Education for Teachers.*

28. Donald R. Moore and Arthur A. Hyde, *An Analysis of Staff Development Programs and Their Costs in Three Urban School Districts* (Chicago: Designs for Change, January, 1980).

29. H. G. Vonk and Robert G. Brown, "The External Doctorate in Education: Growing Criticism and Crisis," *Phi Delta Kappan* 60 (November 1978): 176-79; Peter Cowden and Frederick Jacobs, "The External Degree and the Traditions of Diversity and Competition," *Phi Delta Kappan* 60 (April 1978): 559-61; H. G. Vonk and Robert G. Brown, "A Diller, A Dollar, A Saturday Scholar," *Phi Delta Kappan* 60 (April 1978): 570-72; and Gene I. Maeroff, "College Without Walls," *New York Times*, February 4, 1979, p. E9.

30. See Robert K. Merton, *Social Theory and Social Structure* (New York: Free Press, 1968).

31. For examples, see Neal Gross, Joseph B. Giacquinta, and Marilyn Bernstein, *Implementing Organizational Innovations* (New York: Basic Books, 1971) and Joslin, "The Effect of School Context on the Implementation of an Innovation."

32. Herriott and Gross, *The Dynamics of Planned Educational Change.*

33. W. Timothy Weaver, "In Search of Quality: The Need for Talent in Teaching," *Phi Delta Kappan* 61 (September 1979): 29-32, 46.

34. Teacher resistance to performance-based evaluations as a basis of pay differences (merit pay) is based on a number of factors. The most obvious, of course, is that few teachers believe administrators would be objective in evaluations and they are not convinced peer evaluations would be any more effective. There is, in addition, another reason to resist performance evaluations and merit pay. Most proposals for merit pay are based on such miniscule salary differences ($25 to $500 per year) that one has little to gain from a positive evaluation and one is rightly insulted by a negative evaluation.

35. See Lortie, *Schoolteacher.*

CHAPTER V

Current Patterns of Staff Development

KENNETH R. HOWEY AND JOSEPH C. VAUGHAN

The Historical Context

Staff development did not play an important role in the life of schools in the early stages of public education in this country. Until and throughout most of the nineteenth century, the relatively minimal preservice education provided by normal schools first and later by teachers' colleges and other institutions of higher education was viewed as sufficient to provide the knowledge and skills necessary to sustain professional staff throughout their careers. This was due in large part to the fact that technological or other advancements in knowledge were minimal and the rather narrow emphasis in the schools on the acquisition of basic skills and citizenship necessitated little change over time in teaching practice, or so it was perceived.[1] For the most part, schools were viewed favorably by the general public and there was little conflict over their mission as guardians of existing social, cultural, and occupational norms. Although it may be overstating reality to suggest that educators were "one big happy family," it is interesting to note that the original membership of the National Education Association, founded in 1870, contained not only teachers, but teacher educators, principals, and superintendents under one umbrella organization. It was not until almost the middle of this century that separate organizations were created to represent what by then had come to be the divergent and sometimes conflicting interests of these and other educational constituencies.[2]

While the scientific and technological advances of the late nineteenth and early twentieth century introduced much new content into our schools, instruction in basic skills remained at the core of the

schools' mission and staff development consisted mainly of introducing new information to staff while maintaining much the same
pedagogical practices. Even with the advent of new educational
theories, such as those espoused by Dewey in the early twentieth
century, most teacher education activities, whether preservice or in-
service, focused on dispensing information *about* these theories rather
than using them as a mode for teacher education or modelling their
application in elementary and secondary school classrooms. In fact,
there was little systematic study of what teachers actually did and,
therefore, little organized knowledge upon which to base rationally
organized preservice or in-service programs to address their pedagogical needs.

Probably the first comprehensive study of teachers' activities was
the Commonwealth Teacher Training Study in 1929. That study and
a survey of practices in teacher education by the U. S. Office of
Education in 1933 were key first steps in the generation of knowledge
but they were neither intended to nor did they bring about changes in
practices in teacher education. This rather undisturbed state of education was, however, torn asunder by the Depression and the emergence
of a diversity of radical ideologies that confronted society in general
and schools in particular.[3] For perhaps the first time, the rather
sheltered existence of schools and teachers was changed drastically and
the roles of teachers were enlarged to the extent that social, cultural,
economic, political, and other factors became more highly visible parts
of their lives.

An obvious means to introduce this new "knowledge" and show
teachers how to work with that knowledge in practice was staff
development activities. This is not to say that staff development
became a massive movement of the post-Depression era but, rather, to
note this as a basic point of demarcation where teachers and other
educational staff were being asked to participate in new roles and
schools were forced to expand their missions to explain and combat or
defend social and political views that had previously been of little
concern. Thus a precedent was established. Education was no longer
the relatively tranquil arena it had been for so long. The changes in
society were much more evident and staff development took on new
potential significance as one process for responding to that change in
schools.

Once the precedent was established, schools and school staffs were increasingly called to change as new crises emerged. The decision in *Brown vs. Board of Education of Topeka* in 1954 introduced harsh social realities into the school and classroom and to educational personnel ill-prepared to address them. After the launching of Sputnik in 1956, the cry for an upgrading of mathematics and science curricula led to major emphases in those areas and accompanying massive staff development programs (for example, the NDEA summer programs for teachers). Throughout the 1960s and 1970s, social and political activism created an even stronger need for awareness of cultural diversity and interpersonal relations that schools attempted to meet through training in human relations and similar activities under the banner of staff development.

Incidental to those changes but crucial to the expansion of staff development activities was the practice of tying both salary increments and, in more recent years, various forms of continuing certification to the completion of postbachelor credits, usually in the form of graduate work. Another common pattern was for teachers to pursue in-service work in a district program that had received state department of education approval as an alternative or complement to graduate courses. Finally, the influence of teachers' organizations in demanding and gaining a voice through collective bargaining in the design and implementation of in-service activities has brought new emphasis to this activity.

The Present Situation in Schools

All of this comes together less than harmoniously with present realities such as public dissatisfaction with perceived declines in test scores, increasing discipline problems in the schools, perceptions of lowered teacher competence among beginning and experienced teachers, and an aging teaching force. There are expanding demands on schools in such areas as mainstreaming, desegregation, and bilingual education and, at the same time, declining fiscal resources with which to address these demands. Symptoms of these conditions of conflict are found in the heightened sense of competitive rather than cooperative relationships, in many instances between teachers and administrators as well as between educational professionals and the general public. Other overt manifestations of the fiscal stress (reductions in the teaching force, diminished aid and resources, and enlarged class sizes) only serve to compound the situation.

It should also be noted that the volatile economy that is with us for the short term, at the very least, provides a residue of problems for schools. Not the least of these will be the broadened expectations noted above. Even the most restrictive "back-to-basics" orientation cannot remain oblivious to the growing problems laid at the doorsteps of schools because they have not been reconciled elsewhere. Additional financial resources to address these problems in places other than schools seem highly unlikely. The tension produced by these increased demands and the way in which they are responded to will have a great deal to say about the shape and manner of future staff development. This is a critical point in discussing contemporary staff development patterns. Shifts in expectations of schools have been dramatic over the past three decades.

The situation of being asked to do more with less in our schools presents several alternative courses of action. First, schools could carry on largely as they now do but with an increasingly obvious limp. Second, they could increasingly accommodate special or categorical needs. For example, extended-day and extended-year concepts could become more common as efforts to respond to special needs, perhaps on a pay-as-you-go basis. Third, they could say "no" to many demands, revise present curricula, and more clearly define the limits of public schooling. One strong possibility, already a trend in the 1980s, may be that while the dialogue about the mission of schools will be sharpened, the school curriculum may demonstrate new dimensions of elasticity, and unfortunately superficiality, in response to increasing demands.

The projection here, if that possibility comes to be, is that the most common response will be the need to see the task of teaching, especially at the elementary level, as a more collaborative and complementary endeavor than it is at present. The increasing realization that a single teacher simply cannot be all things to all people will likely forge more cooperative teaching arrangements within schools. The limited support for educational and social services will lead, in many urban communities especially, to a closer working relationship between schools and other youth service agencies and to a clearer delineation of responsibilities. In considering the implications of this possibility, one could suggest the following about staff development in the future: (a) it will increasingly become an endeavor pursued in relatively small working groups to focus on more specific needs; (b) it will increasingly focus on teachers becoming more expert in fewer domains; and (c) it is likely to be viewed increasingly (and eventually validated) as a rather natural and common form of cooperative functioning that can be embedded in the job, that is, *joint problem solving, curriculum development, and structured collegial observation and feedback within the school context.*

In summary, it is not suggested that current and common modes of in-service work targeted for larger groups of individual teachers who largely teach independently of one another or activities concerned with an entire school faculty cannot be helpful and will not continue. Indeed they will. It is suggested, however, that a positive consequence of the present difficult times and those envisioned for the immediate future may well be a growing rejection of normative "band-aid" and general tactics. Such efforts will increasingly be viewed as unacceptable when compared with the magnitude of the challenges and there is likely to be a discernible evolution to more continuing, cooperative, and on-the-job forms of staff development.

The Nature of Staff Development Today

Considering the realities and possibilities cited above, let us look at the scope and nature of staff development as it exists today. First, it is important to understand that the magnitude of the staff development enterprise in schools in the United States may well be underestimated. For example, a recent study of three urban school districts, with high, medium, and low reported levels of staff development activity, showed expenditures attributable to staff development ranging from $1000 to $1700 per teacher per year. These were not all recognized as staff development costs by the districts and, in fact, exceeded their estimates of such expenditures by fifty to sixty times. It was found that many expenditures difficult to estimate in terms of specific dollar figures (for example, time of administrators, teachers, and substitute teachers; salary increments attributable to staff development; costs of district-sponsored courses) were being used in a very fragmented and uncoordinated fashion.[4] School, district, state, and federal program efforts were going on concurrently with little if any sense of how one related to another or how they fit into any type of overall plan. On a national scale, recent survey results indicate that there is perhaps one person with some staff development responsibility in the educational enterprise for every seven teachers.[5] Although these persons may not provide direct staff development, their job descriptions suggest some responsibility for this activity and also suggest that even in more difficult times there is no lack of personnel resources with which to address the situation.

Since there appear to be considerable resources available for staff development, can one assume that such activities are a frequent and continuing part of the lives of teachers and other staff members? Interestingly, the national survey already noted indicates quite the opposite. Teachers invariably reported that they participated in relatively small amounts of staff development during the course of the preceding school year. The great majority reported that they engaged in various forms of staff development not more than once a year, although they reported that staff development generally was either an excellent or a good idea. Perhaps even more revealing were the perceptions of teachers, administrators, teacher educators, and the general community regarding the quality of staff development in schools. Only 25 percent felt it was in good or excellent health, while 30 percent saw it as less than adequate or poor and the remaining 45 percent were but lukewarm in their assessments. It should be underscored that just as there is considerable variation from one school to another in this large and diverse country, there is also considerable variation in staff development practices. There are exemplary practices and there is considerable wasteland.

Perhaps most devastating, the "evidence" that staff developers have about the effectiveness of their programs is anecdotal in most cases; it is based on measures of participant satisfaction and not on degree of changed teacher behavior or increased student learning. What emerges then is a not so pleasant picture of a potentially well-supported (in terms of resources) enterprise that is fragmented, not frequently engaged in on a continuing basis by practitioners, not regarded very highly as it is practiced, and rarely assessed in terms of teacher behavior and student learning outcomes.

Moreover, persons who are responsible for organizing and implementing staff development activities are frequently doing so only on a part-time basis, as they typically have other major responsibilities[6] and have received little special training for their role in staff development. There are practically no higher education offerings aimed at improving personnel responsible for staff development. While it is recognized that personnel both internal and external to the school can be helpful in various ways, there is ample evidence that external personnel are perceived as less able to provide necessary job and site-specific forms of help.[7] However, internal school personnel are infrequently given training to aid them in their responsibilities for staff development and only recently have we even begun to investigate systematically what seems to comprise effective characteristics and behaviors of staff developers.[8]

In examining why staff development is in its present situation, frequently cited criticisms can probably be placed within the following general statements:

1. Classroom-relevant content and easily adaptable instructional strategies are too infrequently presented. Instructional content and practices are often espoused that do not adequately take into account the specific student, school, or classroom context of the participants.

2. Little continuity and coordination exists between or among staff development offerings and it is difficult if not impossible for participants to see how apparently unrelated in-service activities will in any basic way allow them to do a more effective job of helping their students learn. The issue of whether or not staff development is actually intended for the primary purpose of improving teaching and student learning or for a more complex set of purposes is considered by Schlechty and Whitford in chapter 4 of this volume.

3. In-service activities are infrequently related to measures of changed teacher behaviors or student learning outcomes and so teachers rarely receive feedback or are aware of whether or not the in-service program has made any difference in those crucial outcome measures. In most cases, classroom follow-up is nonexistent in staff development activities. Without the incentives of a comprehensive and well-conceived in-service effort targeted toward really making a difference in the lives of teachers and students, teachers are not likely to commit their energies to authentic involvement. These shortcomings are frequently cited as reasons for having staff development participants, whether they are teachers or other personnel, integrally

involved in the planning and implementation of activities from their inception. While there are logical and political (through teachers' organizations) reasons for such participation by teachers, the psychological underpinning provided by responsible and accountable involvement should not be underestimated as a significant reason for teacher involvement.

4. Staff development is often presented and perceived as a way to correct a deficit rather than as a normal growth experience. Also, little attention is paid to the preferences in learning style or stage of development of the educational staff member. Thus, we have the situation where the teachers or other staff participants are not only under suspicion by the public as not doing their jobs adequately but they are also often mandated to participate in an in-service program of an externally determined nature which does not adequately consider the individual's present skills or knowledge. Despite recent attempts to consider adult stages of development,[9] and individual attitudes and behaviors toward a particular desired in-service focus,[10] the norm in structuring appropriate staff development activities continues to be a largely deficit, undifferentiated group approach.

5. Too many times the in-service activity focuses solely on the teacher as the responsible party for improving instruction without sufficient attention to other organizational, social, and political factors in the school and school community. There are many other factors that bear on the instructional process. Yet the teacher is often treated as an isolated influence on instruction. There is little consideration of the teacher's interaction with other teachers, principals, aides, and parents. Moreover, the support systems, which recent research tells us play such an important role in determining instructional effectiveness, are often ignored or inadequately addressed in staff development plans. Thus participants frequently leave staff development activities with a false impression of their own independent importance in determining instructional practices and become increasingly frustrated and disillusioned when that independent action is insufficient to accomplish the intended outcome.[11]

Perhaps the major general criticism that can be levelled at staff development today is one that many participants would not articulate or perhaps even be aware of. This criticism has to do with the fact that much current staff development does not take into consideration the increased knowledge we now have about effective teaching and, to a lesser extent, effective staff development. This leads us to a discussion of what we *do* know.

Empirical and Theoretical Bases for Improving Staff Development

Despite the inadequacies that can be enumerated with regard to the conduct of staff development today, we do have a knowledge base to provide direction for more effective practices. Discussion of theoretical and empirical underpinnings for staff development is provided in considerable detail elsewhere in this volume. However, we feel it imperative to provide here a brief overview of the factors that we believe should be considered in thinking through major issues. We shall point out some of the recent investigations that bear on those factors and attempt to cue the reader to sources of information that we view as crucial to the improvement of staff development.

As stated above, perhaps the most serious criticism that could be levelled at staff development today is that it generally fails to consider much of what we have learned about effective teaching and, to a lesser extent, what we have learned about the content and processes of effective staff development.

The considerable research results on the teaching of basic skills at the elementary level provide one example. Even though there are consistent research findings that point to patterns of teaching behaviors that are effective in increasing student learning in elementary reading and mathematics, we would contend that the vast majority of in-service offerings (or preservice courses, for that matter) do not utilize those results as the content or even part of the content that is offered teachers. Ironically, this situation often exists when those responsible for planning and implementing the staff development are attempting to be responsive to the expressed needs of the participants. If neither the staff developers nor the participants are knowledgeable about the current knowledge base on effective teaching in a given area, they can end up being "successful" in terms of responding to an expressed need but, in fact, suggesting instructional techniques inappropriate for inducing desired student learning. In short, steps must be taken to ensure that participant or provider "needs" are not just "wants" but are supportable by the available knowledge base as being conducive to effective instruction.

There are many sources to which staff development planners can turn for information on effective teaching techniques as the *content* of staff development. A reasonable place to begin might be the examination of the results of the Beginning Teacher Evaluation Study (BTES), a comprehensive multiyear study of second- and fifth-grade reading and mathematics. The BTES served in many ways as a forerunner of subsequent studies using variations on the BTES methodologies to replicate the work and expand the investigations to other grade levels, types of students, and subject areas. The BTES is also an example of a study that incorporated the crucial dissemination phase of translating the findings into a form that could be of practical use to educational practitioners. *Time to Learn*, a volume containing a summary of the BTES research procedures and findings (and a comparison of results with those found in other related research), also contains separate chapters written by a teacher, principal, university teacher educator, school staff developer, and others who discuss the practical and policy implications of this research.[12] There are also other useful summaries of the research findings on effective instruction in the basic skills in the elementary grades,[13] as well as an evolving set of studies that extend this work to the junior high level.[14] Virtually all of these works focus on the importance of the teacher as manager of instruction and on what the teacher can do in planning and implementing classroom instructional activities more effectively.

A growing number of research activities are also concerned with factors external to the classroom that influence the nature of instruction. These works run the gamut from examining the entire ecosystem of a school[15] to assessing the role of the principal as a facilitator of conditions conducive to effective instruction.[16] They constitute a valuable and essential complement to the "process-product" research on effective teaching as content considerations for staff development activities.

While there is less of a "hard" base of evidence about effective staff development *processes*, there is no lack of theoretical bases around which one may begin to conceptualize designs. In a few instances, some of the above referenced researchers have gone on to test experimentally the possibility of using the results of research on effective teaching as the basis for in-service programs. Examples are seen in the work of Stallings,[17] Good and Grouws,[18] and Anderson,

Evertson, and Brophy,[19] all of whom have been successful in documenting both changes in teacher behaviors and enhanced student outcomes.

There is also an emerging body of knowledge relative to the importance of individual and group attitudes about current use of "innovations" that are the content of staff development activities. The basic premise is that it is crucial for the staff developer (or person introducing an innovation) to know where the participants (or "users") are in terms of their feelings and present usage in order to match better the content (innovation) with existing individual, group, and contextual conditions.[20] The central point is that the content must be considered within the context of local policy and practice as well as staff attitudes about and use of the content being proposed.

Much more activity exists in what we are calling explorations of the rational bases for staff development. Theory building evolving out of rich and comprehensive descriptions and analyses of present practice and outcomes is one such exploration. While such activity requires subjective judgments about the meaning of events and outcomes, it provides us with a way to propose alternative staff development processes that can be tested in a quasi-experimental or experimental fashion. These explorations also require that we carefully examine research and theoretical work from sectors outside education that have analyzed human functioning and interaction within social organizations and to compare and contrast these analyses with what we know about what happens in our schools. In pursuing this line of reasoning, one obvious aim is to learn more about what may comprise effective staff development processes.

A second crucial aim is to gain necessary insights into the logical "next-steps" of how to follow through on staff development activities with the appropriate supportive actions and structures to ensure maximally effective adoption or adaptation of acquired knowledge, skills, attitudes, and behaviors in existing or modified school and classroom contexts. The contextual influences of the individual, school, and school system are addressed in the three previous chapters in this volume. Our intent here is to reemphasize how important such considerations are to any thinking about effective staff development.

With respect to the specific issue of what comprises our rational and theoretical bases for determining effective staff development processes, there are additional sources to which one could turn for guidance. Valuable works by Edelfelt and Lawrence,[21] Joyce and Showers,[22] and others have examined what were admittedly incomplete reports of prior research and evaluation and have proposed frameworks within which effective staff development could be structured. Several other recent volumes are collections of various perspectives on the "best thinking" about effective practices and range from topics such as the interaction of staff development with organizational development[23] and other contextual factors to how to go about evaluating whether or not a particular proposal has reasonable potential for succeeding in both accomplishing its objectives and having those objectives make a worthwhile contribution to the sponsoring agency.[24] One other invaluable resource is the document resulting from a National Institute of Education conference in 1982 on synthesizing research results from the last decade on topics including staff development, effective schools, instructional management, teacher selection, recruitment and conditions of employment, classroom organization, teacher decision making, and innovation and instructional technology in the classroom.[25]

We have only briefly mentioned key sources of information relative to what we know or theorize about staff development today. Specific research projects are also beginning to yield preliminary results on the behaviors exhibited by staff developers that are perceived as effective, the extent to which we may be able to reinforce and develop those behaviors as a means to improve staff development,[26] and the role "coaching" can play as a part of in-service training.[27] While research will never provide answers to all the questions about or provide remedies for all the issues that surround staff development activities, we have begun to build a substantive knowledge base. This knowledge base is being developed across a wide range of topics and disciplines rather than simply focusing solely on the process of staff development.

Some Evolving Principles of Effective Staff Development

While it is not our task to review and discuss in any detail the findings and implications of all studies related to or concerned with staff development, we feel it appropriate to identify principles that have emerged from this work that should be useful as one thinks through the implications of alternative designs for staff development. These principles are not meant to be all-inclusive. Others could be reasonably proposed, as well as modifications of those we present here. Our intent is merely to review some of the more crucial factors to be considered in designing and implementing effective staff development and understanding their impact. On the basis of our interpretation of available evidence, we propose the following:

1. *Interactiveness.* Staff development must be considered in terms of how it interacts with other sets of mediating variables such as factors related to adult development and learning, social norms in schools, organizational and managerial patterns, and rewards and incentives. Pedagogical change must be understood as an interactive function dependent upon corollary changes of both a personal and socio-organizational nature.

2. *Comprehensiveness.* Clear conceptualization and delineation of the why, where, when, and how, as well as the what of staff development is essential. This refers to the need to consider the place of an individual activity in some overall plan toward accomplishment of specified objectives. Planners, participants, and providers must all be cognizant of this "bigger picture."

3. *Continuity.* Staff development must be viewed as an incremental process requiring reinforcement through continuing follow-up and feedback. One-time activities are not effective in changing teacher behaviors.

4. *Potency.* This includes the need for both relevance and practicability. Participants must be able to see or be convinced of the power of staff development to make a significant difference in a matter of personal or professional importance to them. They must also be convinced that adoption or adaptation of acquired behaviors, skills, attitudes, or knowledge in the school and classroom will not result in loss or reduction of something more important to them.

5. *Provision of support structures and personnel.* Related to success in all the other considerations discussed in this section is the necessity of providing appropriate support to counteract the individual isolation and programmatic fragmentation that often exists in schools. These support mechanisms should provide visible evidence to participants of the commitment of the school or the school district to accomplishment of the objectives for staff development.

6. *Documentation.* In order to make valid judgments about the impact and viability of any staff development effort it is essential that provisions be made to document thoroughly the planning, implementation, and outcomes of all activities. Outcome measures must include measures of changed teacher or other staff behavior and, to the extent possible, must be considered in view of outcomes in students' learning.

Some Operational Examples of "Successful" Staff Development

We have discussed major problems associated with staff development and have also examined some of the sources of information and resultant principles available to us on how to go about improving present practices. Are there schools or school districts that have already begun to address these problems and have applied sound and defensible principles in designing their staff development efforts? We believe so, and we also believe that it is important to describe what they have done in order to show that the search for improvement is not a futile quest. Their efforts suggest that the problems are not of such magnitude that they cannot be overcome. One of the issues that must be confronted here is that of the criteria by which "success" can be judged. In the first case we describe, a research project was the source of information. That research applied the criteria of student academic achievement, student attendance and program completion (not dropping out of school), and community support as measures of success. Schools were rated as more or less successful and compared also on the basis of high or low staff development activity. The description presented deals with the nature of staff development, the contextual conditions in schools that were rated as more successful, and how these practices and conditions differed from those in the less successful schools. All schools studied were in an urban school system under recent court-ordered desegregation.

The other three descriptions are not presented with the same type of supportive research data. They are, nonetheless, seen as "successful" by virtue of their coherence in terms of employing empirically supported principles such as those enunciated earlier and the positive regard given to those principles by participants in the programs. Participant involvement and support is strong and the programs are consistently rated highly in evaluations. To varying degrees, they also have forms of outcome data that they utilize in designing and revising their efforts. The truth is that very few, if any, programs have conclusive evidence of the impact of their efforts on changing teacher and other staff behavior or increasing student learning. One legitimate reason for this is that no appropriate and feasible methodology exists for exact tracking of these relationships on any large scale. Those who have done it have done so on a limited basis with tight experimental controls and at a relatively high cost. The development of this methodology is certainly a high priority need for the future but that does not mean that we must wait for that methodology before making some interim judgments based on the experience of wise practitioners and whatever research data are available. That is what we feel we are doing in presenting the following descriptions. The diverse approaches employed, the rational soundness of these approaches, and the excellent local and national reputations they enjoy seem to us to be reasonable substitutes for what would admittedly be preferable data about teacher and student change and growth. Thus, these descriptions are presented not as unequivocal examples of effective staff development but as examples of programs that have gone beyond the typical activities to incorporate what appear to be desirable practices.

CHARACTERISTICS OF SUCCESSFUL STAFF DEVELOPMENT PROGRAMS
IN URBAN DESEGREGATED SCHOOLS

The first description comes from a research project sponsored by the National Institute of Education. Data were obtained through nineteen weeks of interviews, observations, and document reviews in the "successful" schools.[28] Little (the principal investigator) described the school as a workplace, going beyond a presentation of discrete activities. Basically, she found that in the more effective schools there were norms of collegiality and continuous improvement among faculty and administrators. "Collegiality" was defined as expectations and structures for shared work and shared responsibility, while "continuous improvement" was seen as expectations and structures for rather normative analysis, evaluation, and experimentation within the schools. Little discusses the manifestation of these norms in terms of teacher and principal behaviors and interactions.

The following, excerpted from one of the project reports, describes three critical elements (work relationships, the role of the principal, and the nature of district staff development) that seemed to differentiate the more successful schools from the less successful:

First, successful schools were distinguished by certain kinds of work relationships among teachers and between teachers and administrators. In those successful, adaptable schools, staff were more likely to engage in four "critical practices" in their work with one another; school improvement is most surely and thoroughly achieved when:

a. Teachers engage in frequent, continuous, and increasingly concrete and precise talk about teaching practice (as distinct from teacher characteristics and failings, the social lives of teachers, the foibles and failures of students and their families, and the unfortunate demands of society on the school). By such talk, teachers build up a shared language adequate to the complexity of teaching, capable of distinguishing one practice and its virtues from another, and capable of integrating large bodies of practice into distinct and sensible perspectives on the business of teaching. Other things being equal, the utility of collegial work and the rigor of experimentation with teaching is a direct function of the concreteness, precision, and coherence of the shared language.

b. Teachers and administrators frequently observe teaching, and provide each other with useful (if potentially frightening) evaluations of their teaching. Only such observation and feedback can provide shared referents for the shared language of teaching, and both demand and provide the precision and concreteness which makes the talk about teaching useful.

c. Teachers and administrators plan, design, research, evaluate, and prepare teaching materials together. The most prescient observations remain academic ("just theory") without the machinery to act on them. By joint work on materials, teachers and administrators share the considerable burden of development required by long-term improvement, confirm their emerging understanding of their approach, and make rising standards for their work attainable by them and by their students.

d. Teachers and administrators teach each other the practice of teaching. In the most adaptable schools, most staff, at one time or another, on some topic or task, will be permitted and encouraged to play the role of instructor for others. In this way, the school makes maximum use of its own resources.

Second, these work relationships were in certain powerful ways influenced by the perspectives and practices of the principal. Principals were able to stimulate or strengthen teachers' participation in collegial work or their commitment to the careful scrutiny and improvement of practice by:

a. *Announcing and describing* expectations for collegial and experimental work, particularly at important occasions such as the first staff meeting at the beginning of the year, then frequently and on various occasions thereafter to confirm and specify the desired interactions among teachers. The principal must imagine the desired behavior, then describe it concretely as the principal's expectations for life in the school.

b. *Modeling or enacting* the desired behavior, by asking staff for evaluation of the principal's performance, by providing useful, concrete observations of classes, by seeking out teachers to talk about practice, by contributing to the preparation of materials, by giving time while asking for time.

c. *Sanctioning* the announced and modeled behavior in the allocation of resources such as released time, in required or formal evaluations of teacher performance, by visible and public praise for collegial or experimental efforts, by tolerating and absorbing inevitable failures encountered in experimentation, and so on.

d. *Defending* the norms thus established from countermovements within the school and from impositions from outside the school, from parents, the district, and others. Courage is likely to be crucial to this defense. Equally important, and more malleable, is skill in translation and reconciliation which deflects some blows, softens others, and negates yet others by finding commonalities of interest and intent among presumably opposing demands.

Third, district-sponsored programs of staff development have been most influential where they have combined a "good idea" (content that reflects the strongest of current theory and research on instruction) with an approach that deliberately and consistently fosters precisely the kinds of staff working relationships described above. Staff development that is collaborative introduces habits of shared work on the improvement of practice; staff development that is school-based and that engages teams or groups of staff in learning and testing a set of ideas builds commitment to the stringent examination of practice; and staff development that is staged over time (a year or more) permits the progressive, cumulative development of understanding, skill, and confidence and builds staff commitment to continuous improvement.[29]

Clearly, the specific administrator-staff relationships that exist in these school *buildings* go beyond what is generally found in a vast majority of settings. Next we look at how several school *districts* have structured exemplary staff development efforts.

STAFF DEVELOPMENT IN MONTGOMERY COUNTY (MD.) SCHOOLS

The program in Montgomery County (Md.) exemplifies a comprehensive and coherent approach. Growth activities are provided not only for teachers but also for administrators, support staff, and civil service personnel. Staff development is related to explicit performance expectations for persons in each role category. Multiple forms of diagnosis and assessment ranging from self-report inventories to pupils' test scores and observations of performance are utilized in developing interrelated goals for (a) the district, (b) each school, and (c) each individual. A key facet of the Montgomery County program is a teacher competency training program comprised of a related series of courses that focus upon specific skill development. Design components for these training sequences include an empirically based rationale, explicit assumptions undergirding the goals and activities, explicit outcome objectives, multiple resources, and an annotated bibliography. Demonstration teachers are also employed in developing model videotapes to be employed in the training. Teachers are selected and trained to serve as instructors in specific programs based upon the quality of their own teaching, their competence as students when they participated in the staff development activity, and their willingness and ability to work with their peers.

The teacher competency program is but one of several options available to teachers in Montgomery County, but it illustrates well several attributes of staff development found to be effective by teachers and school-based teacher educators. The emphasis on skill development (derived from observation of job performance); the opportunity for demonstration, then controlled practice with eventual classroom application, and the involvement of teachers in all aspects of the process are but three of these principles that guide the efforts in Montgomery County.

STAFF DEVELOPMENT IN LINCOLN (NEB.) SCHOOLS

The Lincoln (Neb.) Public School Staff Development Program is another example of a comprehensive and systematically planned effort that interrelates individual, school, and district goals. These goals are developed and priorities set in order to promote teacher growth on a long-range, consistent, and incremental basis as opposed to a short-term, crisis-intervention approach. There have been multiple efforts in Lincoln to analyze learning styles and individual developmental patterns. At the same time, organizational development strategies are commonly employed in an effort to examine systematically the effects of district and school structures, norms, and policies on teacher growth. Thus, each of three interacting dimensions—patterns of adult growth, dimensions of organizational functioning, as well as teacher education or pedagogical strategies—are reflected in the Lincoln scheme.

Perhaps one of the most unique features of the Lincoln approach is the multiple ways in which teachers are involved in all facets of staff development. A Helping Teaching Cadre is one example of this. In this scheme, highly qualified teachers are selected each year and prepared to assume leadership roles. These teachers still have a teaching assignment but are released from some responsibilities each week to work with their colleagues. The selection criteria and temporary nature of the assignment have contributed considerably to the credibility of these persons in this role. It also provides different teachers a new and challenging opportunity each year. At any given time up to 100 teachers in the Lincoln District are engaged in staff development responsibilities.

The Lincoln approach is especially noteworthy for its ongoing, developmental nature and its centrality and integration into the instructional programs of the individual schools. Continuing assessment of the staff development program relative to student goals underscores the efficacy of the program to both the teacher and to those in the community. The program is viewed as able to make a difference and this is the primary base for its fiscal and psychological support.

STAFF DEVELOPMENT IN JEFFERSON COUNTY (COLO.) SCHOOLS

The Jefferson County (Colo.) design is characterized by its attention to multiple needs and goals and multiple role groups. Activities are designed not to focus solely on further pedagogical development but on increasing job satisfaction and providing opportunities for career development and role changes as well. There is an emphasis on promoting growth in all personnel and not placing a disproportionate responsibility on the individual teacher. The continuing development of the building principal is stressed, as it is for those in district-level roles, and even those in policy-formulation roles, namely board members and interested community persons. For example, efforts have been directed toward the community to assist interested parties in better understanding some of the complexities attendant upon publicly supported formal education and to examine ways in which they might be more integrally involved in charting future directions. Likewise, goals have been established by school board members to enhance two-way communication and their decision-making ability.

A Staff Development Academy that works closely with the local education association sponsors a number of activities guided by principles demonstrated to be effective in practice. A structured observation and analysis procedure allows a staff development team (including other teachers) to provide multiple perspectives about instructional interactions of interest or concern to specific teachers. Frank and open discussion of specific teacher and student interaction is promoted in a nonthreatening form. Teacher strengths as well as concerns are enumerated throughout this process and it is accompanied by clearly articulated support for the teachers as they move into new growth areas. Alternative courses of action and experimental teaching are promoted through this structured, collegial exchange. It is conducted in the natural setting of the classroom.

Other noteworthy efforts sponsored by the Academy include assessments of critical factors in the school that contribute to the health of the organization, and emphasis on demonstration and opportunity for practice in staff development, as well as a personal resource bank that allows teachers to be matched with other teachers in a variety of reciprocal helping roles.

The Role of Higher Education in Staff Development

Conspicuous by its absence in these brief descriptions of practices and the earlier discussions of principles of effective staff development has been reference to the role of higher education institutions and personnel. The major reason for this is that staff development has been largely the domain of local districts and more recently teachers themselves through teachers' centers and their strengthened professional organizations. Those in colleges, schools, and departments of education have been involved in the continuing education of teachers and other staff primarily through general courses and graduate programs.

What role might members of the higher education and teacher education community assume beyond offering these courses and programs for individual teachers? We believe there are a number of things that those in higher education can do. Roles and responsibilities will obviously vary as types and sizes of colleges and schools of education vary. The over 1200 institutions of higher education having some teacher education mission range frome one- and two-person faculties to large research-oriented colleges with programs for many types of educational personnel and their potential contributions will undoubtedly vary accordingly.

Certainly high on the list of priorities would be more joint efforts with those in schools to study systematically specific variations in staff development. For many, staff development remains largely an undifferentiated and little understood phenomenon. There are, however, a variety of well-delineated approaches, some of which have been depicted here. There is a need for systematic investigations of how and why these occur and of their impact. In addition, there are numerous other approaches, including teacher centers, clinical supervision models, techniques for organizational problem-solving and development, advisory approaches, collaborative research activities, and a host of other structured training formats designed for specific purposes. There is no shortage of opportunities for those with research and development orientations to help shape and study specific modes of staff development. The end result would be not only an increased knowledge base about these alternatives but, perhaps more importantly, the development of the capacity of institutions of higher education and local education agencies to investigate and understand staff development issues in the future. Schools presently have limited expertise in such matters while institutions of higher education, especially those with more capacity for research and development, are nonetheless known to be less than prodigious in their production of knowledge.[30] Thus, the interests of both institutions could be well served by such a mutual undertaking.

A second potential role for institutions of higher education would be in working with schools in developing programs for preparing specialists in staff development. The eventual significance of this effort should not be underestimated. Currently, one of the apparent major reasons that there are not more powerful ongoing programs of staff development in districts and schools is that no one person is charged with well-defined responsibilities and authority. Often, even when there is such responsibility and authority, the person's training and skills may be lacking. It is even more rare to find an individual with such skills at the individual school building level. It is equally apparent that in the vast majority of cases the building administrator's staff development role is a quite limited one despite evidence of its crucial influence.

Perhaps the most important of all in a long-range sense would be the opportunity for teacher education institutions to work with local education agencies in ensuring closer and more coherent articulation between preservice and in-service education. A logical emphasis for increased development and investigation initially would be the period of transition into beginning teaching where that lack of articulation is so obvious. This period of beginning teaching has been described as crucial to the formation of attitudes and expectations of teachers who choose to stay in the profession as well as being a major factor in the choices of those who choose to leave to go to other fields. However, basic issues of shared responsibility have yet to be even marginally addressed either in terms of necessary assistance to teachers during their beginning years or the most effective preservice preparation for them. Some conceptual work has been done in identifying and analyzing key concerns of a theoretical and operational nature,[31] but a systematic approach to the issues seems very much warranted in the face of public dissatisfaction with the disheartening data on the ability levels of new teachers.[32]

Summary

The current status of staff development practices is one of flux and uncertainty. Pressures are building to supplement or supplant long-accepted in-service practices with processes that are more school-focused, classroom-relevant, and collaboratively planned and implemented. The content of these processes will have to address needs of teachers and other educational personnel that go far beyond needs associated with a traditional view of the classroom as solely an academic setting.

Clearly, the task of understanding and utilizing the potential of staff development for school improvement and professional and personal growth is a major endeavor. Appropriate roles for school and higher education personnel, as well as the roles of other potential contributors such as state departments of education, teacher and other professional organizations, educational service agencies, community representatives and parents, have not been investigated in any systematic or comprehensive fashion. Resources are uncoordinated and underutilized. Support systems, the backbone of any change effort, have been neglected. Little effort has been made to determine the ways in which staff development can really make a difference in changing teacher or other staff behaviors and what those changed behaviors might mean for student learning. Public demand for accountability from the schools is passed along to "underprepared" staff developers who are nonetheless asked to improve their practices and to understand the consequences of their actions within other school and community influences.

Yet there is reason for optimism. We now know much about what constitutes effective teaching, especially in instruction in basic skills in elementary and junior high schools. We have also taken initial steps toward beginning to understand how to look at the ways in which teaching techniques interact with other contextual factors in influencing the effectiveness of schools and how those effective schools maintain or enhance effective instruction. We also now have a limited knowledge base about effective principles of staff development as well as the initiation of creative and sound thinking about how to consider staff development as an integral part of any effort to develop the school program.

Perhaps most significantly, we have a situation where all education constituents are faced with declining fiscal support for public education and a clamoring for improvement in schools. The need for better use of existing human and monetary resources and systematic consideration of how improvement can best be achieved is undeniable. For both schools and higher education institutions that train and provide personnel for those schools, it is clearly a case of "we must all hang together or surely we shall all hang separately." It may well be the case that these negative circumstances will provide the impetus that complacency never did. The tools are here to begin building a strong foundation for the future. It is our responsibility to choose wisely their present use and future improvement.

FOOTNOTES

1. Bicentennial Commission on Education for the Profession of Teaching, *Educating a Profession* (Washington, D.C.: American Association of Colleges for Teacher Education, 1976), pp. 20, 26-27.

2. Ibid., pp. 67-68.

3. B. Othanel Smith, *A Design for a School of Pedagogy* (Washington, D.C.: U.S. Government Printing Office, 1980), p. 1.

4. Arthur Hyde and Donald Moore, *Making Sense of Staff Development: An Analysis of Staff Development Programs and Their Costs in Three Urban School Districts* (Washington, D.C.: U.S. Government Printing Office, 1982), pp. 105-7.

5. Bruce R. Joyce, Kenneth R. Howey, and Sam J. Yarger, *ISTE Report I: Issues to Face* (Syracuse, N.Y.: National Dissemination Center, Syracuse University, 1977).

6. Hyde and Moore, *Making Sense of Staff Development*, p. 105.

7. Joyce, Howey, and Yarger, *ISTE Report I: Issues to Face.*

8. For example, see JoAnn L. Vacca, *Establishing Criteria for Staff Development Personnel* (Washington, D.C.: National Institute of Education, U.S. Department of Education, 1981).

9. Sprinthall's work (chap. 2 of this volume) illustrates one approach. For a general discussion of issues in using adult developmental theory as one basis for staff development, see Sharon Feiman and Robert Floden, *A Consumer's Guide to Teacher Development* (E. Lansing, Mich.: Institute for Research on Teaching, Michigan State University, 1981).

10. See Gene E. Hall, *Using the Individual and the Innovation as the Frame of Reference for Research on Change* (Austin, Tex.: Research and Development Center for Teacher Education, University of Texas at Austin, 1979) for an overview of one approach.

11. Much of what has come to be known as the "effective schools" literature offers additional insights into other influences on the quality of instruction. See, for example, Wilbur B. Brookover, *Schools Can Make a Difference* (E. Lansing, Mich.: College of Urban Development, Michigan State University, 1977); Ronald R. Edmonds, "Some Schools Work and More Can," *Social Policy* 9 (March 1979): 28-32; Ralph A. Hanson and Richard E. Schutz, "A New Look at Schooling Effects from Programmatic Research and Development," in *Making Change Happen?* ed. Dale Mann (New York: Teachers College Press, 1978); Kenneth Howey, "Successful Schooling Practices: Perceptions of a Total School Faculty" (San Francisco: Far West Laboratory for Educational Research and Development, 1980); Michael Rutter, Barbara Maughan, Peter Mortimore, Janet Ouston, and Alan Smith, *Fifteen Thousand Hours: Secondary Schools and Their Effects on Children* (Cambridge, Mass.: Harvard University Press, 1979); George Weber, "Inner-City Children Can Be Taught to Read: Four Successful Schools" (Washington, D.C.: Council for Basic Education, 1971); Edward A. Wynne, *Looking at Schools: Good, Bad, and Indifferent* (Lexington, Mass.: D. C. Heath, 1980).

12. Carolyn Denham and Ann Lieberman, eds., *Time to Learn* (Washington, D.C.: National Institute of Education, 1980).

13. See, as one of many examples of his summaries, Barak Rosenshine, "Content, Time, and Direct Instruction," in *Research on Teaching*, ed. Penelope L. Peterson and Herbert J. Walberg (Berkeley, Calif.: McCutchan Publishing Corp., 1979), pp. 28-56. A particularly straightforward and practical look at several key studies is offered in Jane Stallings, "How Useful Are the Findings from the Research on Teaching," in *Proceedings of the Changing Teacher Practice Conference*, Report no. 9017, ed. Maria E. Defino and Heather Carter (Austin, Tex.: Research and Development Center for Teacher Education, University of Texas at Austin, 1982), pp. 5-24. See also, Donald Medley, *Teacher Competence and Teacher Effectiveness* (Washington, D.C.: Association of Colleges for Teacher Education, 1977).

14. See Thomas L. Good, *The Missouri Mathematics Effectiveness Project* (Columbia, Mo.: School of Education, University of Missouri, 1980), and Carolyn Evertson, "Differences in Instructional Activities in High and Low Achieving Junior High Classes" (Paper presented at the annual meeting of the American Educational Research Association, Boston, 1980).

15. The series of reports from the project funded by the National Institute of Education on "Ecological Perspectives for Successful Schooling Practice" (NIE-G-78-0103) at the Far West Laboratory for Educational Research and Development, San Francisco, provides descriptions of this approach. Volume I represents an overview with an additional six volumes examining specific issues such as activity structures, teachers' role systems, student perceptions, and classroom interaction.

16. The consensus of opinion on the importance of the role of the principal in effecting change and improving instructional practices in schools is overwhelming. Studies as diverse as the previously cited "effective schools" work and Hall's studies of change, as well as the study by Judith Warren Little discussed later in this chapter, all emphasize the critical nature of the principal's role.

17. Jane Stallings, Margaret Needels, and Nicholas Stayrook, *How to Change the Process of Teaching Basic Skills in Secondary Schools: Final Report* (Menlo Park, Calif.: SRI International, 1979).

18. Thomas Good and Douglas Grouws, "The Missouri Mathematics Effectiveness Project: An Experimental Study in Fourth-Grade Classrooms," *Journal of Educational Psychology* 71 (June 1979): 335-62.

19. Linda Anderson, Carolyn Evertson, and Jere Brophy, "An Experimental Study of Effective Teaching in First-Grade Reading Groups" *Elementary School Journal* 79 (March 1979): 193-223.

20. Hall, *Using the Individual and the Innovation as the Frame of Reference for Research on Change*.

21. Roy Edelfelt and Gordon Lawrence, "In-service Education: the State of the Art," in *Rethinking In-service Education*, ed. Roy Edelfelt and Margo Johnson (Washington, D.C.: National Education Association, 1975), pp. 9-14.

22. Bruce Joyce and Beverly Showers, "Improving In-service Training: The Messages of Research" *Educational Leadership* 37 (February 1980): 379-85.

23. A variety of perspectives on these issues is offered in Betty Dillon-Peterson, ed., *Staff Developmental/Organizational Development* (Alexandria, Va.: Association for Supervision and Curriculum Development, 1981).

24. David Berliner and Gary Fenstermacher, *A Conceptualization of Staff Development Evaluation and Implementation* (Washington, D.C.: National Institute of Education, 1982).

25. The results of this conference will be the subject of a Spring, 1983 issue of the *Elementary School Journal* and the individual papers will be made available in a single volume by the National Institute of Education, U.S. Department of Education, at approximately the same time.

26. As one example, the work of the Research in Teacher Education (RITE) project, funded by the National Institute of Education at the Research and Development Center for Teacher Education, University of Texas at Austin, includes examining the impact of strategies for changing behaviors of staff developers.

27. A project sponsored by the National Institute of Education at the Center for Educational Policy and Management in Eugene, Oregon (Transfer of Training: The Contribution of Coaching) is examining the potential of "coaching" techniques in aiding classroom implementation of desirable instructional behaviors.

28. Judith Warren Little, *School Success and Staff Development: The Role of Staff Development in Urban Desegregated Schools* (Washington, D.C.: National Institute of Education, 1981).

29. Judith Warren Little, "Finding the Limits and Possibilities of Instructional Leadership: Some Possibilities for Practical and Collaborative Work with Principals," Project Report (Washington, D.C.: National Institute of Education, 1981), pp. 1-3.

30. Egon Guba and David Clark, *Research on Institutions of Teacher Education, Volume III: An Instructional Self-Report on Knowledge Production and Utilization Activities in Schools, Colleges, and Departments of Education* (Bloomington, Ind.: RITE Project, Indiana University, 1976).

31. Frederick McDonald and Patricia Elias, *Study of Induction Programs for Beginning Teachers: Executive Summary* (Washington, D.C.: National Institute of Education, 1982).

32. See W. Timothy Weaver, "In Search of Quality: The Need for Talent in Teaching," *Phi Delta Kappan* 61 (September 1979): 29-32, and Phillip C. Schlechty and Victor S. Vance, "Do Academically Able Teachers Leave Education? The North Carolina Case," *Phi Delta Kappan* 63 (October 1981): 106-12.

Part Two
CASE STUDIES OF
STAFF DEVELOPMENT PROGRAMS

CHAPTER VI

Tensions in Teaching Teachers the Skills of Pedagogy

JUDITH E. LANIER

In structuring the writing task for this chapter, the volume editor requested a focus on a "real life" staff development experience that had been directed toward the improvement of skill in teaching. Having examined the literature and noted an overabundance of success stories, the editor encouraged attention to various problems and difficulties that were experienced, in addition to the more positive aspects. Given this request, the first section of the chapter describes a particular staff development program and the contextual factors that tend to make the case in point unique. The second section of the chapter addresses the difficulties and problems that were encountered in the development and operation of the program and attempts to distinguish constructive from nonconstructive problems. The third and last section discusses what was learned from the experiences and compares and contrasts these learnings with some of the existing staff development literature.

The staff development program that is described evolved out of a series of staff development efforts that were initially developed in the late 1960s and early 1970s. The initiatives were motivated by perceived staff development needs on the part of a university and a school district. Though their cooperative efforts originally received partial support from various federally funded projects over the years, the continuing staff development program that evolved is now supported by the participating school district and the university and is not dependent upon external resources.

Section one includes descriptive information on the historical evolution of the concern of the university and of the school district for staff development, the subsequent nature of their collaboration, motivations for participation, purposes, resources, and general operation of the staff development program itself. The pragmatic structure of the model is seen to be of central importance, since it provides a set of enabling conditions for dynamic and constructive, though certainly not problem-free, staff development directed toward the improvement of teaching practice.

The essence of the second and third sections is suggested by the title of the chapter itself. It communicates an emphasis on tensions, tensions that seem to arise rather consistently when staff development activities involve both school and university personnel and focus on the improvement of their respective teaching abilities.

A commitment to professional reciprocity and opportunity for shared reflection on the part of school and university educators is at the heart of the staff development experience that is described. The tensions that accompany this particular case thus center on the different perspectives, expectations, and characteristics of the school teachers and university teacher educators who came to construct and participate in the staff development program. The tensions that developed do not appear unique to this particular case, however, for they center around classic differences in view regarding theoretical versus more practical knowledge and skill that appear important for increased effectiveness in teaching. Some of the positive and negative consequences of these tensions are discussed, since they have implications for research and practice in future staff development efforts. They also suggest some means for making educators' theoretical and practical views more compatible and complementary.

A University-School Collaboration: Some Particulars of the Case

Staff development is usually associated with attempts to improve the teaching competence of elementary and secondary school professionals. This case may therefore be somewhat unusual in the sense that the effort was designed to improve concomitantly the teaching competence of *both* school and university personnel: elementary teachers *and* teachers of prospective elementary teachers. Typically, staff development programs for these two sets of educators are designed and implemented independently of one another; in-service programs are planned for practicing teachers, and sabbatical leaves are provided for university professors. But the staff development program for advancing "Excellence in Elementary Education" (referred to as Triple-E or EEE) sought to capitalize on the interdependence of these two sets of professionals and improve the teaching of both groups simultaneously. It did not begin this way, however, and a brief reference to the antecedents of the program is a necessary part of the description.

SOME EARLY RELATED EFFORTS

The circumstances that gave rise to the Triple-E (EEE) Staff Development Program grew out of a tradition of cooperative staff development ventures between a college and school district that were geographically close. The university professors were frequently called upon in the 1950s and 1960s to provide typical in-service instruction for the classroom teachers. Then, in 1968, in response to the growing challenges of teaching in urban school settings and university students' increased dissatisfaction with college instruction, an effort to provide staff development for a number of university professors was proposed and arranged.

The staff development project provided for cooperative arrangements between the school district and the College of Education and allowed teacher educators to assume classroom teaching responsibility in one of the district's urban elementary schools. Project REFUEL was primarily a staff development effort for enriching the experiential background of teacher educators.[1] The university professors had the opportunity to teach half-time for a full semester in an urban elementary school with a culturally diverse student population. The professors' university teaching loads were adjusted accordingly, as were those of the classroom teachers. As originally conceived, it was hoped that Project REFUEL would operate as a faculty exchange: the professors would teach in the elementary schools, and the elementary teachers would assist in teaching prospective teachers at the university.

A total of twenty-nine different professors taught half-time in elementary school classrooms over the two-year life of the project. But the exchange was never fully realized as the majority of classroom teachers did not elect to come to the University for exchange teaching. Though several teachers did actually teach in some of the under-graduate methods classes and some supervised student teachers, most of them preferred to stay at the elementary school and use their out-of-class time for curriculum and instructional materials development. The project was concluded in 1970, but a number of the collegial relationships that had developed during the course of the project encouraged further cooperation.

In 1971 a number of the teacher educators and teachers who participated in Project REFUEL joined together to design an elementary education component for the Trainers of Teacher Trainers (TTT) Project. Though the University and the school district had received U. S. Office of Education support for a TTT project in 1969, the initial focus was entirely on training teacher educators for secondary schools. Well known to many and revealed by the title, the TTT projects were meant to improve the competence of college-level professors who taught prospective teachers.[2] The university, the school district, and the funding agency accepted a proposal for an elementary education addition to the TTT effort and thus enabled an elementary component of TTT to be added just a year after Project REFUEL had ended. This effort became a second precursor for the model EEE staff development project that eventually evolved.[3]

The Elementary TTT Project provided support for university doctoral and postdoctoral fellows, school district personnel, and community representatives. These persons were to cooperate in the development and provision of learning opportunities that would likely improve the competence of teacher trainers. Like all TTT projects, it focused on "parity inputs,"[4] a term derived from the range of persons each of whom typically has only partial input into the preparation of teachers: liberal arts professors, graduate students, professors of education, classroom teachers, school administrators, community representatives, and prospective teachers themselves. Like all TTT federally supported efforts, the emphasis was on broad and democratic participation, with a 1960s egalitarian emphasis.

The Elementary TTT Program had an advantage over the secondary program in that its designers had the opportunity to learn from the struggles and problems that had arisen during the first two years of operation of the secondary program. What eventually came to be a common difficulty for many TTT projects across the nation[5] was a clear problem in the early years of the secondary program. The widely diverse set of participants experienced substantial difficulty in developing common purposes, coherence in program design, and unifying principles. Excessive time and energy were expended in trying to reach

agreement on a program that would improve the professional competence of the diverse array of persons who prepare teachers. While
experience in schools and the community was naturally encouraged,
participants differed strongly on what the nature of the experience
should be and what reasonable outcomes might be expected. The
continuing argument and disagreement inhibited progress in staff
development and resulted in frequent negative encounters.

In an attempt to avoid the development of a similar situation in the
emerging Elementary TTT Program, its designers built in a potentially
unifying factor, something outside of their individual interests for
which all participants would share responsibility. They built into their
training program a process and a product outcome that was indirectly
related to their own staff development; together they would develop
and operate an experimental program for preparing prospective teachers.

The importance of the TTT overall program goals and the
particular implementation strategy adopted by the elementary project
should not be underestimated. The subsequent approach and general
attitude toward staff development which evolved was heavily influenced by this relatively novel approach. The basic rationale was
that shared deliberations and decision making relative to the knowledge
and skills that prospective teachers need to acquire and develop would
be educative to the diverse "experienced" participants. Their varying
perspectives about what was important for effective teaching, combined
with the interdependent need to achieve mutual understanding and
agreement on what and how newcomers would be taught, would press
them to take each others' respective views seriously. Further, the
participants could express their views with minimal anxiety, since their
discourse would focus directly on what *others* (that is, prospective
teachers) needed to teach effectively, and only indirectly on what they
themselves might need to teach effectively.

Thus, in the summer of 1971, the university professors, graduate
students, school teachers, school administrators, and community representatives gathered together with dual goals: the product goal of
improving the manner in which trainers of elementary teachers
performed their professional duties, and the process goal of jointly
planning and implementing a new and hopefully improved approach

to teacher preparation. The TTT focus on parity, combined with the participants' shared responsibility for an actual cohort of prospective teachers, pressed the diverse group into an intensely collaborative effort. The summer planning could not afford to disintegrate into lengthy and abstract discussion and argument on the present weaknesses of teacher trainers and the many things they needed to know and do in order to be less pedantic, irrelevant, and theoretical. An entering group of forty undergraduate students would arrive in the fall to begin a teacher preparation program that had to be judged appropriate by the full though diverse set of TTT participants.

The planning began with a critique of the traditional teacher preparation program offerings. Alternative approaches and potential improvements were considered and designed. Resource constraints and institutional barriers were examined to see if they could be overcome. The various desired learnings were analyzed for purposes of deciding which participants could best facilitate the learning, and responsibilities and roles were defined and assigned on this basis. The obvious need for all project participants to share in the complicated task of preparing prospective teachers became apparent.

As the school and community participants came to see and acknowledge important roles for themselves in teacher preparation, they also began to see themselves as teacher trainers, and in this light, they too became learners in the TTT staff development project. This is not to imply that the classic "we-they" issues did not arise with their predictably frequent and troublesome consequences, for they did. But the continuing pressure created by the entering group of undergraduates consistently encouraged reasonable and professional resolution of differences. The we-they issues had to be consistently resolved within the larger contextual question of "Well, then, what will we do when the students arrive?"

The teacher preparation program that resulted emphasized progressively complex and intense field experiences that were substantively related to the university-based instruction. Systematic linkages in time and curriculum were created for teaching the undergraduates their subject matter content and methods and their pedagogical knowledge and skills. Opportunities for observation, demonstration, and practice of the desired learnings were designed and provided by the various participants. These efforts forced a continued negotiation and understanding between university and school personnel about the "oughts" of elementary school curriculum and instructional practice.

The Elementary TTT Program was operated in two schools. It involved twenty professors, five graduate students, twenty-nine teachers, three community representatives, two principals, and two cohorts of forty undergraduate students each. The funding for the project ended in the spring of 1973, with the total demise of the USOE federally sponsored TTT effort.

The national evaluation of the TTT project reports indicated that this particular project was one of the seven highest-ranked in the nation.[6] It was thus selected for site visits and here again evidenced strong success in meeting TTT goals. Describing the project, Provus noted that "this is the institution about which Harry Passow reported that all of the goals were reached—probably more so than at some of the other institutions visited." Guba and Passow also noted the particularly strong role of the public schools.[7] This evidence is not cited for laudatory purposes, but rather to indicate the strength of the university-school relationship that was achieved.

It was with this background that the EEE staff development program for professionals concerned with effective elementary teaching was constructed in 1973. As the TTT program ended, intrinsic motivations were strong to forge an alternative staff development plan that would allow for the continued professional growth of the elementary teachers and teachers of elementary teachers. Although the federal funding that provided needed resources for the release of professional staff was gone, the participants were committed to continue what had come to be a valued effort. In the summer of 1972, six of the elementary school teachers and four of the university teacher educators met to devise a plan for continuation.

THE EMERGENT STAFF DEVELOPMENT PROGRAM: TRIPLE-E (EEE)

Ostensibly, the school and university educators originally came to work together with the primary goal of increasing the professional competence of teacher trainers; and although this goal was apparently achieved, much more had come from the experience than was initially considered. The teachers and the teacher educators had begun to recognize a basic interdependence. Further, respective conceptual and experiential differences had come to be viewed as important ingredients in deciding what constituted skill and effectiveness in teaching. Thus, the professional staff development of teachers and teacher educators was now dependent upon significant portions of available time for collegial sharing. But the financial support for acquiring released time for teachers and teacher educators was lost with the cessation of federal support. Further, the model teacher preparation program they had collaboratively developed and operated, and for which they naturally felt a major commitment, was about to be terminated, sending the two student groups of forty prospective teachers back into the standard university program. The intrinsic motivation that had developed for continuing their own professional growth through sustained inter-action, combined with their loyalty and pride in the teacher preparation program was apparently strong enough to generate a solution to the problem of lost support for released time. Recognizing that the needed time for interaction could not productively be added to their already heavy set of professional commitments, however, the school and university teachers again turned to the teacher preparation program for their solution.

The two groups of undergraduate students had entered the experimental preparation program as freshmen and, as a consequence, in the fall of 1973, forty students in one group were in their junior year and students in the second group were in their sophomore year. They had observed and worked with the elementary classroom teachers since the first term of their first year of college. In addition to the general education and subject-field major and minor requirements taken by all undergraduates, these students were required to take a heavier than usual set of requirements for their professional studies in pedagogy. Their program plan included experience in schools each week of every term throughout their undergraduate years, with gradually increased amounts of responsibility in both time and teaching functions. By the time these prospective teachers would *enter* their senior year, therefore, they would have acquired more practice-teaching experience than is typically acquired by graduates of traditional teacher education programs at the *end* of their senior year. Hence, it was reasoned, a EEE senior student should be "prepared," in the conventional sense, for a beginning teaching assignment. Yet with one year remaining for continued study and still richer supervised teaching experience, perhaps they could assume additional classroom teaching responsibilities that would permit the teachers and teacher educators to continue their respective collaboration and staff development.

The basic structure for the EEE program subsequently came to be built on such an arrangement. The undergraduate program continued in 1973-74, although for that year only the extra time needed for cooperative planning and operation had to come from "after school hours" on the part of the teachers and teacher educators. With the advent of the 1974-75 school year, however, the new program containing the released time provision moved into place. The first group of EEE undergraduates had become senior interns and were able to share the classroom teaching responsibilities more fully with the cooperating teachers.

Two senior interns were teamed with each cooperating teacher in the participating schools. In the fall term, each member of these three-person teams alternated in the role of lead teacher. Then one intern assumed the bulk of the teaching responsibility for the winter term, and the other assumed it for the spring term. In this way, the interns acquired experience in both team-teaching and a relatively self-contained teaching situation. At all times, the cooperating teacher maintained ultimate teaching responsibility, in the sense of approving the goals and strategies proposed and implemented by the interns. But through the effort-sharing arrangement, each cooperating teacher was able to acquire regular time during the school day, away from the youngsters in the classroom, for professional staff development. The formal time made available for teachers and teacher educators to work together in groups was equivalent to two half-days a week. Twenty teachers originally participated, though the number of participants subsequently increased through expansion of the undergraduate program and cooperative arrangements that were made with the Teacher Corps Project.[8]

Over the years, the program operated in nine different schools. Participation at the various school sites ranged from total staff involvement (all teachers and the school principal) to teacher teams of four to ten members. Changes occurred over the years in the configuration of intern assignments, but the basic structure of using the teacher preparation program as an integral part of the staff development effort remained in place. Carefully selected prospective teachers, who were screened through their early experience in the schools and had the continuing opportunity to work closely with their school and university teachers (who were also learners in this case), were central to the effective operation of the program.

The staff development program that came to be designed included large- and small-group exchanges and work sessions that took place on the two half-days in which the teachers were released from their classrooms. On the other days of the week, it included opportunities for individualized observation, demonstration, practice, and feedback in applying the knowledge and skills being learned. An on-site staff development room was made available in each of the participating schools for the large- and small-group work. Teams of teachers and teacher educators subdivided their small-group activities around subject fields that they elected to work on for the year. In the first year, this included a reading and language arts emphasis, a mathematics emphasis, and two social studies areas—one that emphasized multicultural education and one that emphasized social-emotional education. The large-group activities centered on readings and discussions of psychological and sociological literature that had potential implications for curriculum and instruction for elementary school youngsters. The program remained dynamic in that continuing adaptations were made in response to participant problems and preferences that called for regular negotiation and resolution.

Tensions: An Integral Part of Professional Staff Development for School and University Educators

Tensions consistently arose as the university and school personnel sought to reach agreement and achieve compatible working relationships in their mutual efforts to improve their own skill in teaching and the learning of their school and university students. The various definitions of "tension" all seem applicable as descriptors of the experience: "the act or action of stretching; either of two balancing forces causing or tending to cause extension; a state of latent hostility or opposition between individuals or groups; inner striving, unrest, or imbalance, often with physiological indication of emotion; a balance maintained in an artistic work between opposing forces or elements; a device to produce a desired tension, as in a loom."[9]

The opposing forces that appeared to cause the stretching and extension of the two professional groups were their differing views relative to the skills of pedagogy. The practical views of the classroom teachers and the theoretical views of the university teachers were in frequent opposition to one another, provoking both cognitive and affective disagreement and unrest.

The Triple-E staff development program did not begin, however, with a valuing of tension and unrest. The program simply maintained the broad and general goal of working toward Excellence in Elementary Education (EEE). The school and university teachers who collaborated to design and implement the staff development effort to improve their respective teaching abilities maintained an interdependent relationship that was sustained in large part by the program for prospective teachers. The teacher preparation program, in fact, might be viewed as the *device* that produced the desired tension, since it brought the opposing forces together in a manner which permitted the maintenance of balance.

The interdependence was concrete and real in terms of the potential influence that each set of teachers was able to exert over the other's students. The classroom teachers naturally worked closely with the students of the university teachers. These *prospective* teachers (that is, the university students) were under frequent and direct tutelage of the elementary classroom teachers, who were credible and significant others to them. What the university students came to observe, be told, and rewarded for by the classroom teachers had potentially powerful learning effects. Understandably, the university teachers wanted the elementary teachers to model and reinforce the learnings that they judged to be important and appropriate. Similarly, the university teachers (the teacher educators) and the prospective teachers had close and continuing contact with the classroom teachers' students. What the elementary students came to observe, be told, and rewarded for by the university teachers would also have strong effects on pupil learning. Thus, the elementary classroom teachers wanted the university teachers to be consistent with their teachings as well.

This mutual desire to have each set of teachers, elementary *and* university, interact in a compatible and complementary manner with each other's students, necessitated awareness of and negotiated agreement on preferred learnings and approaches to instruction. The elementary and university teachers therefore needed sufficient time and opportunity to learn about each other's understandings and preferences relative to effective teaching. Further, they had to have sufficient time and commitment to resolve whatever differences they had relative to their respective views about what would constitute acceptable teaching practice for each other's students. The two half-days a week together provided the time for the needed learning and negotiations, although a number of early agreements were needed to guide the design and operation of the program itself.

The two groups of teachers agreed that they should begin with a serious examination of the extent to which they held common views on the goals of elementary schooling. If they shared a common commitment to the broad goals of elementary education, their subsequent planning for narrower goals and more limited teaching units for their students would likely be productive of more fruitful negotiations. They also agreed, up front, that if disagreements could not be resolved about the priority goals of instruction for elementary learners, the views of the classroom teachers would assume priority; they were, after all, professionally responsible for the elementary learners. The teacher educators thus agreed that they would consistently teach their university students to teach *what* the classroom teachers judged appropriate, as long as the teacher educators had the opportunity to know first about the intended goals and to challenge or suggest alternatives if they chose. Following a serious exchange of views, however, it was understood that the classroom teachers had the ultimate authority in this regard.

In terms of instructional methods, however, a slightly different initial agreement was reached. Once instructional goals were decided, the teacher educators and supervised prospective teachers would have the opportunity to select and employ whatever instructional methods they judged appropriate, even though their choice might differ from what the classroom teacher would select. This too was agreed to with the understanding that the classroom teachers had the opportunity to know first about the intended strategies and to challenge or suggest alternatives if they chose.

Thus, although eventual agreement on instructional goals was assured, differences relative to instructional practices were accepted. Though in actuality the classroom teachers held veto power here as well, they essentially agreed to honor the university teachers' judgments relative to appropriate instructional strategy and method. If the classroom teachers felt "sure" that the university teachers' plans were not appropriate they could reject their proposals, although this never occurred. As with the relationships of trust that were established through working together on prior programs, these early agreements and assurances may well have been critical to the participants' subsequent ability to sustain constructive interactions in light of the trying and consistent tensions that were experienced.

DIFFERING VIEWS ON THE SKILLS OF PEDAGOGY

The issue of what constituted skill in teaching naturally arose on numerous occasions and in many different forms and settings throughout the program. As indicated earlier, the tension seemed to be created by the tendency for teachers to focus on the concrete and practical aspects of teaching and the teacher educators to focus on the more abstract and theoretical aspects.

The teacher educators, in the main, held the view that *the* most important pedagogical skills were imbedded in the exercise of informed professional judgment and decision making. The teachers, on the other hand, held the view that the most important pedagogical skills were imbedded in the performance of smoothly orchestrated routines and actions. This difference in view provoked intense debate about what was appropriate preparation activity for the prospective teachers and what was appropriate activity for the staff development seminars and work sessions themselves.

For staff development activities, the teacher educators wanted to share and examine the knowledge that they thought should inform teachers' professional judgment and decision making. The teachers, on the other hand, wanted to discuss particular practical problems they were encountering and find out what they should do about them.

The group's prior general agreements helped structure the tactical response to this difference in preference. They would have full group study and discussion of the disciplinary and pedagogical knowledge that held possible relevance for the general goals and instructional practices of elementary teaching, and they would have small-group application and problem-solving sessions directed toward the identification of potentially effective teaching practices in selected subject-matter areas. Questions about relevance and practical applications of knowledge would be appropriate and encouraged in both contexts.

As the staff development sessions got underway, however, the classroom teachers were often uneasy and skeptical when discussions focused on general principles and abstract ideas related to effective teaching practice. Although the teacher educators verbally described numerous concrete examples of how the principles could be applied, the teachers frequently drew from their own experience and cited numerous examples of how they had tried to apply the particular principle before—and how it had failed them; or they would describe complicating factors that prevented its concrete application in the first place (for example, "Our principal would never allow it," or "The student's parents would object," or "We don't have the resources"). By noting multiple exceptions *or* problems in application, the teachers seemed to disparage the worth of a principle, implying that to be worthy of consideration, it should work in all cases.

The teacher educators often felt frustrated and "put on the spot" with such responses. They countered with the argument that skill in *professional* teaching was, in fact, *deciding* when exceptions to generally appropriate rules were desired or necessary in particular situations. The teacher educators gave elaborate explanations for this view, describing the inevitably probabilistic nature of human behavior and the standard requirements of *professional* activity (thinking and judging in light of prior knowledge and experience) in contrast to *technical* activity (doing as one is told or shown).

The teachers, however, tended to view these explanations as scapegoats or excuses for the teacher educators' refusal to tell them what they should do to solve particular problems. A number of teachers thus argued that the teacher educators probably needed more practical experience actually teaching and opportunities to demonstrate the "how-to's" and "so-what's" of their conceptual principles and ideas. The teachers implied that the teacher educators should be experts and should be able to tell them what to do. The teacher educators tried to explain that they could not fulfill this expectation because they did not have sufficient knowledge of the requisite particulars (for example, knowledge about specific individual student characteristics and the unique configurations of their peer groups). Thus, they could only suggest alternative possibilities that might be helpful when appropriately adapted for and tried in the teachers' classrooms. Not persuaded by their teacher educators' arguments, a number of the teachers countered with the classic Missourian response—"You'll have to show me."

Such a challenge both threatened and frustrated the teacher educators. In addition to being nervous about stepping into the teachers' classrooms and showing them how it should be done, they were basically philosophically opposed to being put in this position. They did not believe that there was *a right way to do it*, nor did they believe that classroom teachers should continue to look to "outside experts" to tell or show them precisely what to do. The teacher educators wanted the teachers to think seriously and critically about the ideas they put forward, and then they wanted them to devise reasonable means of applying and evaluating the applications in their own classrooms.

Thus, the teacher educators appeared comfortable in the belief that their advice was *appropriately tentative* and removed from particular, specific situations. But the teachers, on the other hand, seemed to interpret this stance as a sign of weakness, an indication that the teacher educators *really did not know*. The disagreements relative to this matter were not trivial. The teacher educators saw their credibility and their philosophy about effective teaching at stake. Their response was an adaptive one, rather than a compromise, but full agreement was never reached among the group of teacher educators themselves.

The majority of the teacher educators agreed that the appropriate strategy to employ was one of partial accommodation to the teachers' expectations. They would "show" the teachers how some of the principles might be applied by doing demonstration teaching in their classrooms, but the teachers would be asked to participate in the exercise as joint planners and subsequent coaches and evaluators of the instructional experience. Such a plan was threatening to some of the teacher educators and a number chose to defer the experience, although the majority of them saw it as a way of maintaining credibility and reinforcing their belief that the essence of professional teaching was the considered application and reexamination of principles of effective practice.

The teacher educators made consistent and eloquent arguments that the science *and* art of teaching are found in the examination of pedagogical knowledge and the creative design and practical application of the selected understandings. Their attempts to get the teachers to share this view was a slow and gradual process, and it naturally resulted in a mixed set of responses.

The readings and presentations that the teacher educators brought to the staff development sessions were clearly valued by many teachers, but simply tolerated by others. A number of the teachers also appeared to express discomfort with the reduced level of physical activity that they encountered as they shifted from active teaching to the staff development sessions. Mental activity alone, that is, "just" thinking and discussing ideas, appeared to be insufficient. A number of the teachers brought "doing things" to the discussion sessions. Some brought knitting, crocheting, and needlepoint, while others brought construction paper and scissors for making bulletin-board letters and designs. As a matter of habit, the teachers might have felt the need to be busily engaged or at least productive of something concrete. On the other hand, it may have been that the ideas and discourse alone provoked a sense of guilt ("I am not working hard or accomplishing enough"), or a sense of boredom ("This is dull and thus a waste of my time"), or a sense of anxiety ("This challenges my existing beliefs and practices"). Nevertheless, the "doing things" were disconcerting to the teacher educators, who saw them as distractions to the discourse. They put up with it, however, since the teachers did actively participate and did *say* that they valued the exchange of ideas.

The teachers' response to doing that to which they were unaccustomed was not unlike that of the teacher educators. Though some teacher educators clearly valued their direct elementary teaching experiences, a number merely tolerated them and admitted halfheartedly that the challenges provided a unique opportunity for important learning. But in fact, the practical application lessons were usually threatening and sometimes disappointing for the teacher educators. A fair summary would suggest that the exchange of concrete classroom experience with the teacher educators, like the exchange of abstract ideas with the teachers, was not generally received with great enthusiasm.

The planning and discussion sessions related to the learning experiences needed by prospective teachers carried a similar theme. The teachers argued that their own teacher-preparation programs had been too theoretical. Their programs had not provided knowledge that helped them exercise "informed professional judgment" as teachers.

Teacher educators needed to recognize that when you were "in the trenches" and "on the firing line," you needed to be able to act expeditiously, efficiently, and effectively. Time was always of the essence in teaching, and teacher educators did not appear, from the teachers' point of view, to understand this reality. Thus, for example, the teachers argued that the teacher educators' expectation and requirement that the prospective teachers prepare elaborate lesson plans was unreasonable; they would never have the time to do this when they became *real* teachers.

The teacher educators countered that they *did* understand this reality; that they required prospective teachers to plan initially in a laborious manner, since such planning increased the neophytes' confidence and mental degrees of freedom in being able to handle the unfamiliar and unexpected events that would occur during their early teaching experience. Further, the organized thought processes built into the written planning exercise would eventually become habituated, leaving the prospective teacher capable of carrying them out in rapid, nonwritten forms. Such differences in view were expressed repeatedly as discussions occurred and decisions were made regarding what pedagogical skills were needed by prospective teachers. The teachers continued to emphasize the practical skills of doing, while the teacher educators stressed the conceptual skills associated with general pedagogical knowledge and its logical extension and application in practice. Yet, both in spite of and perhaps because of these experiences, the teachers and teacher educators valued their shared activities. The classroom teachers' enthusiasm for serious study and analysis of pedagogical knowledge was always less than that of the teacher educators; and, similarly, the teacher educators' enthusiasm for obtaining direct elementary classroom teaching experience was always less than that of the teachers. But they shared an enthusiasm for thinking together, creatively and critically, about teaching activities that would be consistent with their mutual understandings of pedagogical theory *and* practice. Shared instructional development and planning was clearly valued by both groups, although these efforts too occasionally met with disappointing results.

A primary example of frustration in this regard grew out of one of their most rewarding exchanges, one which directly produced a valued outcome from their shared staff development activity. In the context of examining the extent to which they shared agreement on the curricular goals of elementary education, the participants engaged in a lengthy conceptual analysis of various approaches to curriculum design and decision making. The collective group of teachers and teacher educators studied and critically examined the strengths and limitations of pre-packaged, linear curriculum programs that supposedly determined *for* teachers what and when particular objectives should be taught. A set of general decision rules and guidelines for selecting appropriate objectives from prepackaged lists was subsequently jointly developed. They had designed, piloted, revised, and were not only implementing and evaluating their work, but were teaching the prospective teachers to use it as well. In the midst of this effort, the school district mandated a prepackaged management-by-objectives (MBO) instructional pro-gram for teachers that required immediate and consistent use by all teachers in the district. If the teachers were to accept and use the district's new MBO system, it would necessitate the abandonment of their own guidelines, general decision rules, and process of decision making. Further, it would require acceptance of a system that they had come to judge as basically flawed. Predictably, the teachers and teacher educators were discouraged; if they accepted the mandated system, their recent and intense staff development effort was essentially a waste of time.

Somewhat unpredictably, however, the teachers responded with renewed criticism of the teacher educators. Through this experience, the teachers had again acquired evidence that the university educators were simply perpetuating an unreal, idealistic concept of what con-stituted skill in teaching. What good did it do to conceptualize professional skill in teaching as "the exercise of informed professional judgment and decision making" when it was rarely encouraged and frequently denied in the real world of practice? The required manage-ment-by-objectives system was further evidence that teachers were technicians, not professional decision makers. Knowledge acquired and decision-making tools developed through their joint staff development efforts were irrelevant. The teachers again had support for their view of what constituted the most important pedagogical skills for teachers; they were not imbedded in thinking, but in the performance of smoothly orchestrated management routines and actions. The teacher educators fought the teachers' ready retreat to their formerly strong position. They convinced the teachers that together they could approach and likely convince the central administration to allow an exception to the general policy that required conformity on the part of all district schools. The teachers and teacher educators requested and obtained permission to meet with district administrators so they could plead their case with sound pedagogical knowledge and logical argument. The meetings were held, but permission to deviate significantly from district policy was not allowed. The teacher educators had to agree with the teachers—under certain very practical circumstances, the teacher educators' views about the realities of teaching were apparently unrealistic.

Such learnings were not easy, but they broadened the perspectives of the professional teachers and teacher educators in important ways. Their challenges to one another's views provoked continuing tension and conflict. Although the profit margins appeared extremely narrow at various times, the experiences apparently produced more benefit than cost, for the participants maintained their shared commitment to the EEE staff development program.

COMMON VIEWS ON THE VALUE OF RECIPROCITY AND REFLECTION

The EEE staff development program for teachers and teacher educators has been characterized as being filled with tension—tension provoked by (a) ongoing differences and disagreements relative to what constitutes effective teaching for elementary and university students; (b) repeated challenges to one's professional credibility and authority; and (c) continued pressures to negotiate and adjust one's preferred plans and activities in order to accommodate the needs and interests of others. Sufficient rewards had to be inherent in the program to counterbalance the incessant presence of the more negative aspects of these tensions. If countervailing positive forces (that is, actual gains for each group) did not exist, continued support for and participation in the program would not have been sustained.

Apparent gains for teachers. One of the most clearly realized benefits for the classroom teachers appeared to be their newly acquired "freedom" to pursue professional improvement. The staff development program was not the typical after-school experience that occurs when teachers are already fatigued and overloaded with stress. Nor was the program like most during-school experiences that occur by either dismissing the youngsters or hiring substitute teachers. When students are dismissed, many teachers worry about the decrease in instructional time and wonder if their staff development gain is worth the students' loss of opportunities to learn. In the case of paid substitutes, teachers worry about the possibility that classroom chaos will develop, resulting in both a loss of student learning and a decrease in scarce financial resources at the district level. Paid substitutes also require a substantial amount of advance planning on the part of the regular classroom teacher. In the EEE program the teachers were not required to make elaborate advance preparations for released time. The university interns, who were intimately familiar with classroom routines and expectations and who were trusted and judged qualified by the teachers and teacher educators, assumed a significant portion of the teachers' regular duties. The classroom teachers in this case thus acquired an authentic form of physical *and* mental freedom from regular classroom responsibilities and the worry that classroom instruction would not proceed productively without them. The provision of two half-days a week on a continuing basis, freed from the incessantly pressing demands of classroom interaction with youngsters to pursue professional staff development that might increase their proficiency and skill in teaching, was a recognized benefit to the classroom-weary teachers.

The presence of other persons concerned about their own and each other's staff development was also a benefit, as was the presence of new thoughts and ideas about effective teaching. Elementary teachers generally work in relative isolation from their professional peers. A common result of this isolation is a sense of loneliness and gradual disassociation from the intellectual habits of abstract thought and analysis. The opportunity to engage in collegial discourse and shared reflection upon one's professional practice was, overall, perceived as a benefit. An excerpt from responses to interview questions about the various aspects of the program indicated the general recognition of this gain:

Gosh, just having somebody to talk to, and having somebody tell me some neat things that I've done, which had to come from me before because nobody else is really interested in what I do here. But also the negative feedback—I can't know what I'm doing if nobody ever suggests how I can get better. I guess it wasn't just the negative feedback, though; it was the information I got at classes that helped me know what I needed to change in myself. Actually all three things were valuable.[10]

Another gain, closely related to the former, was the very practical help that came from the added number of adults in the classroom. Both the teacher educators and the prospective teachers helped with tutoring particular youngsters, supervising playground activity, making or modifying instructional materials, getting ready for PTA, and other such forms of special assistance. This practical form of help was also valued, in addition to the observation, demonstration, or practice teaching responsibilities they assumed. But a number of the teachers summed up the help as more importantly mental than physical; as one teacher put it, "Another head to look at the situation and try to figure out what the problems are and what might be done about them is *most* helpful."[11]

Another gain for the teachers in this case was an increased sense of self-respect and importance. The emphasis upon and recognition given to the critical nature of their work with prospective teachers was reassuring. While they had known all along that student teachers tended to value their practice teaching experiences above the other learning opportunities provided for professional preparation, it was a confirmation and a compliment to have the university personnel affirm the importance of the school experience. By working intensively with the teachers, the teacher educators acknowledged and communicated the importance of the supervising teacher's role.

Similarly, the collegial stance taken by the teacher educators was a departure from the more standard university-school relationship in staff development, where an elevated status is usually accorded to university participants. Typically, teacher educators are the helpers (givers, tellers, showers) and teachers the ones in need of help (takers, listeners, learners).[12] Both groups, in this case, were helpers and both groups were being helped. Both were seen as having knowledge and expertise in differing but important areas relating to gains in teaching effectiveness. The subordinate role so often structured for teachers in staff development was replaced with one of collegial status.

Finally, in addition to obtaining the benefits of increased and authentic free time for staff development and respect for the importance of their present professional roles and expertise, the classroom teachers acquired an increased voice *and* choice in determining the direction and operation of their staff development program. Although numerous efforts have been designed to give teachers more serious input into identification of their needs and preferences for staff development activity, most of them continue to carry major limitations on teacher choice.

The laundry-list approach to needs assessment often forces choices from a set of meagerly described topical options. Informed choice is difficult at best and majority interests tend to dominate. Once topical commitments are made, opportunities for negotiated change and modification are rare. Further, state and federally supported staff development efforts carry a predetermined assumption of what teachers need and thus constrain choice relative to goals; although locally selected strategies may be more open to choice in such cases, these too can be heavily constrained by "deliverable" requirements.

Choice is always limited by the knowledge and availability of options. Opportunities to explore a wide array of alternatives, some of which may appear questionable or unfamiliar at the onset, can be an important part of extending opportunities to learn. The presence of ongoing openness and flexibility to modify the directions one has originally "chosen" can therefore be a particularly important factor. One of the reasons many teachers value the more "open" teacher centers may be partially attributed to the presence of this important form of choice.

The EEE staff development program gave teachers the opportunity to exercise choice that is typically unavailable to them. They were able to pursue interests as well as needs and explore the familiar as well as the new. They were able to shape and determine both the goals and the means of their staff development experience, although their judgments were admittedly affected by negotiation. But constraints were minimal, and choices to pursue and change selected courses of direction throughout the program were present. Staff development topics and times and instructors were changed in response to perceived needs and preferences. Presentations, readings, discussions, active and reflective work time, observations, and practice opportunities with and without systematic feedback were all allowed and arranged. The issues, problems, and subjects pursued changed within and across the years as the teachers exercised more self-determination and choice than they had experienced heretofore regarding professional staff development.

Thus, the benefits to teachers that came in the form of increased professional time, assistance in the classroom, collegial exchange, respect for their work, and choice in regard to staff development were a part of the experience. These gains, blended with the teachers' expressed beliefs that they were growing in their enthusiasm for and effectiveness in teaching appeared to constitute the benefits that made the tensions worthwhile.

Apparent gains for the teacher educators. The benefits to the teacher educators, on the other hand, seemed to be less obvious and powerful. Instead of acquiring freedom in the form of some release from the requirements of their regular duties, they lost degrees of freedom. The increased time and task demands that resulted from their close work with the classroom teachers were not compensated by comparable reductions in their professional responsibilities and workload, although other benefits did accrue.

The teacher educators did receive a modest extrinsic reward for their additional work in the form of some added remuneration. The university administrator responsible for recommendations regarding salary adjustments valued the program and saw that the university participants were not penalized, but were rewarded financially for their serious time and work commitments to the program. This benefit was person-dependent and variable, however, as this "extra duty" compensation was not a part of the college's merit evaluation policy.

In the form of intrinsic rewards, the teacher educators were recipients of numerous accolades from the prospective and classroom teachers who were impressed with and appreciative of the university teachers' courage and commitment to the teacher preparation and staff development programs. It was clear that the teacher educators experienced an increase in their professional credibility and in turn perceived this as a consequence and benefit of their participation.

The teacher educators also expressed a belief similar to the elementary teachers relative to the benefits of professional growth. They thought that they were more effective in their teaching because of the learning that took place through their staff development activities. It is unlikely, however, that this intrinsic reward, even combined with the modest financial and social approval rewards, would have sustained the extra tension they encountered.

The major benefit described by the participating teacher educators was their satisfaction in developing and teaching in a coherent and internally consistent undergraduate program for prospective teachers. Teacher preparation programs at most colleges and universities are known for their fragmentation and lack of curricular articulation. The excessive difficulties encountered in correcting this problem at the university level are legion and continue to defy even the most dedicated academic reformers. Thus, the ability to develop and operate a teacher preparation program that fostered coherence in program offerings, and actually permitted teacher educators to *see* their university students apply their learnings while teaching real elementary school youngsters, was a powerful source of reinforcement. The opportunity to witness their students' growth and refinement of teaching knowledge, competence, and skill was a clear intrinsic reward for the teacher educators; their apparent success in "making a difference" was satisfying. The help they received from the teachers in this regard was also clearly recognized and valued, for the teacher educators knew that they could not have done it alone.

Participants' descriptions of perceived learnings. Various aspects of the EEE staff development experiences and outcomes have been described by participants. The six teachers and four teacher educators who provided the initial leadership for the program published a brief description of their early goals, worries, and impressions of the value of the program.[13] A subsequent description and publication of what was being learned focused on staff development considerations and approaches that appeared important when research results are used in deciding on the effectiveness of teaching practice.[14] Two additional publications summarized some of the teachers' and teacher educators' joint efforts to increase effectiveness in teaching reading[15] and fostering constructive social-emotional behavior in youngsters.[16] A more recent publication focuses on a set of general observations and beliefs regarding staff development that the teacher educators most closely associated with the program have come to hold.[17] The theme that runs throughout these descriptions focuses on the importance of reciprocity and reflection.

The reciprocity that the EEE participants describe refers to in-kind exchanges between school and university educators, while the reflection refers to their thoughtful consideration of each other's unique professional views. Reciprocity comes in the form of shared teaching and assistance with one another's students, but as importantly, it is in their mutual willingness to *listen* and *see* and *consider* seriously each other's experience and perspective on the theoretic and practical aspects of teaching. Reflection comes through the active thinking that occurs as ideas are formulated, expressed, allowed to come up against new experiences and views, and then reformulated to "reflect" the new insights and understandings that result.

The benefits that apparently accrue from the reciprocity and reflection contained in the EEE program, seem to be powerful enough to outweigh the negative aspects associated with the tensions that arise when school and university educators work and study together. It is also possible that the particular set of tensions that the reciprocity and reflection provoke is highly important to effective staff development for *professional* educators, since it effectively "marries" the theoretical and practical forms of knowledge and expertise.

Staff Development and Some Reflections on Our Learnings

The EEE staff development experience reflects a number of pedagogical ideas about effective teacher learning and the subsequent improvement of teaching practice. Several lessons learned from the experience are consistent with the existing staff development literature and support increasingly accepted practice. Some of the learnings are less visibly represented in the contemporary literature, however, and suggest the need for additional thought and inquiry.

THE EEE EXPERIENCE AND RELATED RESEARCH

The conduct of staff development as a school-site effort was judged as obviously necessary by the EEE participants. They observed, as did McLaughlin and Marsh,[18] Williams,[19] and Little,[20] that the importance of the school site for professional development was related to the efficacy of collective and collegial problem identification and study.

The attention to and emphasis upon intrinsic professional rewards was also acknowledged by the EEE participants. Hutson[21] and Berliner[22] both identified the importance of this factor in their reviews, citing the work of Berman and McLaughlin,[23] Fullan and Pomfret,[24] Lieberman and Miller,[25] and McLaughlin and Marsh.[26]

The freedom to adapt instruction to their own classroom situations, with opportunities for extended practice time and coaching by observers who could provide feedback, was also seen as important by EEE participants and others who have studied similar situations.[27] Hutson argues that the design of such programs is and should be necessarily complex and ambitious.[28] This argument is supported by the EEE experience and the findings of McLaughlin and Marsh who suggest that learning of the kind found in staff development programs is an adaptive and heuristic process—a form of professional learning that is both long-term and nonlinear.[29]

Hutson's observation that staff development "should follow a developmental, not a deficit model" was also supported by the EEE experience.[30] While noting that the developmental model is not widely accepted or well understood, Hutson suggests that it is one in which "teachers are seen as being skilled professionals who bring unique abilities and positive attitudes" to the program.[31] The developmental model characterizes teachers as being constructive and open to professional growth that is related to a natural human process of adaptation and change. The deficit model, on the other hand, represents the idea that teachers have generic weaknesses which must be "fixed" or compensated for by outside agents. The "developmental style of inservice" characterized by Feiman and Floden includes opportunities for teachers to engage in close observation and dialogue about the experience of teaching.[32] Teachers focus on action and meaning, and serve as interpreters of educational phenomena, with the expected outcomes of increased self-awareness and the capacity to learn from experience. The EEE participants also supported the importance of these views.

The EEE experience reflecting major tensions between practicing professionals and their academic counterparts from the university is supported by the literature on professional education in a variety of fields. Scholars who have studied other professions and their respective subcultures of professional education have noted the "constant politics of the several parties to professional education"—a continuing tension that appears related to the issue of balance between theory and practice.[33] Thus the tensions experienced by the teachers and teacher educators who worked so closely together could have been anticipated.

Such tension has been viewed as a constructive force, however, and is important to the cognitive developmental theories of teacher education, as advocated by the Minnesota Project of Deliberate Psychological Education.[34] This approach to changing teachers' ego developmental level borrows heavily from Piaget's concept of equilibration or cognitive conflict resolution.[35] Experiences that provide people with new roles often reveal inadequacies in old assumptions and patterns of thinking which are resolved through equilibration.[36]

Herbert Thelen has pointed out that the tension and conflict between views expressed in a group seeking solutions to problems releases an energy which eventually can produce a new resolution.[37] The tension, therefore, plays a constructive role in a continuous dialectic process of learning. Thelen sees this as the essence of the democratic group process, the primary benefit of collaboration between people of differing views. Viewed in this light, the conflict between teachers and teacher educators is not as important as the *process* of negotiating and renegotiating the social meaning of teaching. Hence, the tension that frequently arises can be viewed as an important part of eventual synergistic resolution. But these process dimensions alone may be insufficient when considering various explanations for the learning that might have occurred.

THE EEE EXPERIENCE AND QUESTIONS FOR FURTHER STUDY

Theories about tension and dissonance are suggestive of opportunities for important growth and learning, but the EEE experience implied that the *substance* of the differing perspectives provoking the tension might be of comparable importance. The EEE participants came to the view that careful consideration and relatively balanced attention to the following areas of "study" had a synergistic effect on the professional growth they seemed to experience through staff development: (a) the formal, abstract, and theoretical knowledge that is related either directly or indirectly to teaching; (b) the concrete and practical knowledge that is related to teaching; and (c) the frequently obscure and "thorny" nature of the relationship between the two forms of knowing.

The need for serious attention to the "practical" side of teaching is well established,[38] but the need for continued attention to formal educational knowledge and theorizing is less frequently recognized in the staff development literature. Wilson,[39] Peters,[40] and Fenstermacher[41] have written about the potential value of this learning for teachers, although, as Feiman indicates, it is "a form of educational scholarship that many consider impractical and not directly relevant to the improvement of teaching."[42] The EEE participants found its *indirect* value to be an important part of their professional staff development, however.

Recall that the EEE participants were engaged in an ongoing assessment of the apparent worth of presumed advances in educational knowledge and technique, a necessary exercise if they were to make appropriate judgments about what teachers needed to know and do to teach more effectively (whether the teachers were themselves, in this case, or the prospective teachers they were preparing). This requirement urged a critical examination of the ideas they used, the assumptions they made, and the arguments they advanced. When formal knowledge was considered, it was consistently examined in light of the purposes, consequences, and context of teaching. When problems of teaching practice were considered, they were typically examined in light of the formal knowledge that might shed some possible light on the various resolutions that could be tried. Thus, it is fair to say that there was a flexible interplay between the theoretic and practical knowledge that might be viewed as important and helpful to teachers.

Peters suggests the development of courses that are organized around a common core of relevant, fundamental, and practical problems that are reflective of modes of inquiry in the separate disciplines.[43] Apparently more doubtful about the importance of existing theory for teachers, Wilson recommends more deliberate, clear, and serious discourse on the problems of teaching practice.[44] Although a formal "problems course" as such was not developed (apparently suggested by Peters to protect teachers from potential exposure to "irrelevant" disciplinary knowledge) and discussions of formal knowledge were not avoided (as Wilson implies they should be), the EEE participants appeared to value and support the rational forms of thinking urged by these scholars.

Discussions sometimes grew out of material selected by teacher educators for its apparent general importance to education (for example, studies of child development, teacher expectations, the changing nature and structure of American families, the complex organization of modern institutions including the school). Other times discussions grew out of practical problems and interests of classroom teachers (for example, How can one motivate youngsters to read? How does one help apparent underachievers? How can one encourage greater respect among youngsters of different races?). Thus, the teacher educators made the initial judgments about the formal knowledge that they thought *might* be worthwhile and then let their shared examination and discourse with teachers determine whether or not it was useful in helping them understand and think better about the problems and practice of teaching. The teachers, on the other hand, made the initial judgments about the concrete problems that they thought were worth serious attention, and then let their shared examination and discourse with teacher educators determine whether or not they could justify actions in light of public and general criteria, rather than by personal and unexamined preferences alone. The prevailing approach was continually to use conceptual tools in examining fundamental beliefs and ideas, whether they emanated from formal *or* practical knowledge. The movement was back and forth, from the abstract to the concrete, and from the practical to the theoretic. Questions of how much attention and when to shift attention from one emphasis to another were continually open for consideration and negotiation.

Issues of differential emphasis and curricular articulation between theory and practice have been seriously addressed in regard to initial teacher preparation for some time. Dewey's 1904 essay on "The Relation of Theory to Practice in Education" is a prime example of this historical problem.[45] Those responsible for professional education in other professional fields continue to wrestle with similar theory/practice issues as well.[46] Yet the question of balance between the more formal and the practical forms of knowledge for teacher development does not emerge as a particularly critical one in the contemporary literature. It may be that the question has been decided, in the main, in favor of the obvious need of teachers to satisfy the immediate classroom demands for concrete skills and practical activities. If such is the case, it may be unfortunate, since it could inhibit the advancement of knowledge relative to the question of what teachers need over time.

Furthermore, it may reflect a fundamental conception about the conduct of teaching that downplays the potentially important intellectual and professional aspects of the occupation itself. After studying education for the professions of medicine, law, theology, and social welfare, for example, Hughes made the following observations in his report to the Carnegie Commission on Higher Education:

No profession does its teaching without implanting its philosophy concerning the aspects of nature, society, culture, and knowledge involved in its work. Part of that philosophy is a set of convictions about what knowledge and what skills are most important. The prestigious specialties are thought to require *both* more theory *and* more practice than does general practice. But as one comes to the lower ranks of the occupations called paraprofessions, the emphasis is put on *practical skills*.[47] (emphases added)

Fenstermacher has made an eloquent plea to researchers relative to our "need to know more about what teachers need to know." He also indicates how important the more thoughtful areas of knowing may be to teaching performance:

If a new idea is thought worthy of serious consideration by practicing educators, then it may be that before we can reasonably expect teachers to modify their performance, three things must happen: (1) the teacher is given the opportunity to study the evidence and argument on behalf of the new idea, as part of the process of adopting new intentions or modifying old ones; (2) the teacher is helped to understand how features of the existing setting may be controlled in ways that facilitate expression of new or modified intentions in performance; and (3) information is available that shows what features of the setting not under the direct control of the teacher must be altered in order to encourage teacher performances based upon new or revised intentions. An important task for future research in teacher education is to aid the teacher in answering the question: What, in the setting in which I work, must be different before I can do this new thing well? The allocation of research talent to this question is predicated, of course, on an affirmative answer to the question of *whether this new thing is worth doing at all*.[48] (emphasis added)

The experience of the EEE participants, both teachers and teacher educators alike, left them in general support of Fenstermacher's views as expressed above. They found that various aspects of formal and practical knowing were important for the exercise of professional skill in teaching. The teachers and teacher educators also learned that it was possible to learn effectively from one another, though it was provocative of continuing tension. The continued tension was likely tolerated and sustained because the participants maintained effective interpersonal relationships and received sufficiently powerful rewards for their continued participation in the program itself. But future research is needed to reveal better understanding of the factors that appear to make the very real human travail tolerable, in light of the tension that apparently accompanies shared staff development for school and university teachers.

The EEE participants also found that the tendency of school-based educators to be narrowly and excessively concerned with the practical, and university-based educators to be narrowly and excessively concerned with the theoretic, could be constructively modified through shared and sustained discourse and experience in matters relating to the improvement of teaching practice. Future empirical work could investigate the viability and generalizability of this observation.

The EEE participants also described apparent gains in *both* their theoretical and practical perspectives, as a result of their opportunities to "test" abstract ideas in practice and "test" their practical ideas in theory. They reported perceived benefits from analyzing the apparent problems of both theory and practice; when generalizations were not helpful, for example, was it the fault of the general principles or was it the fault of an inappropriate test in practice? Although the participants *claimed* that such searching analysis was helping them become more effective teachers, was it really, and if so, in what ways?

Finally, a host of questions are raised about the efficacy and means of achieving a better balance between formal and practical knowledge for professional education. It is generally accepted that professionals need knowledge of theory and knowledge of practice, and, as difficult as it may be, it is desirable to have these knowledges compatible and complementary for purposes of professional education. But, it is also generally acknowledged that efforts intended to develop constructive relationships between the distinctive areas of theoretical and practical knowing have, for the most part, been less than successful. This general failure may be partially attributable to insufficient appreciation and compensation for the inherent tension that arises when professionals with more theoretical views interact with professionals with more practical views.

The occupational endeavors of university academics naturally lead to the acquisition and development of formal knowledge and expertise, just as the occupational endeavors of practicing professionals lead to the acquisition and development of practical knowledge and expertise. Since their chosen occupations have brought each of them to pursue and be rewarded for interactions with relatively different forms of knowing, it may be naive to assume that they *should* enjoy or feel compelled to learn about the various underpinnings and intricacies of each other's experience. Because academic and practicing professionals are not compatible in some *natural* sense, however, does not imply that they should not be brought together for purposes of professional education and staff development. If both forms of knowledge and expertise *are* important, and if their effective integration strengthens both the theoretical and practical knowledge, as has been assumed, it seems important that professional educators continue to study and search for potentially effective means of encouraging and sustaining interactions between the two groups.

To do this, professional educators will have to do more than simply write about the problem of the theory-practice "gap." It will not remedy itself with time, nor will members of either group be apt to assume responsibility for the remedy, even though each keeps suggesting that the other should. It may well take members of both groups working together and studying what happens and why it happens, as they struggle to increase their respective effectiveness in teaching.

Summary

This chapter has described a specific staff development program that was intended to improve concomitantly the teaching ability of public school *and* university educators. A major unifying and facilitating aspect of the program was the presence of, responsibility for, and dependence on a preparation program for prospective teachers. One way of thinking about the staff development program is to consider the practicing teachers and teacher educators as the primary beneficiaries of the program and the prospective teachers and elementary students as the secondary beneficiaries. Though the elementary school students were the major responsibility of the practicing teachers and the university students were the major responsibility of the practicing teacher educators, the shared and interdependent responsibility for providing consistent and appropriate instruction to both student groups demanded a careful and critical examination of their intended ends and means of teaching.

This need for shared understanding and agreement provoked intense articulation of and reflection upon the teaching goals and processes important for elementary youngsters and the teaching goals and processes important for prospective teachers. Both the practicing teachers and teacher educators were thus required to state and re-examine their beliefs and practices as they related to the skills of pedagogy needed for effective elementary educators. A process of negotiation and renegotiation of what constitutes the appropriate goals and processes of education was set in motion.

Many aspects of the model presented here are supported by the growing body of staff development literature, but other aspects suggest the need for further research. The contributions of this staff development experience to the professional growth of the participants calls for additional study, and similar programs could readily be designed and examined where school and university educators are mutually dedicated to improving their teaching competence.

Perhaps the major implication suggested by the EEE staff development experience is that we should reexamine the growing tendency to confuse teacher *needs* and teacher *wants*, whether the teachers are from the university *or* from the elementary school. The teacher educators' desire to avoid close interaction with practical experience and the classroom teachers' desire to avoid serious interaction with more formal intellectual activity may simply be escapes from an unpleasant form of tension, a tension that is basically healthy and generative of more fruitful staff development.

Although it involves a larger collective, the "marriage" of school and university teachers who share a commitment to the improvement of elementary education may be analogous, in some important ways, to the institution of marriage between individuals. Keyserling defined marriage as "a state of tragic tension."[49] Believing that each individual is predominantly a solitary being, he argued that efforts toward "communion" were bound to be "riddled with conflict between self-interest and duty to one's partner, between personal ambition and social obligation, between the idea of marriage as a union of two people and the reality of both parties remaining at their core separate entities." Although these inherent conflicts led Keyserling to describe marriage as a state of tragic tension, it did not lead him to reject the relationship. Rather, he argued that the tension promoted "self-development," since it allowed persons to "develop along different lines."[50] Thus, in the end he cast marriage as hazardous, but not *necessarily* tragic. It could be beautiful, but *"only* beautiful if its tragic components were calculated and understood."

School and university partnerships, like those of individuals, appear to have similar hazards and conflicts. Perhaps if these tensions also come to be better "calculated and understood" they can help school and university partners realize improved relationships and more effective staff development.

FOOTNOTES

1. Leland Dean, "Project REFUEL (Relevant Experiences for Urban Educational Leaders): A Program of Michigan State University," unpublished manuscript, 1969.

2. Malcolm M. Provus, *The Grand Experiment: The Life and Death of the TTT Program as Seen through the Eyes of Its Evaluators* (Berkeley, Calif.: McCutchan Publishing Corp., 1975), p. 21.

3. The EEE or "Triple-E" title for the new program was selected because it implied similarity to, but distinction from, the earlier TTT program. Its acronym was drawn from the program's broad goal of advancing elementary education.

4. Provus, *The Grand Experiment*, p. 3.

5. Ibid., p. 147.

6. Ibid., p. 43.

7. Ibid., p. 125.

8. As a consequence of the reciprocal and functional relationship that was forged between the EEE and Teacher Corps programs, published accounts of the work appear under the auspices of both or either of the two projects.

9. Henry B. Woolf, ed., *Webster's New Collegiate Dictionary* (Springfield, Mass.: G. and C. Merriam Co., 1977).

10. Quotation taken from transcriptions of taped interviews with teachers and reported in an unpublished paper by Henrietta Barnes, Michigan State University, 1978.

11. Ibid., p. 16.

12. Henrietta Barnes and Joyce Putnam, "Professional Development through Reciprocity and Reflection" (Presentation at the annual conference of the American Association of Colleges of Teacher Education, Detroit, February 1981). ED 205 472

13. Barbara Ataman, Henrietta Barnes, Cathy Colando, Judith E. Lanier, Perry Lanier, Roberta Peto, Carol Pratt, Joyce Putnam, Diane Rouse, and Erma Whiting, "Improving the Professional Growth Opportunities of Elementary Teaching Person-

nel," in *Inservice Education: Criteria for and Examples of Local Programs*, ed. Roy A. Edelfelt (Bellingham, Wash.: Western Washington State College, 1977), pp. 31-37.

14. Henrietta Barnes, Joyce Putnam, Donna Wanous, "Learning from Research Adaptation," in *Adapting Educational Research: Staff Development Approaches*, ed. Lee Morris (Norman, Okla.: Teacher Corps Research Adaptation Cluster, University of Oklahoma, 1979), pp. 39-64.

15. Gerald Duffy, "The Lansing School District/Michigan State University Developmental Reading Program," in *The Five Dimensions of Demonstration*, ed. Keith A. Acheson (Norman, Okla.: Teacher Corps Research Adaptation Cluster, University of Oklahoma, 1977), pp. 66-75.

16. Henrietta Barnes and Mary Samuelson, "Social-Emotional Education: An Inservice Program," in *The Five Dimensions of Demonstration*, pp. 88-101.

17. Henrietta Barnes and Joyce Putnam, "Professional Development through Inservice That Works," in *School-Focused Inservice: Descriptions and Discussions*, ed. Kenneth Howey, Richard Bents, and Dean Corrigan (Reston, Va.: Association of Teacher Educators, 1981), pp. 215-30.

18. Milbrey W. McLaughlin and David D. Marsh, "Staff Development and School Change," in *Staff Development: New Demands, New Realities, New Perspectives*, ed. Ann Lieberman and Lynne Miller (New York: Teachers College Press, 1979).

19. Richard C. Williams, "A Political Perspective on Staff Development," in *Staff Development*, ed. Lieberman and Miller.

20. Judith W. Little, "School Success and Staff Development in Urban Desegregated Schools: A Summary of Recently Completed Research" (Paper presented at the meeting of the American Educational Research Association, Los Angeles, Calif., April 1981).

21. Harry M. Hutson, Jr., "Inservice Best Practices: The Learnings of General Education," *Journal of Research and Development in Education* 14 (Winter 1981): 1-10.

22. David C. Berliner, "The Elementary School Teacher as Learner" (Paper presented at the meeting of the American Psychological Association, Los Angeles, Calif., August 1981).

23. Paul Berman and Milbrey W. McLaughlin, *Federal Programs Supporting Educational Change, Vol. 8: Implementing and Sustaining Innovations* (Santa Monica, Calif.: Rand Corp., 1978).

24. Michael Fullan and Alan Pomfret, "Research on Curriculum and Instruction Implementation," *Review of Educational Research* 47 (Spring 1977): 335-97.

25. Ann Lieberman and Lynne Miller, "The Social Realities of Teaching," *Teachers College Record* 80 (September 1978): 54-68.

26. McLaughlin and Marsh, "Staff Development and School Change."

27. Ibid.

28. Hutson, "Inservice Best Practices."

29. McLaughlin and Marsh, "Staff Development and School Change."

30. Hutson, "Inservice Best Practices," p. 8.

31. Ibid.

32. Sharon Feiman and Robert Floden, *A Consumer's Guide to Teacher Development*, Research Series no. 94 (East Lansing, Mich.: Institute for Research on Teaching, 1981).

33. Everett C. Hughes, Barrie Thorne, Agostino M. DeBaggis, Arnold Gurin, and David Williams, *Education for the Professions of Medicine, Law, Theology, and Social Welfare: A Report Prepared for the Carnegie Commission on Higher Education* (New York: McGraw-Hill Book Co., 1973), p. 16.

34. Joseph E. Bernier, "A Psychological Education Intervention for Teacher Development" (Doct. diss., University of Minnesota, 1976).

35. Richard C. Sprinthall and Norman A. Sprinthall, *Educational Psychology: A Developmental Approach* (Reading, Mass.: Addison-Wesley, 1974).

36. Sprinthall and Sprinthall, *Educational Psychology*. For extended discussion on the contributions of Piaget and of Deliberate Psychological Education related to the developmental model of teacher education, see Feiman and Floden, *A Consumer's Guide to Teacher Development*, pp. 11-18.

37. Herbert A. Thelen, *The Classroom Society* (New York: John Wiley and Sons, 1981). See also, Bruce Joyce and Marsha Weil, *Models of Teaching* (Englewood Cliffs, N.J.: Prentice-Hall, 1972), chap. 2, "Group Investigation."

38. Berliner, "The Elementary School Teacher as Learner."

39. John Wilson, *Educational Theory and the Preparation of Teachers* (Windsor, Berks: National Foundation for Educational Research Publishing Co., 1975).

40. Robert S. Peters, *Education and the Education of Teachers* (London: Routledge and Kegan Paul, 1977).

41. Gary D Fenstermacher, "What Needs to be Known about What Teachers Need to Know," in *Exploring Issues in Teacher Education: Questions for Future Research*, ed. Gene E. Hall, Shirley M. Hord, and Gail Brown (Austin, Tex.: Research and Development Center for Teacher Education, 1980).

42. Feiman and Floden, *A Consumer's Guide to Teacher Development*.

43. Peters, *Education and the Education of Teachers*.

44. Wilson, *Educational Theory and the Preparation of Teachers*.

45. John Dewey, "The Relation of Theory to Practice in Education," in *The Relation of Theory to Practice in the Education of Teachers*, Third Yearbook of the National Society for the Study of Education, Part 1 (Bloomington, Ill.: Public School Publishing Co., 1904), pp. 9-30.

46. Hughes et al., *Education for the Professions of Medicine, Law, Theology, and Social Welfare*.

47. Ibid., p. 15.

48. Fenstermacher, "What Needs to be Known about What Teachers Need to Know," p. 43.

49. See Hermann Keyserling's interpretation in Joseph Epstein, *Divorced in America: Marriage in an Age of Possibility* (New York: E. P. Dutton and Co., 1974), pp. 42-45.

50. Ibid.

CHAPTER VII

Curriculum Implementation and Staff Development as Cultural Change

THOMAS A. ROMBERG AND GARY G. PRICE

There has been a long history in the United States of moral imperatives for schools to change their practices. The reasons for those imperatives have varied, but the ongoing obligation to change has not.[1] Under this constant pressure to change, it has become a tradition in education to make change by adopting or developing a new curriculum. Implicit in that tradition is an assumption that the adoption or development of a new curriculum is the easiest or best way to change school practices.

Although the adoption of new curriculum materials may involve only minimal changes in school practices, it is nevertheless a form of change that is visible to parents and other groups pressing for change. Many teachers view the pressures for change as illegitimate. As unwilling partners to much change, teachers are sometimes attracted to changes of window dressing (for example, purchasing a revised text series adorned with new, four-color pictures). Such prophylactic changes help to fend off those seemingly illegitimate pressures to change.

Thus, teachers are often cast as defenders of curricular traditions. That role is not all bad, because curricular traditions are important. In the first place, curricular traditions are inevitable facts of life in schools. Furthermore, they do have the virtue of bringing rational order

The material in this chapter is based upon work supported by the National Institute of Education under Grant No. NIE-G-81-0009 to the Wisconsin Center for Education Research. Any opinions, findings, and conclusions or recommendations expressed are those of the authors and do not necessarily reflect the views of the Institute or the Department of Education.

and predictability to schools (for example, teaching a year of geometry to fifteen-year-old students).

However, legitimate changes are made difficult to implement because they challenge curricular traditions that have outlived their usefulness. As satirically narrated by J. Abner Peddiwell in his classic, *The Saber-Tooth Curriculum*,[2] traditions such as a course on "saber-tooth-tiger-scaring-with-fire" sometimes outlive their usefulness (that is, "scaring-with-fire" continues to be taught even after saber-tooth tigers have become extinct). Today, interpolation of logarithms is still being taught, even though calculators and computers have replaced its use in all aspects of engineering. And elementary statistics is often taught using obsolete (precomputer) paper-and-pencil computational shortcuts that interfere with statistical insight. Demands for new educational programs that challenge the curricula of schools must be examined and, if valid, must be met. For example, the demands of scientists and mathematicians to have school programs that reflected their disciplines were authentic in 1957. Funding of the "modern" science and mathematics programs by the federal government led to the curriculum reform movement of the 1960s.

In similar manner today, the microprocessor "chip" and the blossoming worldwide technological revolution in computing is now demanding the attention of schools and is generating an everbroadening need for both computer literacy and mathematical literacy. These needs create pressure for innovation in schools. Also, advances in computing are making possible instructional innovations such as rapid tailoring of drills,[3] complex diagnostic procedures,[4] and two-dimensional simulations.[5] Instructional technologies like these provide another type of pressure for innovation in schools. Again, both new curricula and new instructional procedures need to be—and will be—developed and implemented.

In summary, efforts to change curricula in schools must be viewed as natural phenomena the impetus for which comes from personal, professional, community, and other social sources. Curricula that respond to legitimate pressures need to be developed and implemented. However, the successful implementation of such programs will not just happen. Our purpose in this chapter is to examine the problems involved in planned curricular change with particular reference to staff development in schools.

To that end, we first attempt to shed light on the differing perspectives about a curriculum. Second, we will characterize curriculum innovation in terms of its effect on school life. In particular, we want to draw attention to the need to consider the culture of schools. Third, we will discuss sources of information on the diffusion of innovations, and present various theoretical models of the change process. From that discussion, we will identify some of the problems of implementing change, including those factors that make educational innovation so difficult. Fourth, based on this knowledge of planned educational change, we will offer a set of recommendations concerning the staff development needs for curriculum implementation. Finally, we will present an example from a school district that has developed a curriculum monitoring procedure that meets our recommendations.

Curriculum

The notion basic to this section is that a curriculum is an operational plan detailing what content is to be taught to students and how the students are to acquire and use that content. One's perspective of curriculum is due in part to one's distance from the act of learning. As Goodlad pointed out, a curriculum can

be viewed from many different vantage points and at several levels of generality or specificity. For a student, the curriculum is what he perceives to be intended for him in his courses and classes, including assigned readings, homework exercises, field trips, and so on. For the teacher, it is what he intends for the students; at one level of insight, a perceived means for changing student behavior. For teachers (and administrators) in concert, the curriculum is the whole body of courses offered by the institution or all planned activities including besides courses of study, organized play, athletics, dramatics, clubs, and other programs. For citizens and policymakers, the curriculum is the body of educational offerings available to whatever groups of students or kinds of educational institutions concern them. For a philosopher, theologian, or educational reformer, the curriculum might be in the learnings to which groups of students, in his judgment, should be exposed. All of these perspectives concern themselves with end products in the form of intended learnings.[6]

This is somewhat analogous to industrial planning. Corporate operational plans are viewed quite differently by assembly-line workers and members of the board of directors. Although production operations are carried out only at the assembly-line level, planning takes place at several levels. As distance from actual operation increases, plans are less specific and show a greater emphasis on general structure and relationships. Similarly, planning in schools takes place at several levels. For clarification, four levels of curriculum planning are identified in Figure 1—design, blueprint, concrete interpretation, and utilization.

LEVEL	EDUCATIONAL PLANNERS (AND ANALOGUES IN INDUSTRY)	NATURE OF PLANS
Design	National Committees (Board of Directors)	General Specification of Needs and Priorities
Blueprint	Publishers and Curriculum Groups (Vice President)	Package of Curriculum Materials—texts, materials, software
Concrete interpretation	Local Curriculum Committees (Shop Foreman)	Guidelines to Teacher for Sequencing Topics and Grouping Children
Utilization	Teacher or Instructional Team (Worker)	Lesson Plans

Fig. 1. Levels of curriculum planning

The design level is analogous to that of a board of directors in corporate planning. From the perspective of this level, curriculum is considered the general course of study—an outline of the content to be covered, specifying the needs and priorities to be served. The main topics to be covered are mentioned, but little is said about instruction. In education, planning at this level is usually done by national committees.

The next level of planning, the blueprint or vice-presidential level, goes beyond the bare outline of content to a carefully detailed listing of what is to be covered, what order is to be followed, and what resources can be used to achieve the intended learnings. The curriculum becomes a detailed set of specifications. The expected interactions are central to the planning; however, the way the interactions are to take place is not spelled out. Most texts can be considered operational definitions of a curriculum at this level.

The third level of curriculum planning, the concrete interpretation or shop-foreman level, goes beyond specification of materials and resources to specification of how humans should use and interact with those materials and resources. Here a curriculum becomes "the organization and sequence of a subject matter in which statements about the subject, methods of teaching, and the activities of the learners are intricately interrelated to form a single entity."[7] Both what is to be done and the way it is to be done are spelled out. The key to this conceptualization of the curriculum is the elements other than content and objectives that are included in the detailed planning.

The last level of curriculum planning, the utilization level, involves those interactions each child actually takes part in. The curriculum here is an individual set of lesson plans that must be developed in terms of the specific instructional setting. The focus is now not on what or how but on whom.

Thus, since the intended learnings remain fixed, a single curriculum can be viewed as a different set of operational plans at each of these levels. The thing that varies over the levels is the specificity of the plans.

This matter of the perspective one takes in relation to a curriculum has been raised for two reasons. First, it illustrates the variety of views on the subject. Second, it underscores the fact that, while different persons have different curricular perspectives, it is the teacher who has the final say about what is actually taught. That fact makes teachers' perceptions of a new curriculum critical to the determination of whether and how it is implemented.

Culture and Change

Our purpose in this section is to examine the problems involved by planned curriculum change. We begin by examining curriculum change in terms of its effect on the lives of persons in schools. We argue that schools have a culture of their own that affects and is affected by efforts at curriculum development. In our experience, to adopt a curriculum change is not necessarily to use it. Moreover, if a curricular innovation *is* used by an adopting school, it is rarely assimilated into the school in the manner intended by the developer. We recommend that curriculum development be considered, in general, as an effort to change the culture of a school, and, in particular, as an effort to change the belief structures and work habits of the school staff.

CURRICULUM CHANGE AS CULTURAL CHANGE

The difficulty of implementing a particular innovation depends on many factors, ranging from the characteristics of the innovation itself to the structure of the culture affected by the change. McClelland discussed how the effective implementation of an innovation may involve different levels of cultural restructuring.[8] The simplest level of restructuring is the substitution of one isolated component of a system for another, such as a change in textbook. If this simplest of changes causes further systemic alterations, such as the purchase of manipulative materials for the classroom, that is a higher level of change. The most complex of all changes deals with values, such as asking teachers to value an active classroom over a quiet one.

This way of characterizing curriculum changes focuses on the degree of restructuring they involve. Arranging curriculum changes on a continuum from least to most restructuring, we have labeled the poles of this continuum *ameliorative innovation* and *radical innovation*. *Ameliorative innovations* are designed (or are perceived as designed) to make some ongoing practice better or more efficient, but do not challenge the values and traditions associated with the school culture. For example, the nonprogrammable calculator as a replacement for the slide rule in engineering classes does not challenge how knowledge of engineering is defined in that culture, or how teachers are to work. Thus, it is an ameliorative innovation.

At the other extreme, *radical innovations* are designed to challenge the cultural traditions of schools, and are perceived as doing that. For instance, "modern mathematics" texts asked schools to define the proper content of school mathematics differently. In another instance, "team teaching" asked schools to develop new staff relationships. The infusion of computers into classrooms, though often marked by ameliorative innovations like computer-mediated drill, will also invite radical innovations like the decoupling of penmanship from composition, wholesale individualization of certain curriculum strands, and the use of dynamic simulations to convey complex concepts. The technologically inexorable infusion of computers will create an especially visible context for the introduction of both amelioratively innovative and radically innovative curriculum change.

CULTURE IN SCHOOLS

Our basic premise is that curriculum development should be planned with the culture of the school deliberately in mind. The need for systematic procedures for disseminating innovations into the culture of schools is evident in the growing literature on school stability. Education in the United States has been remarkably refractory, despite massive efforts sponsored by foundations and the federal government to engineer and implement changes such as team teaching, programmed learning, individualized curriculum programs, modern mathematics, modern science, and open multigraded schools.

In reviewing major educational reform efforts, Goodlad maintains that the work of teachers and students has hardly changed since the turn of the century.[9] Bellack argues convincingly that the most interesting phenomenon of reform is the schools' remarkable resistance to change.[10] Stability, not change, seems to be the dominant characteristic. From an analysis of one reform effort, Romberg states that most change, however well intended, ends up being nominal (with changes in labels, but not practices).[11] From a case study, Gross demonstrated how enthusiasm and dedication are eroded in a very short time, after which practitioners revert to old habits.[12] In a review of the modern mathematics movement, the Conference Board of Mathematical Sciences was forced to conclude that modern mathematics was not a major component of contemporary education in the United States, and that there was no evidence it had even been given a fair trial.[13]

To discuss the culture of schools, we will follow the sociological notions used by Popkewitz, Tabachnick, and Wehlage in their examination of exemplary Individually Guided Education (IGE) schools—a part of the IGE Evaluation Project.[14] "First, school is a place of work where students and teachers act to alter and improve their world, produce social relations, and realize human purposes. Second, schools are places where conceptions of knowledge are distributed and maintained. . . . Third, schools contain an occupational group whose conduct gives legitimacy to the forms of work and knowledge that enter into schooling. Often that group uses the slogan 'professional' to establish its status, privileges, and control."[15]

These three institutional dimensions—work, knowledge, and professionalism—were used because they direct attention to the social assumptions and values that underlie school practices and constrain the implementation of innovations. By our definition, *radical innovations* challenge basic assumptions about work, knowledge, and professionalism.

Work. First, school should be seen as a place of work. Children in schools are doing work when they do assignments, manipulate objects such as microscopes, build things in an industrial arts class, and answer questions on a test. Teachers in schools are doing work when they take attendance, plan lessons, lead discussions, read stories, and evaluate children's performance.

The nature of school work becomes apparent when we look at the initial school experiences of children. Apple and King showed that kindergarten children are taught particular distinctions between work and play.[16] Work was what the teacher gave directions for children to do. Accordingly, children perceived work as coloring, drawing, waiting in line, cleaning up, and singing. The definition of work did not concern specific accomplishments but instead concerned the motivation of the activity. Play activities were those permitted only if time allowed, only after children had finished assigned work. Classroom work was related to certain classroom social relations. All work activities were compulsory, done simultaneously by children, and directed toward identical products. The purpose of classroom work was always defined by the teachers. Diligence, perseverance, participation, and obedience were paramount as evaluative criteria.

In a similar vein, Jackson characterized the teacher as one whose work involves being a supply sergeant, a dispenser of special privileges, an official timekeeper, and a traffic manager.[17] The need to control great numbers of individuals in schools produces a form of spectatorship in which students spend much of their time waiting for the teacher's directions. Although these aspects of schooling may not be viewed fondly by teachers, they are nonetheless embedded in teacher training, school architecture, and definitions of professional competence.

Some computer-based innovations challenge traditional conceptions of school work. Altered conceptions of students' work are involved when students turn their attention to a computer display, whether they do so as consumers of a program or as programmers. The work of teachers is also changed to include diverse new responsibilities like scheduling computer use, interpreting computer output, learning certain uses of a computer and its peripherals, helping students to use computers, and tolerating the absorption many students exhibit when interacting with a computer.

An innovation can sustain, modify, or otherwise interact with conventional patterns of work. Consequently, we must consider the relationships between curriculum change and elements of institutional work in order to make apparent the significance of intervention.

Knowledge. The second institutional dimension of school culture concerns the conception of knowledge. Young and others pursuing the sociology of knowledge have characterized schools as institutions that distribute and maintain certain types of knowledge.[18] Young argues that the relationship between teachers and students is essentially a reality-sharing, world-view-building enterprise. As teachers and students interact, they develop a shared vocabulary and shared ways of reasoning which give sense to one another's actions and provide a framework applicable to future experiences. This shared understanding is based upon an implicit value structure that defines "being educated."

Curriculum changes are radical to the extent that they change the knowledge distributed by schools or the way in which that knowledge is distributed. Curriculum changes (if radical) may change the way teachers allocate their efforts (that is, the way teachers work) and they may also undermine conventional notions of what it means to be educated.

Professionalism. The professional position of teachers is our third dimension of school culture. Professional educators are vested with the authority and power to define pedagogical practice. The label "professional" is used by occupational groups to express the belief that they are highly trained, competent, specialized, dedicated, and effectively serve the public trust. But the label is more than a declaration of public trust. It is also a social category that implies status and privilege. The label "professional teacher" signifies not only technical knowledge and service, but also the power of teachers to bestow a social identity upon their clients (students), a social identity that can affect students' subsequent status as adults.

Like other professional groups, teachers use their power to preserve and expand control, and to resist disadvantageous changes in power relationships. For example, in Becker's study of parent involvement in Chicago schools, teachers reacted to parent involvement in ways that preserved their own control and status in the institution.[19]

Much of the bureaucratization of schooling in recent years has been to the benefit of teacher professionalism at the expense of lay involvement. Technical language, increased specialization, and greater hierarchical differentiation of school personnel make the work of teaching seem esoteric and immune to outside influence. For example, in a study of a Teacher Corps project, technical jargon set apart the initiated (teachers, university professors, school administrators) from the outsiders (lay persons from an Indian community).[20] Shibboleths like "competencies," "modules," "cycles," and "learning styles" forced the Indians to look to experts for interpretations of school experiences. The technical language introduced a perception of efficiency and prevented critical scrutiny of educators' priorities and beliefs.

In summary, our argument is that schools are complex social institutions which are not easily altered. The faltering implementation of an innovation into school culture can be examined in terms of its effects on the work of teachers and children, the knowledge dispensed, and the professional position of teachers.

PERSONS IN SCHOOLS

As explained earlier, teachers' perceptions of a new curriculum are critically important. Institutional resistance to innovation can be understood by considering the perspectives held by the persons involved. Their perspectives are important because they govern the way innovations are ultimately used. Innovations are introduced into social situations in which people have beliefs, hopes, desires, and interests, and into institutional contexts that structure actions. The net effect of an innovation can easily be a surface change congenial to existing values and assumptions. Innovations tend to be assimilated into existing patterns of behavior and belief, frequently coming to function as little more than slogan systems that legitimize the values and assumptions underlying the status quo.

If curriculum developers want the essence of their innovation to be implemented, they must assure that its effects on the work of teachers and children, on the nature of knowledge dispensed, and on the professional position of teachers are understood by all persons involved. Innovations not understood in this way have generally failed to endure in a form that would please developers. At best, they have been assimilated into the existing school culture without affecting that culture. If administrators, teachers, the immediate community of the school, or the general public misconstrue the innovation, it likely will be implemented in a distorted form, if at all. This was the fate of many reform programs of the past twenty years.

Our colleagues in the IGE Evaluation Project have documented in rich detail how this fate befell IGE, even in some schools that were reputed exemplars of IGE.[21] One of us was made sadder but wiser to see a similar fate befall *Developing Mathematical Processes*.[22] Other examples abound. The matrix algebra materials of the School Mathematics Study Group[23] and *The Man Made World*[24] are other examples of well-conceived, federally funded projects that were never widely implemented. Despite their virtues, these curriculum changes contradicted certain aspects of conventional school culture. The beliefs of high school mathematics teachers concerning which parts of high school mathematics are indispensable left no room for the intrusion of matrix algebra, a content previously not taught in high school. *The Man Made World*, an excellent introduction to engineering for high school students, was seldom used, largely because no high school teachers regarded themselves as teachers of engineering.

The rejection of *Man: A Course of Study (MACOS)*[25] by religious groups in local communities is an instance where persons other than professional educators have helped make the culture of schools refractory to change. Innovations can even run afoul because they contradict children's beliefs about the nature of work or teacher-child relations. The Au and Jordan study of culture-bound participation structures is a case in point.[26] Questioning strategies used successfully by teachers with white, middle-class children failed with children of Hawaiian background, reportedly because the children attach different meaning to adults' behavior and expect something different of them. Heath's study of a black community in the piedmont Carolinas similarly illustrates how children assimilate school events to the culture of their community.[27]

School administrators', teachers', parents', community groups', and even children's understanding of an innovation and its challenges to the existing culture of schools must be considered when developing and implementing curriculum change.

PLANNED CHANGE

Curriculum development is a form of planned change. The extensive research literature on planned change includes many classic references.[28] In that literature are many attempts to develop guidelines for planning educational change.[29] As noted by Havelock in his review, such models of planned change can be grouped into three main classes: the *research-development-diffusion perspective*, the *social interaction perspective*, and the *user-as-problem-solver perspective*.[30]

The research-development-diffusion perspective, which is associated particularly with Guba,[31] is characterized by a sequence of planned, coordinated activities, a division of labor, and a rather passive target population. This model is often criticized for giving little heed to users' own perceptions of their needs. Also, it fails to recognize the importance of schools in generating worthwhile problems for research and development, as has been noted elsewhere.[32]

During the past decade, many innovations based upon this model were advertised and adopted, then dismissed by teachers as badly matched to the student population of their school system. Hamilton has argued that lack of significant curriculum change is in part due to the inadequacies of this "center → out" development-implementation process. New programs are developed by a few central individuals, who prepare implementation procedures.[33] School staffs, unaware of the problems, assumptions, and alternatives considered in development gradually modify the new program back to fit old habits. In an example offered by Romberg, primary school staffs assigned to new open-plan schools inevitably introduced partitions and other permanent fixtures so that, within a couple of years, the schools operated as if walls were there.[34]

The social interaction perspective is basically sociological in nature, and considers the path taken by a preidentified innovation as it moves through a social system. This model has guided a great deal of empirical research in agriculture,[35] education,[36] and medicine,[37] and emphasizes characteristics of innovators[38] and theories of rejection[39] as well as adoption. Also stressed are important aspects of the social structure, such as group membership and opinion leadership.

The weaknesses of this model include lack of concern with how the innovation is developed and with the adaptations the user may make. While education is a social enterprise, there has been a failure by many to consider the organizational structure of the school.[40] Different curricula make different assumptions about learners, about the system of delivering knowledge to students, and about the technology of the instructional system. Failure to appreciate these assumptions may make adaptation of the new program very difficult.

The *user-as-a-problem-solver perspective* stresses (a) starting with the user's need and its diagnosis, (b) providing nondirective help from outside, and (c) encouraging the user to develop his or her own internal resources and capacity for change. The main drawbacks of this perspective, according to Havelock, are that it puts great strain on the user, it minimizes the importance of outside resources, and it is not suited for large-scale implementation.[41] The possibility of generally applicable guidelines for planned change has been called into question by Broudy, Cronbach, Phillips, and others.[42] In essence, the point is that the social sciences at best produce short-lived generalizations, and at worst, can never generalize beyond the situation studied.

While none of these three perspectives is perfect, each identifies factors that should be considered when planning educational change.

THE OCCURRENCE OF RADICAL CHANGE IN SCHOOLS: STAFF DEVELOPMENT

Ameliorative innovations are commonplace and are readily implemented, so their implementation is seldom a concern of curriculum developers. Radical curriculum development is concerned with a change in the culture of the school. But the crux of the matter is that the developer's view of a radical innovation is ultimately not what matters. Ultimately what matters is the mix of actual responses in a school to the innovation.

From our shared experience in the evaluation of Individually

Guided Education (IGE) and from Romberg's experiences in the evaluations of the School Mathematics Study Group and *Developing Mathematical Processes*, we find it useful to consider the different sorts of school responses to radical innovation that get viewed and labeled as "change."[43] Responses to radical innovations can be loosely divided into nominal change and actual change.

Nominal change. Nominal change is the most prevalent type of response to innovations. It involves adopting nothing but labels. Educators are good at this. If team teaching is in fashion this year, we label groups of teachers as "Team Red," "Team Blue," and so on. Next year, when individualization is in vogue, the new term gets prominence in the school reports. But the routines are not changed. We do not fault school staffs for this strategy. As institutions, schools are under considerable political and social pressure to do things they were never designed to do; nor do they have personnel trained to do them. To maintain political viability or to keep pressure groups at bay, nominal change is often reasonable.

Nominal change is recognized and admitted by practitioners. For example, many principals of IGE schools admitted that they really did not have regular Unit meetings, did not have an operative Instructional Improvement Committee, and did not group and regroup students on a regular basis. All of these features were central to orthodox operation of IGE schools. Reasons or excuses why such practices were not operative were freely offered. Such statements were usually accompanied by a promise or a wish that in the future things would be changed.

Actual change. Actual change occurs where the school staff understand that a radical innovation is expected and attempt to implement it as such. But even when the staff perceive themselves as having actually changed, we must distinguish between different kinds of actual change. We present here a three-part taxonomy that emerged in the IGE Evaluation as a useful way to describe different kinds of IGE implementation.[44] The kinds of actual change are labeled technical change, constructive change, and illusory change.

Technical change describes a situation in which practitioners have adopted not just the labels but also the rituals and routines of a new program. However, this implementation is done without fully grasping or taking to heart the values and principles that guided the development of the program. Technical change is analogous to following the letter of a law, but not understanding its intent.

Technical change is unquestionably actual change at the procedural level, and procedural change is not inconsequential. Most educational programs specify procedures to be followed. For example, in most modern mathematics texts a chapter on sets was added, and often one on other number bases, and so forth. Technical adopters dutifully cover those chapters. However, their coverage is mechanical, done without understanding the purpose of the chapter. Drilling on "base 7" addition facts is not what the authors had in mind. Likewise, in the IGE program, we found schools in which the staff dutifully specified instructional objectives, grouped students according to need, assessed progress, kept records, and so forth. What was missing was reflection, common sense, and an understanding of the purposes of the routines.

Given what Hamilton has characterized as a "center → out" approach to planned change, this shallow form of implementation is understandable.[45] In a center's efforts to convince practitioners to adopt a new program, the "how" of implementation is usually emphasized. The assumptions, practical compromises, and inevitable arguments that were involved in developing the program are not mentioned. Hence, the staff of an adopting school has little sense of the reason for change.

In schools exhibiting technical change, there is a strong sense of efficacy. That is, teachers are convinced that children are benefitting from the innovation in demonstrable ways. Their defense of the program may not cite the developer's broader educational purposes, but will make reference to outcomes other than the teachers' own successful acquisition of vocabulary, rituals, and routines.

Constructive change refers to those instances that most please a curriculum developer. The staff of a school adopting the innovation understands its underlying values and principles, and appreciates its larger educational purpose. The language, rituals, and procedures of the innovation are used in light of that purpose. The staff's grasp of the purpose of the innovation enables schools like this to rise beyond orthodoxy and to construct local adjustments for the purpose of better serving the ends of the program. In schools that have responded to a radical innovation with constructive change, deviations from the letter of the law are sometimes made for the purpose of better serving the intent of law. It is this kind of change that Goodlad and others are seeking.[46] In the IGE evaluation, a few instances of constructive change were found.[47]

In *illusory change* the trappings of a radical innovation, its language and rituals, are adopted, but teachers show no conviction that the effects of the innovation will be demonstrable in their own right. In other words, only ipso facto justifications are given for the innovative program. In such a context, doing a good job becomes equated with trying hard and with employing state-of-the-art techniques, regardless of the net effect on children. Teachers find solace as participants in the innovation. If children are not shown to benefit, then their failure to respond is rationalized as inevitable. In this regard, the developer and the school staff may have discrepant beliefs about the capabilities of children and the kind of knowledge the school should offer them. The developer's innovation gets assimilated into the teacher's world view.

This situation invites slippage of procedures, despite staff sincerity about implementing the innovation. The surface trappings can lead a casual observer to believe that the innovation has been fully implemented, which makes this type of change insidious. Careful and repeated observation in the IGE evaluation revealed that some reputed exemplars of IGE fit this description.[48] As prescribed by IGE rituals, teams of teachers were formed, a team leader was chosen, and team meetings were held at scheduled times. Unfortunately, the team meetings were not devoted to the kinds of activities recommended in IGE procedural guidelines—activities like sharing ideas about instruction and making decisions about how to group and regroup children. The casual observer is not the only one affected by the illusion. Surprisingly, the teachers themselves in these schools believed that bona fide implementation of IGE had occurred.

Distorted conceptions of education can arise in illusory change. Some teachers in the IGE evaluation equated the learning of rituals with being educated (for example, how well children read was not important, so long as they acted like children who could read). Similarly, many educators in the past considered that they were teaching a "modern mathematics" course by adding a chapter on sets. We are particularly afraid that in many schools, *computer literacy* will be approached as nothing more than an additional topic in some mathematics class. Unless computer technology permeates school culture beyond that level, the schools will be deluding themselves about fostering computer literacy. Frankly, we are haunted by the unfortunate prospect of computer equipment being wheeled into a classroom with the announcement, "It's your week to cover computers."

Recommendations

Based on our experience and upon this review, we make three general recommendations. The recommendations are meant to address problems that are commonly, perhaps inevitably, involved in planned curriculum change. The recommendations are couched in the language of a "center → out" orientation with respect to the generation and dissemination of innovations, but they are not limited to that orientation. The problems of planned change and general recommendations for dealing with those problems would be applicable to any strategy for implementing change.

1. IDENTIFY TRADITIONS THAT ARE BEING CHALLENGED

Our first recommendation is that innovators identify cultural traditions that will be challenged by an innovation. This may or may not spark conflict. Perfectly reasonable innovations can be subverted by unexamined cultural traditions that, if they were examined, could be changed. As Popper argued, criticism of a cultural tradition can lead to change, but criticism presupposes that the tradition has been identified and brought to consciousness.[49] Whereas some cultural traditions may be found on examination to have low priority in everyone's eyes, some traditions can be challenged successfully only by explicating and arguing about the trade-offs that they involve with other traditions.

Essentially, this is a recommendation that innovators anticipate the various ways in which a planned change will affect the lives of persons in schools, and give a forthright description of those anticipated effects. Innovators who neglect to do this, we would argue, fail to appreciate the inertia of curriculum traditions in schools and the role of persons in schools (particularly teachers) as defenders of curriculum traditions. Even though a curriculum change may have been developed with its effects on children as the paramount concern, its successful implementation must involve changes in the belief structures and work habits of school staff. It is our experience that belief structures and work habits do not change easily, especially when left unexamined and unchallenged.

For innovators to anticipate the effects of an innovation on the lives of persons in schools, they must be well acquainted with the belief structures and work habits of persons in schools. More generally, they must give ample attention to the culture of schools.

2. DEVELOP A DISSEMINATION PLAN AND MATERIALS TO SUPPORT DISSEMINATION

Our second recommendation is not to abandon proven practices in staff development. There are proven ways of recruiting schools and introducing them to a curriculum change. Among those proven ways are a dissemination plan and materials developed to support dissemination.

Dissemination plan. A dissemination plan divides the process of disseminating an innovation into a sequence of stages, and it provides for the unique requirements of each stage. A simple distinction can be made between an initial *awareness stage* and a subsequent *installation stage.* The awareness stage of a dissemination plan introduces the new program and provides school staff with the information they need to decide whether to adopt or reject the program. Teachers and school leaders will certainly be included in plans to generate awareness of a program. Less obvious but equally important targets are the clients of schools—children, parents, and community groups. Indeed, staff are inadequately informed of the ramifications of a program if they are unacquainted with the prospective reactions of school clients to the changes it will bring.

Providing for the requirements of the awareness stage is a challenging task that few curriculum developers have done well. One problem is the "pollyannaism" of the initiated. Persons who are immersed in a new development and are knowledgeable about it tend to be overly forgiving in their appraisal of it. Besides that lack of objectivity, they also tend to see the virtues of the development as self-evident, and consequently they have a hard time communicating with persons who lack their enthusiasm for the new development.

The new program is initially put into practice during the installation stage. Staff development techniques applicable to the installation stage include in-service training, group discussions, and workshops for teachers on materials development. Group discussions appear to be valuable in helping participants to identify the particular changes that they hope to achieve through the new program.[50] Inasmuch as few innovations survive without the ongoing support of the school principal,[51] it is also important to provide for the needs of administrators, particularly principals.

Staff development techniques should do more than acquaint staff with the program and persuade them to try it. Enthusiasm for a new program is not enough. There must also be training—most typically, in-service training of existing staff. Belief structures and work habits do not change easily or quickly; to change them, a well-designed and unhurriedly executed training program is a virtual necessity. We will not elaborate on features that distinguish effective training programs, but we do want to underscore the importance of staff training as an often neglected ingredient of curriculum change.

Materials to support dissemination. One proven practice in staff development is the provision of materials that support the training of staff to use an innovation. Such materials are typically coupled with a description of how, on a procedural level, the new program is distinct from others that may have preceded it. As described in our earlier discussion, surface procedural differences can easily become the focus of persons who encounter and use the materials. For constructive change to occur, it is necessary for the staff to grasp the purpose of the innovation.

Obviously, then, dissemination materials must go beyond descriptions of procedures and provide a statement of purpose. The dissemination materials of IGE did provide a positive statement of the purposes that motivated that innovation. That "positive sell" approach to recruitment and motivation is evidently successful at initiating a change. However, it often fails to identify how certain aspects of the innovation are intended to remedy what curriculum developers saw as deficiencies of existing practices. If criticism of existing practices (that is, "negative sell") is omitted, radical innovations will soon be deflected and modified to include some features that curriculum developers hoped to supplant.

We recommend that dissemination materials include the "negative sell," in combination, of course, with a "positive sell." Dissemination materials must tell persons what *not* to do (and why), in addition to telling them what they *should* do (and why).

Dissemination materials often overlook the idea that, to make change, something must be given up. We recommend that dissemination materials be explicit about traditions with which the innovation is incompatible. Traditions that the innovation is meant to supplant are obviously in this category. Incompatibilities of that kind are *deliberate incompatibilities*. There can be other traditions that must also be changed if the innovation is implemented, even though the innovation was not specifically designed to supplant them. These easily overlooked *tangential incompatibilities* between an innovation and traditions can disrupt the implementation of the innovation if they are not dealt with explicitly as a part of staff development. To summarize this point, the "hit list" of things that must be given up will include both deliberately incompatible traditions and tangentially incompatible traditions.

3. USE A SYSTEMATIC MONITORING PLAN

Our third recommendation is that a systematic monitoring procedure be planned and implemented for any innovation. To monitor something means to gather information about it at several times. The procedure would monitor the expected effects of the innovation. The term "expected effects" is not limited to student outcomes, which are conventionally monitored. It can certainly include student outcomes, but it should also include other expected effects on the lives of persons in schools. Moreover, it should include the monitoring of anticipated problems.

There is an a priori tone to this recommendation that is deliberate. There is prior specification of what is to be monitored. Things specified to be monitored are the expected effects, and not the unexpected effects. It is difficult to monitor systematically things that are unexpected, so the benefits of systematic monitoring stem mainly from knowledge about prespecified, expected effects. Developments that occur unexpectedly during the implementation of a new program certainly should not be ignored. Our point is simply that awareness of a development is a precondition to focused, systematic tracking of it.

Monitoring and the tracking that it permits of selected aspects of life in schools involves a different conceptual framework (and more data) than conventional pretest-posttest approaches. Campbell and Stanley made a strong case for an interrupted time-series design to study the effects of planned change on single populations.[52] Two measures (pretest and posttest) on a single population simply do not give enough information to demonstrate effects due to implementation. At least four observations (two before implementation and two after) are necessary to distinguish between change due to implementation and change due to natural growth. At least six are needed to discern drift, decay, cycles, and so forth. Obviously, the larger the number of observations, the more we can detect.

As a part of such a plan, we suggest causal modeling to specify the variables to be observed, to identify expected relationships, and to assist in communicating the expected changes. This approach can be used to study the ongoing nature of schooling events, and it permits us to focus on the effects of a change on various characteristics.

If key elements are identified from a causal model, a reasonable monitoring scheme following an interrupted time-series framework can be developed. Our motive is not to advocate statistical esoterica. The kernel of our recommendation is the suggestion that developers attempt to be explicit about the chain of events they would expect to occur, pursuant to implementation of their innovation. Through doing that, they will acquire a better grasp of what phenomena to monitor.

Furthermore, communication with potential users of the innovation may be improved. If a developer provides explicit speculation about diverse effects of an innovation, schools adopting it will be better informed and more likely to show constructive change.

Systematic Monitoring of Planned School Changes: An Example

To demonstrate that our recommendations are plausible, we have chosen to conclude this chapter by examining the efforts of one school district to produce planned curricular change. The Berea (Ohio) City School District serves a working- and middle-class suburban community bordering on Cleveland. It is typical of many districts in that it has experienced a decline in enrollment, a gradual change in population due to outmigration from a troubled major city, and an aging staff with little opportunity for administrative advancement. Yet, its staff is committed to a quality instructional program. In 1975, the district's Board of Education and its superintendent made a commitment to a project called "Curriculum Review."

CURRICULUM REVIEW

The purpose of the Curriculum Review project was to develop a comprehensive scope and sequence of skills and content for kindergarten through grade twelve for all subject areas and to have those curriculum programs understood and implemented by all teachers.

Conventionally separated subject areas (for example, Language Arts, Mathematics, Home Economics) were placed into a five-year cyclical schedule. In each year of the schedule, approximately one-fifth of the subject areas were singled out for intensive review, with each subject area reviewed by an area-specific review team composed of teachers on leave and administrators. The review team for each subject area was responsible for identifying a manageable set of high priority objectives for which teachers in *all* subject areas would be responsible.

The process in each subject area involved formation of the review team, attendance of team members at workshops and seminars, review of current practice, review of pertinent research, selection of top priority objectives, preparation of a program guide for meeting those objectives, reaction to drafts of the program guide by teachers in the school district, reactions of nationally recruited consultants, and formal adoption of the program guides by the Board of Education. It was clearly understood that, once a program guide was adopted, all teachers in all subject areas were to use it as a basis for their classroom planning and instruction. During the year following formal adoption of a program guide (year two), it was expected that all teachers would be helped to understand the program guide. It was also expected that all teachers would incorporate suggestions of the guide into their lesson plans. In the year after that (year three), changes in classroom practice (observable by a supervisor) were expected. Only in the fourth and fifth years of the cycle were the curricular changes expected to manifest themselves in students' behavior (construed broadly to include such things as recreational reading as well as test performance).

At this level of description, the Curriculum Review project sounds typical of many programs developed in other school systems. However, the approach taken to the project was unique in that they attempted to deal with the three recommendations we proposed in the last section.

First, they knew they were challenging many traditions surrounding the professional specialization and autonomy of teachers. Indeed, they were expecting *radical change* on the part of teachers. Although changes in student outcomes were the ultimate goal, they were consciously expecting teachers to change their work habits (and, in turn, the students' work habits). For example, *all* teachers were expected to implement the writing program. This meant that teachers of science, mathematics, shop, homemaking, and so forth were to know the program and its objectives and to implement it by correcting spelling, grammar, and organization of paragraphs in their courses. Similarly, social studies and science teachers (not just mathematics teachers) were responsible for teaching students to interpret data from tables. Thus, although the program developers did not systematically attempt to identify traditions that were being challenged (as we recommend), they were aware that some common habits of teachers would need to be changed. In particular, *all* teachers were responsible for all curricular changes.

Second, they were concerned with dissemination and implementation. In fact, a long-term commitment to the Curriculum Review process was expressed. For each curriculum program, a five-year commitment to implementation was made by all administrators. For each new program, the expected changes in staff planning and teacher behavior were specified, carefully considered, then formally adopted. These expectations became part of staff evaluation. The curricular changes were not viewed as fads. Thus, an implementation plan and materials were made, and staff in-service training was carried out. The school board did not assume that teachers would automatically use Curriculum Review materials. Nor did they assume that improvement in student learning would be a pro forma occurrence. Student changes were expected to occur only with changes in teachers and their teaching. The school board recognized that in the past curricular changes often ended with adoption, publication, and distribution of a guide or manual. Once classroom doors had been closed, the innovation had remained on a bookshelf. The activities of teaching had continued unchanged. Thus, staff development was seen as essential.

Third, systematic monitoring was seen as part of the Curriculum Review process. In each succeeding year after the adoption of a curriculum guide, more information was monitored. This expansion from lesson plans to teachers' behavior to students' behavior reflects a realistic, unhurried commitment to change. The intent was to document actual, gradual change. Evaluation was not a summative judgment external to the implementation, but an integral part of and stimulus for curriculum change.

THE SYSTEMATIC MONITORING PROCESS FOR LEARNING (SMPL) STRATEGY

In 1978, as Curriculum Review programs were being completed, the Curriculum Review staff of the district realized that they must develop and put into practice a self-monitoring scheme. What evolved was a strategy for monitoring and evaluation, which they called the "Systematic Monitoring Process for Learning" (the SMPL strategy).

Traditionally, to evaluate the introduction of a new curriculum or program, schools have relied primarily on assessments of pupil performance. In SMPL, that is still done. However, SMPL also monitors, documents, and assesses changes in teacher and student activities that occur *between* the introduction of a new program and the evaluation of student achievement in a content area. The ongoing process of monitoring maintained an incentive for staff to internalize the changes into their daily routines. District administrators also hoped that the monitoring would provide documentation of any real change that did occur, and that it would help to restore community faith in the ability of public schools to chart, adjust, and reach their goals. The district administrators were confident that the SMPL strategy would demonstrate that each new curriculum program was actually implemented and that the money, time, and effort were indeed worthwhile.

The actual use of the SMPL strategy by administrators and staff involved gathering, summarizing, and analyzing information concerning four basic questions: (a) What related background information is available? (b) How are the new curriculum programs being used? (c) What data describe the processes of student learning in classrooms? (d) Have students reached desired outcomes? Information concerning each of those questions is described below.

Background. The first question addressed by SMPL deals with background information about students, staff, and the community. As a first step, that information needed to be gathered and studied. The context of the new program or curriculum change was examined to identify factors that were believed either to facilitate or restrain implementation. For this question, the staff of each school wrote descriptive summaries of the school's students, staff, and social environment. The staff then decided upon goals for the school and upon means that might be used to reach those goals. The exercise provoked self-analysis, identification of priorities, and reflection on environmental factors that might affect innovation.

Program use. District administrators were determined not to overlook the second question—how programs were being used—because they believed bona fide implementation of new curriculum programs was necessary to improve student outcomes. The administration assumed that student achievement (in particular) would not improve unless three conditions were met.

The first condition is that teachers understand the rationale and philosophy of each new Curriculum Change program. This includes not only a grasp of its content, but also a grasp of its underlying philosophy, its techniques and strategies, and the changes it involves.

The second contention is that targeted aspects of the new program be reflected in teachers' lesson plans and classroom activities. Teachers tend to achieve what they plan; therefore, daily and long-range planning were seen as critical. Lesson plans must include the new content or skills, the new priorities, appropriate materials and strategies, and means of assessing the student growth expected in the new program. In addition, teachers were to work collaboratively to make their daily plans consonant with long-range goals.

The third condition is that teacher-student interactions and student-student interactions should follow certain principles suggested by instructional research. According to the first principle, *structuring*, the teacher should explain in advance the purposes of a lesson and the connection of activities to the purposes. According to the second principle, *feedback*, the teacher should inform students of their successes, strengths, and needs. According to the third principle, *motivation*, the teacher should create a learning environment that is interesting and supportive and one in which mutual respect is practiced by the teacher and students. According to the fourth principle, *individualiza-*

tion, the teacher should assess the needs and interests of individual students, then match students with appropriate activities and resources during instruction. According to the fifth principle, *peer relations*, cooperative peer relations conducive to learning are recognized and fostered by the teacher.

Classroom learning. The third question in the SMPL strategy—gathering data to describe classroom learning—provides monitoring of the actual interaction of the new program with students. The data collected included: (a) *Allocated Time*: How much time is allocated for teaching a new Curriculum Review program? (b) *Engaged Time*: How much student time is actually engaged with a particular skill, concept, or content area? (c) *Quality and the Appropriateness of Teaching Activities*: What activities are basic to the new program? Which activities best develop a skill or teach a concept? Which activities do not work? Which activities involve factors of effective classrooms identified from research?

The collection of such data involved a myriad of monitoring procedures and data sources: classroom observations, work samples, lesson plans, teacher logs or diaries, faculty discussions, grade level and department sharing sessions, regular status report forms, and individual teacher-principal conferences.

Student outcomes. The fourth question—how well students reached desired outcomes—was to be answered unhurriedly. Student outcomes were to be examined only after the district administration had determined that a new Curriculum Review program was implemented as planned. Berea decided that at least three years were needed for this process of implementation. A premature leap to demonstrating student achievement without first documenting significant changes in instruction would presumably have produced little evidence of improvement.

Also, school administrators were well aware that their program goals would not be reflected in standardized achievement tests alone. One goal, for example, was to increase the time children spend reading "classroom libraries." Time spent in free reading was seen as a valuable outcome, regardless of its relationship with performance on standardized reading tests.

Summary. The SMPL strategy begun in 1979 by the Berea Schools is a longitudinal, systematic change model. The monitoring activity is thoroughly integrated with the implementation of newly refined curriculum programs. While initially concerned with changes made by teachers, its eventual concern is with students. Based on the Berea experience, as reported by Langer and Romberg,[53] SMPL has helped improve the educational process in at least six major areas.

1. SMPL has caused principals, staff, and program supervisors to study their implementation plans, procedures, goals, and actions continuously.

2. A detailed examination of planning has resulted in a totally new assessment of teachers' lesson plans. Each school has examined the role of planning. The school system has stressed the need to have new programs reflected in all planning—particularly long-range planning. The quality of lesson plans has improved.

3. Time is now more carefully considered and used. Not only has allocated time been documented, but teachers and principals are more aware of engaged time. In effect, the use of time is now viewed more critically as a key element in learning.

4. SMPL has changed staff documentation of the implementation of Curriculum Review. Every teacher, kindergarten through grade twelve, has set goals in reading, mathematics, written communication, and social studies and provided a status summary of these goals.

5. The relationship of principal to teacher and of principal to staff to program has changed. The use of SMPL has returned to the principal a critical role, that of instructional leader and evaluator. Monitoring the new Curriculum Review program has become a high priority job for the school leadership. As a result, classroom observations have increased, and the staff and principal regularly discuss curriculum and school goals.

6. SMPL has placed curriculum and instruction in the spotlight. It has assured that Curriculum Review programs enter into teachers' thinking and planning. Preliminary data indicate that the new programs are indeed being used and are indeed the basis for teacher planning. Principal, staff, and new programs have merged cooperatively to assure that students are taught according to the priorities of Curriculum Review.

Curriculum implementation and evaluation in Berea has been more than talk, more than promises, and more than educational jargon. It has involved the hard work of perseverance, of setting priorities, of assuring and assessing educational change for the improvement of learning. The community has observed a school system committed to long-range planning, staff development, and systematic improvement through professional monitoring.

Concluding Comment

There is no question that schools are and will continue to be under considerable pressure to change their practices. In particular, changes made by adopting or developing a new curriculum will occur, but the success of their implementation will not just happen. The obstacles that school staffs face in order to make a curriculum change a success are many. To facilitate planned curriculum change, we have made three recommendations based on our analysis and experience:

1. Identify traditions that are being challenged.
2. Develop a dissemination plan and materials to support dissemination.
3. Use a systematic monitoring plan.

Furthermore, to demonstrate that such recommendations are feasible, we have examined curriculum review and monitoring procedures developed in one school district. The culture of a school is more likely to change if our recommendations are followed.

FOOTNOTES

1. Lawrence A. Cremin, *The Transformation of the School: Progressivism in American Education, 1876-1957* (New York: Alfred A. Knopf, 1961); Herbert M. Kliebard, "Education at the Turn of the Century: A Crucible for Curriculum Change," *Educational Researcher* 11 (January 1982): 16-24.

2. J. Abner Peddiwell [pseud.], *The Saber-Tooth Curriculum* (New York: McGraw-Hill, 1939).

3. Richard C. Atkinson, "Ingredient for a Theory of Instruction," *American Psychologist* 27 (October 1972): 921-31.

4. John S. Brown and Curt VanLehn, "Towards a Generative Theory of 'Bugs'," in *Addition and Subtraction: A Developmental Perspective*, ed. Thomas C. Carpenter, James M. Moser, and Thomas A. Romberg (Hillsdale, N.J.: Lawrence Erlbaum Associates, 1982).

5. J. Olin Campbell, "2d Simulation: Educational Breakthrough," *Interface Age* 5 (1980): 86-90.

6. John I. Goodlad, *The Development of a Conceptual System for Dealing with Problems of Curriculum and Instruction* (Washington, D.C.: Office of Education, U.S. Department of Health, Education, and Welfare, June 1966), pp. 2-3.

7. Evan R. Keislar and Lee S. Shulman, "The Problem of Discovery: Conference in Retrospect," in *Learning by Discovery*, ed. Evan R. Keislar and Lee S. Shulman (Chicago: Rand McNally and Co., 1966), p. 190.

8. William A. McClelland, *The Process of Effecting Change*, Professional Paper 32-68 (Alexandria, Va.: Human Resources Research Office, 1968).

9. John I. Goodlad, "Schooling and Education," in *The Great Ideas Today*, ed. Robert M. Hutchins (New York: Encyclopedia Britannica, 1976).

10. Arno Bellack, *Competing Ideologies in Research on Teaching*, University Reports on Education 1 (Uppsala, Sweden: Department of Education, University of Uppsala, September 1978).

11. Thomas A. Romberg, "Systematic Monitoring of Planned School Change" (Invited address at the University of Tasmania, October 1979).

12. Neal Gross, "The Fate of a Major Educational Innovation" (Paper read at the Conference on Improvement of Schools through Educational Innovation sponsored by the Wisconsin Research and Development Center for Individualized Schooling, University of Wisconsin, Madison, October 1969).

13. Conference Board of Mathematical Sciences, *Overview and Analysis of School Mathematics, Grades K-12* (Washington, D.C.: Conference Board of Mathematical Sciences, 1975).

14. Thomas S. Popkewitz, B. Robert Tabachnick, and Gary G. Wehlage, *The Myth of Educational Reform: School Responses to Planned Educational Change* (Madison: University of Wisconsin Press, 1982); Thomas A. Romberg, "IGE Evaluation: Perspectives and a Plan," Working paper no. 183 (Madison: Wisconsin Research and Development Center for Individualized Schooling, 1976).

15. Popkewitz, Tabachnick, and Wehlage, *The Myth of Educational Reform*, p. 11.

16. Michael W. Apple and Nancy King, "What Do Schools Teach?" in *Qualitative Evaluation: Concepts and Cases in Curriculum Criticism*, ed. George Willis (Berkeley, Calif.: McCutchan Publishing Corp., 1978).

17. Philip H. Jackson, *Life in Classrooms* (New York: Holt, Rinehart and Winston, 1968).

18. Michael Young, ed., *Knowledge and Control: New Directions for the Sociology of Education* (London, England: Collier-MacMillan, 1971).

19. Howard S. Becker, "The Career of the Chicago Public School Teacher," *American Journal of Sociology* 57 (March 1952): 470-77.

20. Thomas S. Popkewitz, "Reform as Political Discourse: A Case Study," *School Review* 84 (November 1975): 311-36.

21. Popkewitz, Tabachnick, and Wehlage, *The Myth of Educational Reform*.

22. Thomas A. Romberg, "Developing Mathematical Processes: The Elementary Mathematics Program for Individually Guided Education," in *Individually Guided Education*, ed. Richard Rossmiller, Herbert Klausmeier, and Mary Saily (New York: Academic Press, 1977).

23. School Mathematics Study Group, *Introduction to Matrix Algebra* (Stanford, Calif.: School Mathematics Study Group, 1965).

24. Engineering Concepts Curriculum Project, *The Man Made World* (New York: McGraw-Hill, 1968).

25. Jerome S. Bruner, "Man: A Course of Study," in Jerome S. Bruner, *Toward a Theory of Instruction* (New York: W. W. Norton and Co., 1968).

26. Kathryn H. Au and Catherine Jordan, "Teaching Reading to Hawaiian Children: Finding a Culturally Appropriate Solution," in *Culture in the Bilingual Classroom*, ed. H. Treuba, G. P. Guthrie, and Kathryn H. Au (Rowley, Mass.: Newbury House, 1981).

27. Shirley Brice Heath, "Questioning at Home and at School: A Comparative Study," in *Doing the Ethnography of Schooling,* ed. G. D. Spindler (New York: Holt, Rinehart and Winston, 1982).

28. See, for example, Warren G. Bennis, Kenneth D. Benne, and Robert Chin, eds., *The Planning of Change,* 2d ed. (New York: Holt, Rinehart and Winston, 1961); Ronald G. Havelock, *A Guide to Innovation in Education* (Ann Arbor, Mich.: Institute for Social Research, 1970); Ronald R. Lippitt, Jeanne Watson, and Bruce Westley, *The Dynamics of Planned Change* (New York: Harcourt, Brace and World, 1958); Eleanor E. Maccoby, Theodore M. Newcomb, and Eugene L. Hartley, eds., *Readings in Social Psychology* (New York: Holt, Rinehart and Winston, 1958); Matthew B. Miles, ed., *Innovation in Education* (New York: Bureau of Publications, Teachers College, Columbia University, 1964); Everett M. Rogers, *Diffusion of Innovations* (New York: Free Press of Glencoe, 1962).

29. See, for example, J. Victor Baldridge, *Organizational Change Processes: A Bibliography with Commentary,* Research and Development Memo no. 57 (Stanford, Calif.: Stanford Center for Research and Development in Teaching, 1970); Ronald G. Havelock, James C. Hueber, and Steven Zimmermann, *Major Works on Change in Education: An Annotated Bibliography with Author and Subject Indexes* (Ann Arbor, Mich.: Institute for Social Research, 1969); McClelland, *The Process of Effecting Change.*

30. Havelock, *A Guide to Innovation in Education.*

31. Egon F. Guba, "Development Diffusion and Evaluation," in *Knowledge Production and Utilization in Educational Administration,* ed. T. L. Eidell and J. M. Kitchel (Eugene, Oreg.: University of Oregon Press, 1968).

32. See especially, Herbert J. Klausmeier, "Research and Development Strategies in Education," in *Research and Development Strategies in Theory Refinement and Educational Improvement,* Theoretical Paper no. 15, ed. Herbert J. Klausmeier, J. L. Wardrop, Mary R. Quilling, Thomas A. Romberg, and R. E. Schutz (Madison: Wisconsin Research and Development Center for Individualized Schooling, 1968); Dennis C. Phillips, "What Do the Researcher and the Practitioner Have to Offer Each Other?" *Educational Researcher* 11 (December 1980): 17-20, 24; Thomas A. Romberg, *Examples of the Use of Various Strategies for Relating Research and Development to Educational Improvement Through Individually Guided Education* (Madison: Wisconsin Research and Development Center for Individualized Schooling, 1970).

33. David Hamilton, "Making Sense of Curriculum Evaluation: Continuities and Discontinuities in an Educational Idea," in *Review of Research in Education,* ed. Lee Shulman (Itasca, Ill.: F. W. Peacock Publishers, 1978).

34. Romberg, *Examples of the Use of Various Strategies for Relating Research and Development to Educational Improvement.*

35. Rogers, *Diffusion of Innovations.*

36. Richard O. Carlson, *Adoption of Educational Innovations* (Eugene, Oreg.: University of Oregon Press, 1965).

37. Herbert Menzel and Elihu Katz, "Social Relations and Innovations in the Medical Profession: The Epidemiology of a New Drug," in *Readings in Social Psychology,* ed. Maccoby, Newcomb, and Hartley.

38. Rogers, *Diffusion of Innovation.*

39. Gerhard C. Eichholz, "Why Do Teachers Reject Change?" *Theory Into Practice* 2 (December 1963): 264-68.

40. Charles Perrow, "A Framework for the Comparative Analysis of Organization," *American Sociological Review* 32 (April 1967): 194-208.

41. Havelock, *A Guide to Innovation in Education.*

42. Harry S. Broudy, "Criteria for the Theoretical Adequacy for the Conceptual

Framework of Planned Educational Change" (Paper prepared for the Conference on Strategies for Educational Change, Washington, D.C., November 1965); Lee J. Cronbach, "Beyond the Two Disciplines of Scientific Psychology," *American Psychologist* 30 (February 1975): 116-27; Phillips, "What Do the Researcher and the Practitioner Have to Offer Each Other?"

43. Romberg, "Developing Mathematical Processes."

44. Popkewitz, Tabachnick, and Wehlage, *The Myth of Educational Reform.*

45. Hamilton, "Making Sense of Curriculum Evaluation."

46. Goodlad, *The Development of a Conceptual System.*

47. Popkewitz, Tabachnick, and Wehlage, *The Myth of Educational Reform.*

48. Ibid.

49. Karl Popper, *Conjectures and Refutations: The Growth of Scientific Knowledge* (New York: Harper and Row, 1963).

50. Havelock, *A Guide to Innovation in Education.*

51. Mark A. Chesler, Richard Schmuck, and Ronald Lippitt, "The Principal's Role in Facilitating Innovation," *Theory Into Practice* 2 (December 1963): 269-77.

52. Donald T. Campbell and Julian C. Stanley, "Experimental and Quasi-experimental Designs for Research on Teaching," in *Handbook of Research on Teaching,* ed. N. L. Gage (Chicago: Rand McNally, 1963).

53. James W. Langer and Thomas A. Romberg, "The Systematic Monitoring Process for Learning," *Educational Leadership* 39 (November 1981): 140-42.

CHAPTER VIII

Staff Development for School Improvement

R. LINDEN COURTER AND BEATRICE A. WARD

The view of using schools as a vehicle to initiate or enhance cultural change has been and appears to be a continuing force in society. As a result, schools in the United States have long been and continue to be under constant pressure to change their practices.[1] A consistent and positive motivation in the pressure to change is the apparent belief that change will make schools more effective, more enjoyable places for students to learn. This means that all individuals who are involved (teachers, students, school administrators, parents, and school board members) expect whatever change is introduced more nearly to meet their particular definitions of a successful school and successful teaching and learning than the education program that existed previously. To achieve these ends, at a minimum, change in people as well as in curricular content and instructional procedures and processes may be required. Thus the phenomenon of change for school improvement has a direct relationship to staff development. It is this latter aspect of school improvement that we wish to address in this chapter. First, an attempt will be made to outline the various elements that must be considered to achieve the desired staff development. Then an actual change process as it was carried out in a large urban school district will be presented for consideration.

Some Essential Features of School Improvement

Generally, it is difficult to make a case against school improvement. However, while there are many examples of successful attempts at school improvement, there are also many school improvement efforts that have failed. When there is an "absence" of school improvement, it may lie in part in the frustration of the staff (and students) over a lack of common goal(s) and the apparent feeling of not being capable of

185

doing anything that will significantly and positively impact on student achievement. Principals and teachers often appear overwhelmed (in many cases not admittedly) by the complex requirements of today's educational world—dictates of the federal government, requirements of local boards of education, and on and on. The challenge then is to carry out an improvement process that attends to these complexities and at the same time introduces the changes in people, procedures, and outcomes that are desired.

The title of this chapter already implies that one of the key factors in achieving successful school improvement is staff development. This will be dealt with at length later in our discussion. Two additional factors that also warrant consideration are the perceptions of improvement that prevails and the importance of the school as the place where change occurs. Each is discussed briefly below.

In our view, it is essential that the term "school improvement" not imply a deficiency model but rather an orderly "tuning" process required of all schools and school staffs on a continuing basis. While school improvement implies "change," it should become part of the responsible, ongoing operation of schools. To achieve real school improvement, there must be created a feeling within the teachers, students, parents, administrative staff, support staff, and even board of education members that positive changes have occurred or are occurring and that the school program continues to be strengthened to meet students' needs. Teachers must feel listened to and feel that their role and function are dignified by actions and attitudes of the administration, students, and parents relative to the improvement process. In turn, they must have high expectations for students, believe that students can learn, and know that they (the teachers) are responsible and accountable for providing direct instruction to the students. Students must feel that the work they are expected to do is fair and that the goals set for them are achievable. Above all, they must experience and feel success in their day-to-day learning activities. Parents must understand and support the school improvement efforts. They must feel that the school is open to their involvement and responsive to their questions and concerns. They must know that their children are happy in school and are achieving the acquisition of knowledge and skills at a reasonable and realistic rate of speed. The administrative staff must provide the leadership to insure achievement of the learning goals.

They must assure that a safe atmosphere exists for the students and staff and feel that the school's instructional program is comprehensive and appropriate for students' needs. They must know through personal and direct observation and use of other indicators that each staff member is performing adequately and feels that his or her contributions are valued; that the students feel secure and successful; and that the parents are supportive of the school and their child's "school experience." The school support staff, including volunteers, the office staff, the cafeteria workers, and the maintenance staff and part-time custodians, must feel recognized and valued for their contribution to successful operation of the school. Board of education members must know through direct observation, reports on student achievement, and communications from parents and the administrative staff that the desired orderly improvement of the schooling process is underway. An image of success must permeate all school activities and communications about the school. In other words, "real school improvement" affects everyone and everything involved with schooling, not just teachers.

The power of the school site in the school improvement process has been discussed in several recent studies.[2] Little points out the aspects of the school site that make it so important:

Without denying differences in individuals' skills, interests, commitment, curiosity, or persistence, the prevailing patterns of interactions and interpretations in each building demonstrably create certain possibilities and set certain limits. . . . Most at issue here are the nature and extent of collegial relationships among teachers and between faculty and administrators, and the nature of the stance adopted toward present practice and new ideas.[3]

Hence the school situation can influence the willingness of staff to include an improvement activity in an already busy instructional agenda.

Moreover, as Purkey and Smith note, "the success of a teacher depends upon the job done by other teachers."[4] No single teacher can alone bring about a marked change in education. Thus the notion of the isolated classroom in which a teacher works behind closed doors does not mesh with the view of school improvement that we are applying in this chapter, nor does it respond to what has been learned about effective school improvement. Little emphasizes the need for the school situation to foster a belief that recourse to the knowledge and experience of others is valuable and that shared work and discussion will increase the success of all participants.[5] A "work together" attitude is seen as conducive to the conduct of school improvement efforts that will be both reasonable in scope and expectation and can be accomplished by the people who are involved.

From an instructional standpoint, many teaching and learning theories have been developed, made known and available to, and often thrust upon schools and teachers. Few of these theories have attended to the attitudinal and school factors mentioned above. Possibly as a result, while concepts such as "individualized learning," "open classrooms," and "flexible scheduling" have not "failed" in all situations, no one of them appears to have the general application once thought possible.

To illustrate the ways in which individuals' perceptions and school-level factors may influence the success of an improvement strategy, consider the concept of providing teachers the opportunity to choose their own classroom materials. Not too long ago, this idea was implemented in California under the belief that it would promote creativity and would free the teacher from the need to utilize materials that did not fit his or her instructional approach. For the most part, in our opinion, this strategy has not achieved the desired goals because the necessary perceptions and school-level features were not built in. Rather than promoting a collaborative "working together" stance and building common expectations for school improvement, this strategy is likely to present an individual teacher with a mountain of instructional materials from which he or she must select those that appear to serve best the unique needs of a single classroom. While many teachers are highly skilled in evaluation and selection of instructional materials, many are not. For those who have not developed these skills of analysis, the task may be an unrealistic burden and unless it is specifically planned for at a school level they probably will not benefit from the expertise of others. The end result, therefore, may be a disjointed learning sequence across the classrooms in a school. For students who receive such uncoordinated learning experiences, this strategy may in turn present an unnecessary learning burden. Hence this well-intended improvement strategy may or may not be successful, depending on the degree to which a particular school site is aware of, attends to, and capitalizes on those attitudes, feelings, and school-level factors that support successful ongoing improvement of the schooling experiences of students.

The Need to Change People

The above discussion presented two aspects of school improvement—perceptions and school-level factors—that Griffin suggests comprise part of the context in which school improvement occurs.[6] He talks about a process of "mutual adaptation" in which the setting is changed by both the focus of the improvement and the strategy used to implement the improvement. Likewise, the improvement itself is influenced (and possibly changed) by the setting. Since people are part of this setting, to bring about school improvement frequently requires changes in the ways in which people function, interact, and think. These same individuals may in turn modify the focus and process of the improvement strategy.

Because the teacher serves as the individual at the school level who has the most direct contact with students, the teacher also is the staff person who most often will be required to acquire and implement changes, and who will be most apt to influence the form and outcomes of whatever improvement occurs. Recent research on school improvement supports this view, indicating that the teacher is the pivotal force in the change process.[7] Given that this is the case, these same studies provide insights regarding the requirements of successful school improvement efforts, several of which are relevant to the model presented later in this chapter.

Hall and Loucks indicate that awareness of and attention to teachers' concerns are important aspects of any change process.[8] They introduce the notion that teachers' concerns may range from concern about how an improvement may affect them personally, to a desire to learn more about a proposed improvement, to an interest in "improving" a particular new procedure or process. They also present the notion of "levels of use" of a particular improvement. The levels they identify are nonuse, orientation, preparation, mechanical use, routine use, refinement, and renewal. Griffin suggests that both levels of concern and levels of use need to be considered when initiating a school improvement effort.[9] In order to assure that the professional growth activities undertaken are appropriate to the needs of the individuals who are involved (for example, teachers), he emphasizes the importance of these two factors. He further notes that consideration of these factors makes it possible to determine whether teachers and other staff members, in fact, need to change. As a result, he suggests that improvement efforts undertaken should fit the context in which they are to operate.

Gross, Giacquinta, and Bernstein look at the teacher as a catalyst for implementation of school improvements.[10] They indicate that successful improvement (that is, improvement that matches the intended changes in procedures and processes and achieves the intended changes in student outcomes) depends on the presence of several factors. Among them is the requirement that the innovation be clearly specified. In particular, they underline the importance of specifying any new role requirements for teachers. They also indicate that teachers must be given the experiences necessary to develop any new skills or competencies that are required. They state that teachers need to be committed to the improvement and that they should be provided with whatever materials and equipment are needed. Finally, they point to the importance of school administrators as supporters of the improvement process. They suggest that administrators can help teachers overcome problems that occur. As a result, they judge the commitment of the school principal and other administrators to be as important as that of the teachers.

Tikunoff and Ward look at staff development from yet another standpoint—the individual teacher's view of instruction.[11] They suggest that a teacher, on the basis of preservice and in-service experiences, develops beliefs about what teaching and learning should be like and what the teacher's role is. They propose that these views or orientations may differ from one teacher to another. Building from their own observations of and discussions with teachers, they identify three ways that teachers view instruction. First, there are teachers who see instruction in terms of cause-and-effect relationships. These teachers believe that they have control over the outcomes of instruction and behave accordingly. For example, given a particular instructional problem, Tikunoff and Ward indicate that "cause-and-effect" teachers will consider a range of potential solutions. They will describe and speculate about a variety of possible instructional moves on their part and possible responses by various students in their classes. Based on the results of this reflection, they will select and try out a new instructional strategy, new materials, or some other modification in their classroom procedures or processes. A second group of teachers considers instruction in terms of its technical features (for example, materials, prescribed curriculum, diagnosis and prescription, and instructional objectives tied to measured outcomes). Given a particular problem, these teachers may be expected to apply one of the technical strategies they have acquired. When the strategy is unsuccessful, they will look to others to provide a better alternative. The third group of teachers views instruction in terms of conventional wisdom. Given a problem, these teachers draw from this wisdom. They carry with them a romanticized view of teaching that is more service-oriented than science-oriented. When asked to implement a new approach to instruction, they appear to shape it such that it looks the way they think it ought to be, which may or may not be the form that was intended. Usually, they see forces external to themselves and the classroom as being responsible for most of the problems students have in school.

Tikunoff and Ward suggest that any given school faculty will include one or more individuals who view instruction from one or the other above perspectives. This being the case, they recommend that a single approach to staff development for school improvement may not be successful. Different strategies may need to be used for the teachers (and other staff members) who view instruction in different ways.

Building on the work of other researchers,[12] Tikunoff and Ward also make recommendations regarding the conditions that are necessary if adults are to learn. In terms of staff development for school improvement, they list four requirements for successful education of teachers and other staff members. These include, first, provision of time for guided reflection about the changes that are to be introduced and for integration of these changes in the staff members' repertoires of skill and knowledge. Second, they suggest that the staff members need personal support as well as challenge during the change process. Third, provision of opportunities to try out the new roles that may be required is seen as important. Fourth, continuity of emphasis on a particular improvement, a particular set of goals, and a specific set of desired changes in the behavior of the teachers or other staff members is recommended. Tikunoff and Ward suggest that an effective means for meeting the above conditions for adult learning is through use of a school-based "inquiry process." Within such a process, the entire professional staff at a school identifies goals, collects and analyzes data regarding the extent to which their approaches to instruction meet these goals, and plans ways to improve whatever weaknesses are identified, if any. Throughout this process, the inquiry is focused on the concerns of the school staff rather than on issues that are brought to them from the outside. Linkages between what occurs in one class and instruction in another are studied. In addition, they propose that the initial goal of the inquiry should be analysis for problem-solving purposes rather than evaluation. They note that as the inquiry process proceeds a common vocabulary and common concepts should be developed so all staff members understand the new insights and behaviors that are acquired. Ultimately, they hypothesize that the inquiry process will become a natural part of the decision-making process for a school faculty. When this occurs, they indicate that school improvement should become an ongoing process at that site.

Little adds to the knowledge base regarding effective approaches to changing people by indicating that staff development may prove differentially powerful based on several critical features. Chief among these is collaboration. She writes:

The more collaborative the program, the greater its prospects for demonstrating relevance to individual, school, and district interests, and the greater the prospects that it will exert influence. . . . The more closely that collaboration engages persons in the examination of classroom practices, the greater will be the demands for reciprocity. . . . The greater the reciprocity evident in the interactions between staff development and school personnel, the greater the prospects for influence.[13]

Little further indicates that effective staff development activities foster collective participation of the staff in a school. Individuals are not isolated as the only ones needing to change. The entire school staff is involved. Like Tikunoff and Ward, Little also views as important the attention to shared ideas and purposes and the provision of time to practice whatever improvements are undertaken. She states that successful staff development is less a question of individual development and more a question of organizational change at the school level.

Berman and Pauly reach much the same conclusion based on a study of 293 federally sponsored programs that were trying to introduce improvements in public schools.[14] They particularly support teacher participation in decision making and the need for clarity of goals. They note the importance of school and district level factors.

Jacullo-Noto identifies similar requirements for changing people.[15] She stresses the need for collaboration. She indicates that teachers need to participate in an improvement effort from the earliest stages of needs assessment when the improvements to be implemented are selected through evaluation of the implementation outcomes. She reiterates the importance of support, rewards, and materials that was mentioned earlier. In addition, she presents the notion that teachers need to build an "awareness that they are becoming competent as the staff development experience proceeds."[16]

The findings regarding staff development and teacher change presented above suggest several guidelines for designing and carrying out successful school improvement efforts. These guidelines include (a) the need to consider the differences in instructional orientation and skill and knowledge levels that may exist among the participants, (b) the importance of recognizing that a teacher is a central figure in any school improvement effort, (c) the usefulness of collaborative approaches to school improvement, (d) the recommendation that the change effort be focused at the school level as well as at the classroom level and involve the entire school staff, (e) the suggestion that the ultimate goal of any school improvement effort should be to implant inquiry as an ongoing process in the school, and (d) a reminder that various sorts of support elements need to be provided, such as time, materials, and expert guidance and assistance. The staff development model that follows in this chapter responds to these guidelines. In addition, because the goal of the model is school improvement, the findings of research regarding the characteristics of effective schools are also relevant. A brief summary of these findings is presented next, after which the model will be described.

Characteristics of Effective Schools

A considerable amount of research regarding the characteristics of effective elementary schools has been completed in the past few years. Two reviews of this research were compiled in 1982 as part of a conference sponsored by the National Institute of Education on the implications of research on teaching for practices in schools. In one of these reviews, Edmonds identifies four "correlates of school effectiveness": (a) the strength or weakness of the principal's style of leadership; (b) the instructional focus of the school and the climate of the school relative to instruction and learning; (c) the nature of teacher expectations of pupil performance; and (d) the role of standardized measures of pupil performance in program evaluation in the school.[17] In effective schools, the principal is a strong leader; the school staff, students, and parents stress the importance of instruction and learning; teachers expect students to learn and accept responsibility for producing this learning; and student progress is monitored on a regular basis using standardized achievement tests as well as criterion-referenced measures.

In the second review, Purkey and Smith identify school characteristics that appear to contribute to student achievement by increasing the likelihood that the school will have instructionally efficient and effective classrooms.[18] They suggest that the locus of the educational process is at the classroom level, but the quality of the process at this level may be enhanced or diminished by what occurs at the level above it (that is, at the school level). Based on the research of several individuals, they note that there is considerable overlap regarding the features that seem to be salient in the creation of effective schools.[19] They reiterate the features mentioned by Edmonds: strong administrative leadership, high expectations for students' achievement, an orderly atmosphere conducive to learning, emphasis on basic skill acquisition, and frequent monitoring of student progress. In addition, they note the importance of explicit instructional goals. They cite the study by Armor, who identifies two additional characteristics of effective schools.[20] These are high levels of parent-teacher and parent-principal contact, and ongoing in-service training of teachers in areas related to better achievement of the school's instructional goals. They note that schools in which these features are not in operation can be changed (improved). However, they stress that imposition of change from the top down will not produce fundamental change at the school and classroom level. Rather, the changes that are undertaken must result from faculty-administration collaboration and shared decision making.

Thus the effective schools research points out certain school characteristics that any school staff should attempt to install as they undertake an improvement effort. To implement these school-level features as well as classroom-level changes requires attention both to factors that facilitate changes in people and to factors that support modification at the school level.

A Model for School Improvement

One effort that attempts to respond to the above findings regarding successful staff development and school improvement is the Achievement Goals Program in the San Diego Unified School District. This program was originally initiated as a result of the efforts of a task force comprising elementary school principals, elementary school teachers, curriculum staff and other staff from throughout the school district. In the beginning, attention of the task force was drawn to the evidence emerging from various "time on task" studies and also data derived from a study of the effects of classroom interruptions that had been conducted within the school district. Later, a court order relating to improvement of the quality of education in selected racially isolated elementary and secondary schools within the district provided impetus for moving to a school improvement focus. While the Achievement Goals Program was first conceived as a program aimed at schools with predominantly minority student populations, the results of evaluation in the first year indicated that the program had a more universal application. Hence, during the school year 1981-1982, the program was implemented in reading and mathematics in kindergarten through grade six and in reading, mathematics, and vocabulary for grade seven. Since there is a significant number of Spanish-speaking students enrolled in the district, all reading and mathematics materials and activities are designed to accommodate instruction in both English and Spanish.

The discussion that follows provides an overview of the program and outlines the steps that have been taken to implement the various parts. The ways in which the various staff development efforts respond to the requirements listed above are noted throughout the discussion.

OVERVIEW OF THE PROGRAM

The basic components of the Achievement Goals Program (AGP) build upon recent research regarding time on task, direct instruction, mastery learning, and coping with classroom distractions. Each of these research areas was reviewed and elements were identified that had been found to be most influential in bringing about effective classroom instruction and school improvement. Figure 1 shows the major elements from the four research areas that guided the development of the program.

SAN DIEGO CITY SCHOOLS
CURRICULUM AND PROGRAMS DIVISION

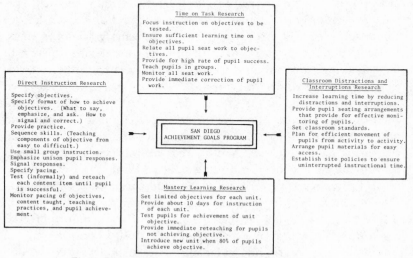

Fig. 1. Research base of the Achievement Goals Program

Since review of all known available instructional materials indicated that no single package adequately supported the instructional program that was proposed, board of education approval was obtained to develop special materials to accompany the staff development efforts that were to follow later. Funds were made available to employ classroom teachers to develop the materials.

Preparation of the teachers for the curriculum development effort served as a beginning staff-development activity. The teachers were introduced to the "cornerstone research" summarized in figure 1. They also were acquainted with the instructional design concepts that were to be employed. These concepts build on a mastery-learning approach in which students are to work through a series of instructional units, each of which is designed to encompass approximately eight to ten days of class time. At the end of each unit, students are to be tested and reteaching materials are to be provided for students who have not as yet mastered the skills and knowledge included in the unit. Students who have mastered the content of the unit are to be provided enrichment activities. After a second testing, all students are to move to the next unit, even though some students may not have achieved the prescribed level of mastery. These steps are illustrated in figure 2. As noted in the figure, students who do not achieve mastery after the second testing receive "reinforcement" instruction at some later date.

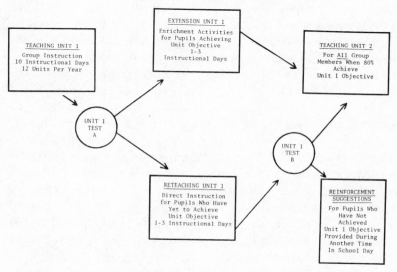

Fig. 2. Unit plan in the Achievement Goals Program

AGP materials were developed during the late spring and summer, prior to implementation in the fall in grades one through six. However, it must be noted that change in the materials is an ongoing part of the program. On the basis of input from teachers, many changes have been and continue to be made in format, suggested teaching times, and materials needed to support each unit.

THE IMPLEMENTATION PROCESS

During the first year, AGP was to be implemented in fourteen elementary schools in the district. The following discussion indicates how what might appear to be a "top-down" improvement strategy was implemented in a manner that facilitated decision making, analysis, and change in individual schools.

School plans. The first step in the implementation process was the development of school plans for carrying out the changes that would be required to introduce AGP in each school. To provide the school principals and vice principals in these schools with the skills and knowledge needed to lead such an effort, meetings were held for a half-day each week during the summer preceding the implementation of the program. These meetings were chaired by the district assistant superintendent responsible for operation of all elementary schools. Discussion topics for the meetings ranged broadly from research reports on successful schools, to scheduling the introduction of the various aspects of AGP, to exploring ways to modify the school schedule to increase time for teaching reading, to listing responsibilities of the site staff for various aspects of program implementation.

This training effort generated several outcomes that proved to be important to the success of AGP at the school level. First, by the conclusion of the summer, the principals and vice principals understood the background for and design of AGP. Second, regular attendance at the meetings of the district program directors, the district program development staff members, the deputy superintendent for instruction, members of the district staff development unit, and the district program evaluation specialists indicated the high priority given to the program by the district's decision makers. Third, it was evident that the weeks of discussion and debate had generated a "team spirit" among the participants. The principals who were to implement the program had formed a support cadre, the members of which could provide assistance and support as the change effort began. Finally, the importance of the role of the principal to the success of the improvement effort had been underlined.

The training program for principals was followed by a two-day seminar in late August. At the beginning of the seminar, the president of the board of education addressed the principals regarding the priority of AGP in the minds of the board members and provided assurance that the board would offer whatever support was needed to insure achievement of the program goals. This further reinforced the importance of the task the principals were being asked to undertake.

A few days after the principals' seminar, and before the beginning of the regular contract year, the classroom teachers who would be implementing AGP were employed to participate in an in-service activity. The agenda included many of the topics discussed by the principals in their summer meetings and at the August seminar. The "cornerstone research" was presented; the requirement of the court order for program improvement was interpreted; the AGP reading and mathematics materials and the instructional sequence were presented in detail; program management plans were discussed, including monitoring of the pacing of instruction; and the assignment of responsibilities to the site staff was discussed.

During the afternoon of each of the in-service days, the site staffs convened at their schools. Under the leadership of the school principal they identified concerns about the program and began joint development of that school's implementation plan. Topics that were discussed included scheduling instructional time for reading and mathematics (and other subjects), homework policy, role and responsibility of classroom aides (in AGP this is limited to monitoring seatwork, recording student progress, and providing reinforcement for student learning), and ways of anticipating, eliminating, or substantially reducing problems that might occur. By the time the regular school year began, the staffs of the participating schools were well informed about AGP (even though some were nervous and apprehensive) and plans were ready to launch the first efforts to change the instructional program.

Implementation support. The development of the instructional materials needed to carry out AGP was discussed earlier. It is important to note here that the materials were developed before the initial implementation activities occurred in the classrooms of the participating schools. In addition, the teachers were provided short review units that were to be used during the first few days of the school year while the regular AGP materials were received, organized, and distributed to the teachers at each school. Thus the teachers were not required to "fill time" waiting for the school district to make available important components of the program.

Another critical ingredient in the successful introduction and implementation of AGP was the provision of resource teachers. Schools were provided one resource teacher for every fifteen teachers who were participating in the school improvement effort. The AGP resource teacher was to provide direct classroom technical assistance and ensure that each classroom teacher would be supported in his or her effort to implement the new instructional strategies required by AGP. Figure 3 gives an example of the form that was used to request and plan the technical assistance provided to each teacher. The goal was to offer individualized assistance, feedback, and reassurance as the teachers were in the process of acquiring and inserting the new instructional procedures into their repertoires. Based on the informa-

SAN DIEGO CITY SCHOOLS
CURRICULUM AND PROGRAMS DIVISION
ELEMENTARY ACHIEVEMENT GOALS PROGRAM

TECHNICAL ASSISTANCE FORM

Teacher_____Grade_____Date_____

Instructional Period: _____Reading _____Mathematics _____Language Arts

Group: = 1 2 3 _____Other_____
(circle one)   (Describe)

Specific Lesson: _____Level _____Unit _____Lesson

Type of Instruction: _____Developmental _____Reteaching _____Extensive
                                                                                      Activity
_____Other_____
                                            (Describe)

Person(s) Conducting Lesson/Activity: _____Teacher _____Aide _____Volunteer

Pacing: On Schedule: _____Yes _____No

Progress chart and schedule of lessons posted and current: _____Yes _____No

_____
(AGP Resource Teacher)

PROGRAM ASSISTANCE AVAILABLE   (OPTIONAL)

To: AGP Resource Teacher
From: _____
         (Name of Teacher)

I would like the following assistance_____scheduling; _____pacing;
_____teaching methods;_____materials; _____classroom management;
_____grouping; _____placement test;_____ reteaching; _____extension;
_____reinforcement; _____testing; _____analyzing tests; _____reviewing
test with students; _____other.

Comments:

_____
_____
_____
_____

Fig. 3. Form for requesting and planning technical assistance

tion presented earlier in this chapter, the importance of this support element from an adult learning standpoint is clear. Further, the fifteen teachers who worked with a particular resource teacher soon coalesced into peer groups that, in the larger schools, facilitated interactions that would have been difficult to generate at the total-school level.

Another critical ingredient of the early success of the program was the assignment of one substitute teacher to each AGP school. The substitutes were trained in the AGP instructional procedures so that when they took over for the regular teacher they could provide a consistency of instruction for the students, who were also learning to work in new ways. The daily presence of these teachers allowed flexibility in that it released regular teachers to work with their resource teacher on specific problems, as well as providing coverage when one of the regular teachers was ill. Essentially, the substitutes became recognized and accepted by students and staff alike as members of the regular staff.

A district parent education program was a third form of support provided to the school staffs. This program included briefing meetings for parents at which AGP was described. Particular attention was given to the sorts of experiences their children would have and how these might differ from the ways they were taught in previous years. The board of education commitment to the program also was communicated. Plans for monitoring student progress were reviewed. In addition to these district-sponsored meetings, each school site developed and implemented its own plans for parent involvement. These plans differed across the schools, but all included procedures for facilitating parent interaction with the principal and teachers.

Implementation activities. AGP implementation began only after teachers, administrators, parents, and school board members had reached a common understanding of the goals to be achieved. As students began to be involved in the program, they too sensed the high interest in the program and the commitment to improving students' learning. Hence the goal focus required for successful school improvement was in place prior to use of the program in the schools.

During the initial period of AGP implementation, the site resource teacher made daily contacts with each classroom teacher. These contacts provided both technical assistance and reassurance. They gave each teacher an opportunity to ask questions, raise concerns, and share successes. As a result, the on-site in-service training provided to each teacher was adapted to his or her unique level of concern, way of viewing the program, and level of skill and knowledge.

Further, inconsistencies or other weaknesses identified by teachers in the newly developed AGP materials were communicated back to the developers. In this manner, problems were addressed quickly and new materials were designed to eliminate them. This process not only upgraded the quality and usefulness of the materials; it also gave all the participating teachers an important role in program design.

Other activities that encouraged input regarding the program and facilitated sharing of ideas and successful implementation procedures included meetings of resource teachers and of school principals. The site resource teachers met every two weeks to discuss program implementation concerns and receive any new program information. These meetings also were attended by the AGP materials developers and other key central district staff. Through their participation, teachers' needs and concerns were communicated directly to the staff members, who were responsible for providing any services and materials that might be needed. The goal was to eliminate as many problems as possible early on in the program.

The AGP principals' meetings also were held every two weeks. These meetings lasted from two to three hours and emphasized management issues that were developing. For the most part, these meetings continued discussion of the topics introduced during the summer seminars and involved the same central district personnel.

Progress of AGP from a school improvement standpoint was monitored in several ways. Evidence of student progress was monitored on mastery charts posted in each classroom. As students successfully mastered unit content and skills, this was recorded on the charts. Regular review of the charts was conducted by the classroom teacher, the resource teacher, the school principal, and the students themselves. In addition, parents received progress information in the form of successfully completed worksheets, which students took home on a daily basis.

Implementation of critical program features was monitored through regular formal and informal observations in each classroom by the school principal and the vice principal(s) in those schools having two or more administrators. The formal observations were reported on forms that were completed by the administrator and discussed with the classroom teacher and the resource teacher (see figure 4). These discussions dealt with two aspects of the program: (a) things that were going well and why; and (b) areas in which improvements needed to be made and what might be done. In addition, the entire staff maintained records of interruptions that reduced the instructional time in the classes and met as a total group to identify and implement methods for eliminating such interruptions.

Progress of AGP likewise was monitored at the school-district level. The deputy superintendent for instruction appointed an AGP steering committee. This committee met every two weeks and, based on input from the AGP resource teachers and AGP principal meetings, reviewed the progress of implementation and established any new support efforts that were needed. Central district administrators, curriculum planners and developers, and program evaluators also discussed program implementation regularly. In addition, progress reports were frequent topics at board of education meetings and some board members exhibited their interest and concern for the program with personal visits to AGP schools.

PROGRAM OUTCOMES

As might be expected, given the implementation strategies outlined above, the AGP school improvement effort has been successful. Early on in the first year, the information that was provided made it clear to everyone in the district—parents, students, teachers, principals, other staff, members of the board of education and the community at large—that AGP had promise for substantial improvement in instruction and student achievement. Further, not only were the initial school sites committed to successful implementation of the program; evidence began to surface indicating that the AGP program principles and approach to school-site improvement were permeating the entire district operation and effecting a change in the thinking and daily operation of many central district staff. Further, the focus and form of teacher-principal interactions and the recognition given to the teacher as the person responsible for providing uninterrupted, high quality, direct instruction changed the perceptions of the staff regarding the form and importance of school-based inquiry. Most importantly, at the end of the first year of AGP implementation student achievement

RECORD OF CLASSROOM OBSERVATION (FORMAL)

Teacher_____   Observer_____   Date_____

Grade Level_____   Time In____ Time Out____

Instruction observed:	____reading	____whole group	Others Present:
	____language	____two group	_____
	____mathematics	____three group	_____
	____other (describe)_____		
Type of instruction observed:	developmental ____instruction	____reteaching	____extension activity
	____other (describe)_____		

			Yes	No
SCHEDULE/PACING	Is the recommended pacing schedule being followed? If no, list the group(s) that are _behind_ schedule.		____	____
PRESENTATION OF LESSON	The _lesson_:	1. was begun promptly	____	____
		2. was appropriately paced	____	____
		3. provided appropriate seatwork	____	____
		4. included district guide and materials	____	____
	The _teacher_:	1. stayed on task	____	____
		2. involved all students	____	____
		3. gave corrective feedback	____	____
		4. gave clearly understood directions	____	____
	The _students_:	1. stayed on task	____	____
		2. understood objective lesson	____	____
		3. received immediate corrective feedback	____	____
		4. responded positively to corrective feedback	____	____
		5. worked/completed seatwork	____	____
MANAGEMENT OF STUDENT BEHAVIOR	Misbehavior and/or inattention was:			
		1. handled effectively and appropriately	____	____
		2. not observed	____	____
	Guidelines for personal and procedural needs of students were understood and followed.			
CLASSROOM ORGANIZATION AND MANAGEMENT	The daily program and schedule of lessons were posted.		____	____
	Minimal instructional time was used for classroom management.		____	____
	Transitions were rapid and orderly.		____	____
	The teacher faced students being instructed and could see the students doing seatwork.		____	____
	Students doing seatwork worked efficiently.		____	____
SUMMARY AND RECOMMENDATIONS	Observed strengths and/or suggestions for improvement of instructional program.			

_____

_____

RECOMMENDED FOLLOW-UP

1. observe demonstration lesson____   3. meet with AGP resource teacher____

2. observe another teacher on site____   4. other_____

COMMENTS: _____

_____

_____

Fig. 4. Record of classroom observation

had improved. Figure 5 indicates the percent of students scoring at or above the publisher's median in reading (the achievement goal set by court order) prior to AGP (1980) and after year one (1981). Figure 6 reports similar data for mathematics. In all areas but reading in grades

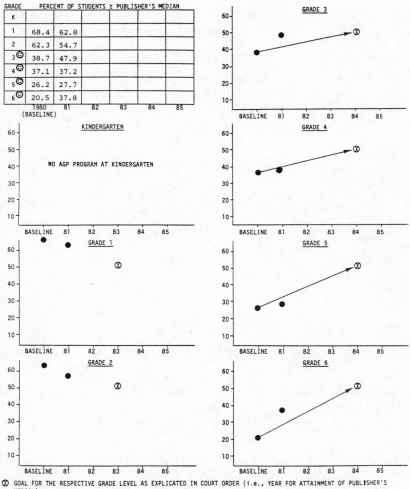

Fig. 5. Percent of pupils scoring at or above the publisher's median
(matched reading data)

one and two, the percent of students above the median increased. It must be noted, however, that the percent of AGP students above the median at the grade levels was above the goal set by the courts in both 1980 and 1981. To further increase students' learning at all grade

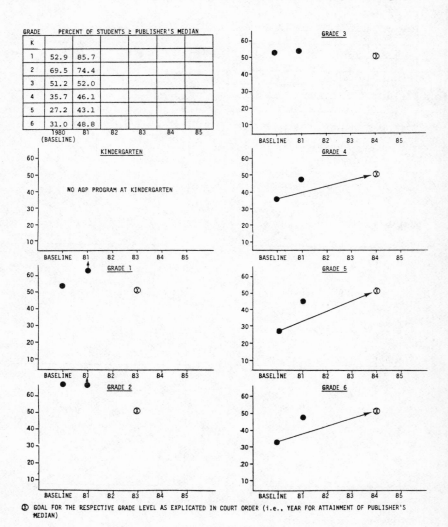

Fig. 6. Percent of pupils scoring at or above the publisher's median
(matched mathematics data)

levels, implementation efforts in year two were designed to maintain the ongoing monitoring and refinement of the program and to resolve procedural problems that had arisen in year one. As noted earlier, during year two AGP was expanded to include classes from kindergarten through grade six in additional schools and grade seven classes for some subjects.

The San Diego experience is a demonstration of an extraordinary effort to secure school improvement through staff development. The success can be attributed to several factors. One is the level of commitment and support for the achievement of the agreed upon objectives that was accomplished across all levels of the school district. Another is the extent to which the implementation procedures included the requirements for successful change efforts.

Upon reviewing the events that preceded the implementation of the program and also those of the first year, the planning, development, and implementation effort may be considered to be essentially a one-and-a-half year staff development function that included daily activities. The concepts on which the program was to be based were new to the staff, the highly structured instructional materials were new, the instructional requirements for teachers called for a style change in most instances, the role of the classroom aides was different, the assignment of AGP site resource teachers was new, and the requirement for frequent and formal classroom observations by the principal, as well as close program monitoring, was a change from past practice for most. Students' daily progress generally was more closely monitored by the teacher than before, and regularly scheduled tests of student progress were administered more frequently than in the past. These elements combined to signal change for all persons with responsibility for or involvement in an AGP school. Concurrently, the AGP implementation procedures required various of the participants to provide guidance, assistance, and support to the others. Further, preimplementation sessions allowed time for reflection on what was to occur.

It is apparent that the San Diego effort likewise compelled the school staffs to put into operation those factors that have been shown to be correlates of effective schools. There were agreed upon program goals, site instructional leadership was provided by the principal, teacher and administrator efficacy were built into the program, appropriate in-service staff development was (and continues to be) provided, and teachers were (and are) required to provide direct instruction to students.

While the characteristics outlined here and expanded upon earlier in this chapter are clearly important to the success of a school improvement effort, the San Diego model also demonstrates that commitment and strong support for the effort by district decision makers, including the superintendent and his staff and the board of education, are equally essential. Moreover, it is evident that "real school improvement" cannot be expected to occur through the conduct of isolated and occasional in-service staff development activities. Staff development for school improvement must be a *process* that involves entire school staffs, including the site administrators, in an ongoing, high-quality effort to achieve well understood and agreed upon goals for school improvement.

FOOTNOTES

1. David B. Tyack, Michael W. Kirst, and Elisabeth Hansot, "Educational Reform: Retrospect and Prospect," *Teachers College Record* 81 (Spring 1980): 253-67.

2. For example, see John Frederiksen and Ronald Edmonds, "Identification of Instructionally Effective and Ineffective Schools" (Unpublished paper, Harvard University, n.d.); Wilbur B. Brookover and Lawrence W. Lezotte, "Changes in School Characteristics Coincident with Changes in Student Achievement" (East Lansing, Mich.: Michigan State University, 1979); Michael Rutter, Barbara Maughan, Peter Mortimore, Janet Ouston, with Alan Smith, *Fifteen Thousand Hours: Secondary Schools and Their Effects on Children* (Cambridge, Mass.: Harvard University Press, 1979); Michael Cohen, "Effective Schools: What the Research Says," *Today's Education* 70 (April-May 1981): 46G-48G; J. Victor Baldridge and Terrence E. Deal, *Managing Change in Educational Organizations: Sociological Perspectives, Strategies, and Case Studies* (Berkeley, Calif.: McCutchan Publishing Corp., 1975).

3. Judith W. Little, "School Success and Staff Development in Urban Desegregated Schools: A Summary of Recently Completed Research" (Paper adapted from Judith W. Little, *School Success and Staff Development: The Role of Staff Development in Urban Desegregated Schools, Final Report* [Boulder, Colo.: Center for Action Research, 1981]), p. 9.

4. Stewart C. Purkey and Marshall S. Smith, "Effective Schools: A Review" (Paper presented at the conference on Implications of Research on Teaching for Practice, Airlie House, Virginia, February 25-27, 1982), p. 6.

5. Little, "School Success and Staff Development in Urban Desegregated Schools," p. 11.

6. Gary A. Griffin, "Staff Development" (Paper presented at the conference on Implications of Research on Teaching for Practice, Airlie House, Virginia, February 25-27, 1982).

7. Ann Lieberman and Lynne Miller, "The Social Realities of Teaching," in Ann Lieberman, ed., "Staff Development: New Demands, New Realities, New Perspectives," *Teachers College Record* 80 (September 1978): 54-68.

8. Gene E. Hall and Susan Loucks, "Program Definition and Adaptation: Implications for Inservice," *Journal of Research and Development in Education* 14 (Winter 1981): 46-58.

9. Gary A. Griffin, "Staff Development."

10. Neal Gross, Joseph B. Giacquinta, and Marilyn Bernstein, *Implementing Organizational Innovations: A Sociological Analysis of Planned Educational Change* (New York: Basic Books, 1971).

11. William J. Tikunoff and Beatrice A. Ward, "Inquiry Is an Unnatural Schooling Activity" (Paper presented at the Annual Meeting of the American Educational Research Association, San Francisco, April 1981), pp. 12-16.

12. See, for example, the chapter by Norman A. Sprinthall and Lois Thies-Sprinthall in this volume.

13. Little, "School Success and Staff Development in Urban Desegregated Schools," pp. 32-33.

14. Paul Berman and Edward Pauly, "Federal Programs Supporting Educational Change: Factors Affecting Change Agent Projects" (Santa Monica, Calif.: Rand Corp., 1975).

15. Joann Jacullo-Noto, "Inside/Outside—Who Are the Experts? Collaborative Staff Development Models" (Paper prepared for the National Institute of Education, Washington, D.C., 1981).

16. Ibid., p. 39.

17. Ronald Edmonds, "Programs on School Improvement: A 1982 Overview" (Paper presented at the Conference on Implications of Research on Teaching for Practice, Airlie House, Virginia, February 25-27, 1982).

18. Purkey and Smith, "Effective Schools: A Review."

19. See, for example, David Armor et al., "Analysis of the School Preferred Reading Program in Selected Los Angeles Minority Schools" (Santa Monica, Calif.: Rand Corp., 1976); Wilbur B. Brookover et al., *Schools Can Make a Difference* (East Lansing, Mich.: Michigan State University, 1977); Ronald Edmonds, "Programs on School Improvement"; Lawrence Lezotte and J. Massalacqua, "Individual School Buildings Do Account for Differences in Measured Pupil Performance" (Occasional paper, no. 6, Institute for Research on Teaching, Michigan State University, East Lansing, Mich., 1978).

20. Armor et al., "Analysis of the School Preferred Reading Program in Selected Los Angeles Minority Schools."

CHAPTER IX

Inquiry as a Means to Professional Growth: The Teacher as Researcher

WILLIAM J. TIKUNOFF AND JOHN R. MERGENDOLLER

It is generally assumed that rigorous scientific research should inform and direct the instructional processes which occur within classrooms. Yet, when teachers and administrators are provided with research findings (generally in the form of thick technical reports), they often throw up their hands in exasperation or confusion. Comments often heard include: "I can't understand this jargon" or "This stuff is too esoteric. Why don't they study something I can use?" or "I can't believe this! It just doesn't sound reasonable." In response to these challenges, researchers and staff developers generally attempt to simplify findings and make concrete suggestions about how the findings can be implemented in the classroom. The implicit assumption is that if educators are exposed to carefully presented and understandable research findings, they will recognize the wisdom of the results and immediately employ them in their daily practice.

We disagree. Moreover, we suggest that the process of translating and implementing research-based recommendations is more complex than one would assume from examining a typical in-service education program. There are several reasons for this.

First, the outcomes of research are not necessarily intended for all audiences. Since educational researchers and funding agencies generally

The authors wish to acknowledge the support of the National Institute of Education, U.S. Department of Education. Many of the thoughts that underlie this discussion result from work begun under Contract NIE-C-003-0108 and completed under Grant OB-NIE-G-78-0203 to the Far West Laboratory for Educational Research and Development, San Francisco, California. However, the opinions expressed here are solely those of the authors, and no official endorsement by the Institute, the Department, or the Laboratory is intended nor should be inferred.

set their own research agenda, the research topics which fall under these agenda may not reflect the concerns of teachers or other educators. As a result, findings from a single study or research program cannot be expected to be perceived as relevant or useful by all research consumers. This is particularly true with studies that are primarily methodological in focus, or which refine well-developed and long-researched hypotheses. Second, since much research involves the testing of hypotheses within a predeveloped theoretical framework, unless one is conversant with the terms and assumptions that make up such a framework, a great deal must be understood before research findings make any sense. This is especially true of research on social cognition and cognitive development. Third, research questions reflect the social and intellectual trends of the times, and it often takes several years to make the journey from research design to implementation of the findings. Consequently, what was once perceived as important may later be considered insignificant. Finally, typical educational research is controlled by funding agencies or professional educational researchers or university professors and generally excludes teachers from the conceptualization and conduct of the research. Teachers are thus trapped in the role of research *consumers* rather than research *creators*. Moreover, the studies teachers are expected to learn from and utilize in their daily instruction are undertaken to answer questions that teachers never asked. Teachers are thus disenfranchised from the research process. As a result, they often perceive typical educational research as confusing, or worse, useless.

To counter this situation, we believe it is imperative to involve teachers in the conduct of research intended for their use. As a result of this involvement, we believe that there is greater probability that the findings will be perceived to be relevant and useful by other teachers. We believe that research skills are among the most powerful in an educator's professional repertoire. When used to analyze and adjust instruction, they provide the basis for developing a deeper understanding of the classroom environment and the process of instruction. Such understanding, we argue, ought to be a major goal of professional staff development.

The development of research skills as a form of professional growth for educators is the topic of this chapter. The discussion proceeds in three parts. First, the nature of research is defined. Then, a research and development strategy that engages teachers in the conduct of inquiry is described. We call this strategy Interactive Research and Development (IR&D).[1] Finally, three variations of the Interactive Research and Development process are discussed. Our concern throughout is with developing an understanding of how engagement in the conduct of research provides rich, valuable professional growth experiences for teachers.

Research as a Process of Inquiry

In the social sciences, the term "research" most frequently is used to denote formal inquiry into social phenomena in order "to establish lawful relations comparable to those of the traditional natural sciences."[2] Formal inquiry in educational research implies utilization of accepted procedures to understand instructional phenomena or to evaluate the effects of a particular strategy or innovation. One can distinguish between "basic" research and "applied" or "naturalistic" research.[3] Basic research is characterized by the testing of hypotheses in a controlled setting, using procedures derived from the physical sciences. Procedures utilized most frequently are quantitative in nature and involve statistical tests of significance. Applied or naturalistic research generally employs systematic observation of naturally occurring social phenomena in a field setting. Such research is often conducted to develop new hypotheses.[4] Procedures are frequently qualitative in nature and strive for "thick description" of social phenomena[5] to obtain the information necessary to establish logical-situational generalizability.[6]

Regardless of the mode of inquiry—"basic" or "applied"—the intent is "understanding, explaining, and predicting people's behavior in their social milieux."[7] Usually this involves stating a problem or a hypothesis, establishing its relationship with what already is known, specifying the procedures to be used for the collection and analysis of data, and identifying the treatment, mediating, and outcome variables. This conceptualization is publicly advanced in a research design. Upon completion of the research, findings are presented in a technical report which thoroughly describes the research procedures and the results obtained. Further reporting typically is accomplished through technical journal articles and presentations at meetings of professional organizations. It then becomes the responsibility of an individual trained in staff development to take these research findings and "package" them in such a way that they can be understood and utilized by teachers.

This process has been described as being linear in that it moves systematically from conduct of the research to using research findings for the development of procedures and materials for use by the intended research consumer. Various aspects of the process have been allocated to specialists: researchers do the research; development specialists develop the training procedures or materials; and staff developers or teacher educators implement these procedures or materials by training teachers in their use. In the linear research and development model, the teacher as research consumer is perceived to be at the receiving end of a product which implements research findings. However, as we have argued, the very act of excluding teachers from the research and development process may explain why research findings heretofore have been difficult to implant in classroom instruction.

It was this assumption which established the rationale for an alternative research and development strategy and led directly to raising two questions: If teachers were included in the process of conducting research and development centered on classroom concerns, could the research and resulting development be more useful for other teachers? And in the process of engaging in conducting formal research and development activities, could teachers gain skills of inquiry which might prove useful for instruction? The result was formulation of a research and development approach called Interactive Research and Development.

Although it employs the same methodological processes and can focus on the same educational issues as the typical researcher-directed procedures described above, IR&D is a research and development strategy which is *team-centered*. All research and development activities are orchestrated and carried out by a team made up of teachers, researchers, and staff developers/trainers. These teams are charged with conducting a rigorous research study by following the steps outlined above. This study must address the *current concerns* of classroom teachers. IR&D is thus a *problem-solving strategy* as well as a research process.

The IR&D team is also charged with creating a staff development program to present their findings to other teachers in such a way that the findings can be of immediate use. These two tasks of research and development are approached *concurrently*. Throughout the research and development process, IR&D teams work *collaboratively*. This means that individual team members are given *parity* in making decisions about the topic to be researched, the methodology to be employed, and the training program to be implemented. The team strives to ensure that each member of the team is given equal status and shares equal responsibility for the team's decisions and actions. During the conceptualization phase of the research and while the team is writing the research design, they are required to respect the *integrity* of the classroom. That is, the research activities must not disrupt the naturally occurring instructional processes they set out to study. Finally, IR&D is considered to be not only a strategy for research and development. It is also an *intervention* process which brings about changes in the ways teachers, researchers, and trainer/developers conceive and manage their professional roles. In the following pages, we shall elaborate this brief sketch and describe the features of Interactive Research and Development in more depth.

Features of Interactive Research and Development

IR&D requires *concurrent* development of research strategies and a training program to disseminate the results of this research. Such a feature enables the IR&D team to select questions for study that can be translated directly into preservice and in-service training, and prevents the conduct of purely "theoretical" or "academic" studies which may be of little value to classroom teachers. Moreover, the focus on concurrent research and development allows procedures for data collection and analysis to be selected which are appropriate for future use in staff development programs. Our experience with IR&D has demonstrated that in-service training programs which enable others to utilize the techniques of inquiry developed by the IR&D team are often more powerful than workshops that promulgate "cookbook" procedures and disseminate research results through handouts.

As we have emphasized, IR&D is a *team* strategy; at a minimum, the IR&D team must be composed of one teacher, one researcher, and one trainer/developer. The purpose of including representatives of all role groups affected by the research and development process at the start is to ensure that all questions and objections which arise during the planning process will be considered from the perspectives of all those who are affected by the research and development effort. Such early involvement of all three role groups prevents the development of a status hierarchy based on "being there first and knowing more."

While the charge to conduct concurrent research and development and the composition of the team are central features of IR&D, the manner in which the team makes decisions about the research effort is also crucial to the establishment of a fully interactive research and development process. Decisions regarding research questions, data collection procedures, and materials development must be made in such a way that the expertise of all team members is respected and acknowledged. When this occurs, *parity* has been established among team members. During the implementation of IR&D, it is important that no single member of the team continually dominates the remaining members. Each team member must be given equal opportunity to propose, plan, and direct the research and development effort. To facilitate such reciprocity among team members, leadership focuses on specific issues and rotates among the team members according to the competencies necessary at various points in the research and development effort. On an IR&D team, no member is accorded higher status than any other member.

To ensure that the research procedures and results authentically reflect the *problems* of classroom teachers, the research questions approached by an IR&D team emerge from the concerns expressed by teachers—both on and off the team. During question formulation, the teachers on the team are charged with talking with their peers to determine what instructional problems are of most concern. Once these questions are identified, the research design must be phrased in such a way that the intent of the study will be easily discernable to other teachers who will participate in the in-service education programs developed by the team. The concern here is to avoid the imposition of research questions formulated by an external researcher—or funding agency—and to provide a responsive forum where teachers are able to have significant impact on the nature of the research conducted in their own schools.

In IR&D, the research methods selected for use by the IR&D team must seek to be unobtrusive so that the *integrity* of the classroom is maintained. We are concerned not only that the research process does not intrude on the daily instruction of students, but also that it acknowledges the complexity of the classroom. To communicate with teachers who deal continually with the complexity of the classroom, research must strive for ecological validity.

Finally, IR&D is not only a research strategy; it is an ongoing *intervention* as well. Although IR&D allows the team members to continue to function within their professional roles, it requires certain alterations in their usual roles, conventional functioning, and expectations. Teachers are encouraged to acquire new ways of thinking about their own classroom problems. Through direct involvement with teachers, researchers can learn to identify new research procedures and methods and become aware of critical research issues they had not previously considered. Similarly, the trainer/developer may acquire new skill and insights into classroom functioning from extended work with teachers, and may be able to design more appropriate in-service education programs.

To carry out interactive research and development that meets the above criteria and at the same time produces rigorous and useful outcomes at reasonable cost is not a simple task. Members of the IR&D team generally make sense of the world in different ways as a result of differences in professional training and experience. While this diversity is to be celebrated, and brings the potential for the team's contribution to exceed the sum of the individual contributions, it does require that conflicting assumptions about the purpose of research and development must be aired, and that effort be expended so that mutually agreed upon goals are established. Because teachers, researchers, and trainer/developers often speak using the words and assumptions proper to their own profession, pains must be taken to ensure that the different members of the collaborative team fully understand each other's concerns. When this occurs, a common vocabulary develops among team members. Words like "variable" or "operationalization" become the property of all team members—not just the researcher. If IR&D is to function optimally, the equal status of all team members must be maintained, and this frequently is demonstrated in the development of such a common lexicon.

IR&D as a Vehicle for Professional Growth

To this point, we have been considering the features of IR&D which make it, in our opinion, a useful strategy for conducting educational research. The same characteristics also make IR&D an important vehicle for professional growth. Such growth can occur in several ways.

First, by being part of an IR&D team, teachers are encouraged to reflect upon their classroom lives, acknowledge problems, and take formal and concerted action to examine further and ameliorate those problems. We believe this practice of self-reflection, problem definition, and intervention required for the formal IR&D inquiry generally spills over into the informal inquiry, which is one characteristic of good teaching. In this fashion, an inquiring "habit of mind" is facilitated by participation in the IR&D process. In addition, teachers gain experience in the conduct of formal inquiry and the use of appropriate instruments and procedures. It is our perception that when teachers begin to understand the "techniques" of inquiry, and practice thinking through problems and selecting appropriate methodological strategies for further inquiry, it often has a more powerful impact on their future classroom practice than exposure to research findings in a series of in-service workshops.

A second benefit from participation in the IR&D process comes from the development of collaboration and discussion skills as a result of participation in the team's planning and organizing meetings. Because team leadership rotates, all team members are given the opportunity to practice agenda setting, group facilitation, and other leadership skills. The development of these skills not only gives teachers an advantage in the classroom; it can also benefit the entire school by facilitating more productive faculty and committee meetings.

Finally, teachers who participate on an IR&D team have at their fingertips the results of the inquiry they are conducting, and are able to apply these findings immediately in their own classrooms. Because of the participants' interest in the findings, they generally desire to "try them out." Following this implementation, other teachers may become interested, and a process of informal implementation may sweep the school and complement the more formal procedures of the in-service training program.

Interactive Research and Development: Three Cases

Thus far we have been describing the features that define Interactive Research and Development and the impact this process may have on the professional development of teachers. In the following sections we turn our attention to three examples of the way in which the IR&D model has been implemented by different teams.

INTERACTIVE RESEARCH AND DEVELOPMENT ON TEACHING (IR&DT)

The initial program of research which elaborated the above theoretical model and evaluated the results was developed at the Far West Laboratory for Educational Research and Development. This program implemented an IR&D strategy at two sites—one an urban setting in California, the other a rural setting in Vermont. The urban site was organized in collaboration with a local educational agency— the San Diego Unified School District. The rural site was conducted in collaboration with a school of education at the state university and a small rural school district. These diverse settings were purposefully selected in order to observe IR&D implementations in different geographical locations and examine the utility of the IR&D strategy with differing institutional arrangements.

The urban site. The urban site was organized in collaboration with the San Diego Unified School District, which serves the ninth largest municipality in the United States and enrolled more than 118,000 students in the year of the study (1977-78). The IR&DT team consisted of four teachers, one researcher, and one trainer/developer. All of these individuals were on the school district staff.

Three of the teachers on the IR&DT team taught kindergarten, first, and second grades in the same elementary school. This school served 400 students, a majority of whom were black or Hispanic. There were also small percentages of Asian and white students. Eighty-five percent of the students were eligible for free lunch, and an additional 13 percent qualified for reduced price lunch. As a result of the student population served, the school received funds from a number of categorical aid programs.

The fourth teacher member of the IR&DT team taught in a combination third and fourth grade class in another elementary school in the same district. This school served 1200 students, 77 percent of whom were white, 11 percent Hispanic, 9 percent Asian American, and 3 percent black. This school was also the site of a district-wide program for gifted students.

The rural site. The rural site included two cooperating institutions—the College of Education and Social Services at the University of Vermont and the Underhill Independent School District. In 1977-78, the college served about 1,000 students, approximately 120 of whom were enrolled in the preservice elementary teaching program. The Underhill Independent School District includes only one school, an elementary school serving students in kindergarten through fourth grade. In 1977 to 1978, the school enrolled 130 students, the majority of whom were white. The faculty was comprised of five teachers including a teacher/principal. Three of these teachers were members of the IR&DT team, which also included one researcher and two trainer/developers who worked in succession with the team.

Focus of the research and development efforts. During the 1977-78 school year, the San Diego Unified School District was attempting to draw teachers' attention to the importance of keeping students "on-task" (that is, engaged in meaningful learning activities). This district-wide concern was reflected in the individual concerns of the IR&DT team members, and they formulated the following question for their research and development activities: What are the strategies and techniques which classroom teachers use to cope with the distractions to classroom instruction and how effective are these techniques? The purpose of the research study, then, was to examine the techniques classroom teachers used to cope with distractions to classroom instruction and to determine how effective these techniques were with respect to: (a) minimizing instructional time lost due to distractions; (b) dealing with distractions at a level which has a minimal disruptive effect on the flow of instruction; and (c) eliminating distractions. Classroom distractions were defined as those events which take the attention of teachers and/or their students off the intended instructional tasks. Coping techniques were defined as verbal or nonverbal mechanisms used by teachers to eliminate a distraction.

Concurrent with conducting their inquiry, the team designed a training program for other teachers. This program featured several components from the research methodology, particularly the data collection techniques developed by the team. In addition, the training design included information about classroom distractions and coping techniques obtained through the team's research study and charged participants with testing the generality of these results in their own classrooms.

Research was conducted in the winter and spring of 1978 in eight classrooms (those of four IR&DT team members and four additional teachers who taught the same grade). The data set included quantitative coding of occurrences of distractions and coping strategies, narrative descriptions of teacher-student interactions, and other relevant context information for each classroom. Two observers collected the data simultaneously, one recording quantitative data and the other developing the narrative description. Data were analyzed in the spring and early summer. Data interpretation and report writing took place over the summer. In addition, the IR&DT team prepared a training design which was reviewed by a national advisory panel. A training program based on this design was implemented in the fall of 1978.[8]

At the Vermont site, the IR&DT team was interested in the effect that teachers' moods could have on teaching performance. Consequently, they focused their research on the following questions: Are there relationships between the mood of the teacher and the teacher's classroom supportive instructional behavior? If so, what is the nature of these relationships? Mood was defined as a state, not a trait. To narrow down the scope of their inquiry, the IR&DT team reviewed extant research on teaching and selected a set of *supportive* instructional behaviors as the dependent variables under study. These behaviors included acceptance, attending, conviviality, cooperation, optimism, engagement, monitoring, pacing, and promoting self-sufficiency.

Research was conducted in late spring 1978 in nine classrooms. None of the participating classrooms was taught by members of the IR&DT team. The data set included narrative descriptions of what occurred in each classroom during the reading lesson as well as narratives documenting the events which occurred at the time of day judged "most difficult" by each teacher, teachers' ratings of their moods by way of an adjective checklist, and observer-teacher interviews. Data were analyzed and interpreted in the late summer, and the research reports were completed in early fall. In addition, a training design was completed during the spring, and, after review of this document by a national advisory panel, a training program was implemented the next fall.

IR&DT participation and professional growth. Participation on the urban or rural IR&DT teams had definite consequences for the professional growth of the team members, and for the social relationships found within the participating educational institutions.[9] Participants on both IR&DT teams increased their awareness of educational options and possibilities available within their own professional roles and daily functioning, partly as a result of their experience of systematic inquiry into classroom processes. This result was particularly notable for the members of the rural IR&DT team. In addition, members of both IR&DT teams became more knowledgeable about and skillful in the process of educational research and development as a result of their IR&DT experience.

Another significant impact of IR&DT participation was on the social relationships of the team members. Although self-contained classrooms and professional norms have historically been associated with teacher isolation, the teacher members of both IR&DT teams related to one another and to the researcher and trainer/developer in atypical ways. Systematic, focused, and interactive inquiry provided avenues for professional communication which had not formerly been part of their job experience. The institutional isolation of elementary school from elementary school, and elementary school from university (in the case of the rural site), was also reduced.

Another impact of participation in IR&DT was an increased belief on the part of the participants that the work of other team members was of value and otherwise prestigious in their immediate workplaces as well as in the broader educational community. The combination of (a) an increased ability to understand the research and development process and (b) the belief that the findings and training programs emerging from their work were worthwhile and perceived positively by others was experienced as a powerful antidote to the sentiments that teachers and teaching are of low status and priority in terms of social action and reward systems at local and national levels.

Finally, IR&DT team membership was associated with significant changes in the professional practices of the participants. Self-reports indicated that participating teachers changed some of their instructional patterns, that researchers learned and demonstrated new research skills, and that trainer/developers revised and reordered certain beliefs and practices regarding teacher education. Some of these changes resulted from adopting the findings that emerged from the research itself; others came from participating in the research process; some followed from interactions with other members of the IR&DT team. There was also an indication that participants began to rely less upon conventional wisdom, and more upon prior research and/or expert testimony as the work proceeded. On both teams, although more markedly so at the rural site, initial discussions focused most frequently on the experiences of individual participants rather than on findings from more systematic inquiries. As the IR&DT process continued, team members (especially the teacher members) began to question one another regarding the empirical accuracy of statements, reports, and hypotheses. This change from a personal to a more theoretical and questioning turn of mind appeared to result both from participation in the IR&DT research process and from the technical assistance provided the IR&DT teams by the Far West Laboratory.

In summary, the original IR&DT study confirmed the hypothesis that engaging teachers in a collaborative program of inquiry with other teachers, researchers, and staff developers has a positive impact on the professional growth and development of all team members. Moreover, the IR&DT experience helped teachers to develop habits of inquiry that are expected to long outlast the original intention. The significance of this initial demonstration of the IR&DT strategy increases when one considers the following two efforts to employ the IR&DT strategy.

IR&D AT TEXAS TECH UNIVERSITY

An IR&D project at Texas Tech university utilized a variant of the original IR&DT strategy to involve university professors in the School of Education, Teachers Corps staff, and teachers in local schools in collaborative research on teachers' instructional problems.[10] This project began with the premise that teachers do not use research findings and practices in their teaching, nor do they look to research as a means of solving educational problems. To examine this phenomenon further and to provide initial data suggesting ways teachers could be encouraged to utilize research results, a study was conducted which sought (a) to determine whether participation in an IR&D project resulted in a significant change of teachers' concerns about the use of research findings and practices in their teaching, and (b) to determine whether participation in an IR&D project resulted in teachers acquiring skills, interests, and attitudes which were likely to promote their future use of research findings and practices in teaching.[11]

The study employed a pretest-posttest, control-group design, with thirteen teachers in the treatment group and eighteen teachers in the control group. Subjects in the treatment group participated in an IR&D intervention sponsored by the local Teacher Corps project. The treatment consisted of approximately ten hours of initial training in general research practices and procedures and in the essential features of Interactive Research and Development as well as membership on an IR&D team. Six teams were formed to mirror participants' research interests and social preferences. Each team consisted of one to three teachers, one university professor who served as the researcher, and one person from the Teacher Corps staff who served as the staff developer. Each team was charged with the responsibility of identifying a research question, conducting a research project using appropriate methodology and design, and collaboratively planning a means to disseminate the research findings.

Data reflecting the impact of participation on the IR&D team were gathered using three questionnaires which assessed: (a) teachers' concerns about and interest in the use of research findings and practices in teaching; (b) teachers' self-perceptions regarding their skills in carrying out research and development; and (c) teachers' favored topics for professional development activities. In addition, open-ended statements were collected about teachers' concerns and feelings related to the use of research findings and practices in their teaching. Finally, informal interviews were used to probe teachers' attitudes about the use of research findings and practices in teaching.

The quantitative data were analyzed using standard statistical procedures, while the open-ended statements were scored and discussed by two independent readers until consensus was reached. Interview data were subjected to an informal analysis.

Based upon analyses of the above data, the following conclusions were reached:

1. Teachers who participated in an IR&D project demonstrated significantly greater changes in concerns about the use of research findings and practices in teaching than those who did not participate in an IR&D project.

2. Teachers who participated in an IR&D project demonstrated significantly higher research, teaching, and development skills than those who did not participate in such a project.

3. Teachers who participated in an IR&D project did not demonstrate significantly higher interest in professional development than those who did not participate in an IR&D project.

4. Teachers who participated in an IR&D project demonstrated a positive attitude about the use of research findings and practices in teaching.[12]

Implications from these results included the following suggestions:

1. The integration of the IR&D process into more traditional programs of staff development may increase the effectiveness of staff development by providing teachers with opportunities to develop research skills.

2. The addition of a university graduate level course using the IR&D process may be an additional means of addressing the research needs of public school practitioners and university research personnel.

3. The amount of field-based research conducted in the future may be increased by the continuation of an IR&D project, in that such a project provides university research personnel with more ready access to public school settings in which to conduct field-based research.

4. The working relationship of university and public school personnel may be enhanced through the continuation of an IR&D project in which persons from both institutions work together to study questions of mutual concern.[13]

In sum, the IR&D project at Texas Tech again demonstrated that the interactive research and development strategy can facilitate professional growth and encourage teachers to turn to educational research findings when confronted with classroom problems.

IR&D ON SCHOOLING (IR&DS)

Beginning in 1980 at Teachers College, Columbia University, an IR&D project has been conducted under funding from the National Institute of Education.[14] This two-year project attempts to replicate the IR&D model in three institutional contexts not previously investigated. The institutional contexts included are:

1. A Teachers' Center. This institution coordinates the work of four teacher specialists responsible for organizing and operating

Teachers' Centers in their respective schools, and a researcher and staff developer/teacher trainer from Teachers College.

2. The Board of Cooperative Educational Services (BOCES), an intermediate education agency serving several school districts. This organization is working with four secondary teachers from two of these districts, a researcher from Teachers College, and a staff developer from the BOCES staff; and

3. A school district. Members of the IR&DS team include four elementary school teachers, a researcher who is a teacher with a completed Ph.D., and the assistant superintendent for curriculum and instruction as staff developer.

All three teams are charged with identifying a research topic of concern to teachers, producing a piece of research, and utilizing findings to facilitate staff development for others. At present, the teams are conducting their research, the design of which was reviewed and critiqued externally by experts in order to assure quality.

During the course of each team's work, the Teachers College staff is collecting data concerning the characteristics of the participants, the nature of team interactions, and the rigor and usefulness of outcomes of the research and concomitant staff development. Combined with the findings from the original IR&DT study, the results of the current study should help determine the characteristics of participants which predict successful IR&D implementations, as well as the nature of necessary technical assistance and resources.

In a preliminary analysis of the IR&DS participants' perceptions regarding research and development, Benjamin utilized some of the same questionnaires employed in the Texas Tech study.[15] Two instruments assessed participants' interest in different professional development topics and activities, while a third tapped teachers' perceptions of their skills in research and development. The final questionnaire required teachers to indicate the major problems they faced as a teacher.

Preliminary analyses of these questionnaires indicated that, in the area of subject matter, participants' interests were highest in the ways students learn (learning styles, motivation, reinforcement, retention) and teacher-student interaction. Other areas of high interest were evaluating student learning, motivating students, new curricula, and classroom management.

In the area of activity types, all teams were most enthusiastic about the exchange of ideas with colleagues and visits to successful programs. These were followed by presentations by knowledgeable people, attendance at professional conferences, and independent study or research (including self-analysis of teaching effectiveness).

As perceived by the teams, the major problems faced by teachers included classroom management, discipline, morale, teacher stress, and instructional techniques. Funding, support, and encouragement also were seen to be of major importance to a majority of teachers.

In the area of research and development skills, all three teams perceived themselves as being more skilled in the planning and conduct of professional development activities than in research on schooling. Areas in which the teachers considered themselves to be most highly skilled were the ability to lead group discussions, moderate meetings, or facilitate constructive interactions among personnel; the ability to prepare instructional materials appropriate to a student's developmental level; the ability to record classroom events accurately and objectively; and the ability to sequence learning activities to facilitate student learning in curriculum or a set of curriculum materials. In addition, teachers felt they were skilled in knowledge of procedures and steps used to develop curriculum materials and were knowledgeable about instructional approaches to be used with these materials. Most team members (with the exception of the researcher) expressed greatest weakness in the areas of research design and statistical techniques.

Although it is too early to draw many conclusions from the IR&DS effort, preliminary results suggest the Interactive Research and Development strategy can be usefully employed in other institutional contexts besides those originally investigated.

Conclusions: Inquiry and Professional Growth

Conducting research to inquire into and resolve instructional problems traditionally has not been perceived as a responsibility of classroom teachers. As a result, much of the educational research conducted to date has gone unused. One way to ensure the usefulness of research is to engage teachers in the research process. By joining a team with a researcher and a trainer/developer, teachers can not only help in the selection of questions to be studied. They also learn skills of inquiry which can aid them in examining and understanding their own teaching. At the same time, an *interactive* process of research and development ensures that appropriate procedures for utilizing the research will be developed concurrently with the conduct of the study. Ultimately, we believe that inquiry skills are valuable tools to be added to a teacher's professional repertoire. Staff development which utilizes the Interactive Research and Development strategy enables teachers to acquire these tools.

FOOTNOTES

1. William J. Tikunoff, Beatrice A. Ward, and Gary A. Griffin, *Interactive Research and Development on Teaching: Final Report* (San Francisco: Far West Laboratory for Educational Research and Development, 1979).

2. Lee J. Cronbach, "Beyond the Two Disciplines of Scientific Psychology," *American Psychologist* 30 (February 1975): 121.

3. William J. Tikunoff and Beatrice A. Ward, "Conducting Naturalistic Research on Teaching: Some Procedural Considerations," *Education and Urban Society* 12 (May 1980): 263-90.

4. Jacob S. Kounin, "Some Ecological Dimensions of School Settings" (Paper presented at the annual meeting of the American Educational Research Association, New York, April 1977).

5. Clifford Geertz, *The Interpretation of Cultures* (New York: Basic Books, 1973).

6. Beatrice A. Ward, "Why Consider Context?" (Paper presented at the annual meeting of the American Educational Research Association, New York, April 1977).

7. Tikunoff and Ward, "Conducting Naturalistic Research on Teaching," p. 265.

8. Grant Behnke, Eugene Labovitz, Janice Bennett, Cynthia Chase, Jane Day, Charlotte Lazar, and David Mittleholtz, "Coping with Classroom Distractions," *Elementary School Journal* 81 (January, 1981): 135-55.

9. Tikunoff, Ward, and Griffin, *Interactive Research and Development on Teaching*.

10. Leslie L. Huling, "The Effects on Teachers of Participation in an Interactive Research and Development Project" (Doct. Diss., Texas Tech University, 1981).

11. Ibid., p. 4.

12. Ibid., p. 68.

13. Ibid., p. 68-69.

14. Gary Griffin, Ann Lieberman, and Joann Jacullo-Noto, *Interactive Research and Development on Schooling, Report I: Initial Description of the Participants and the Three Sites* (New York: Teachers College, Columbia University, 1980).

15. Stephanie Benjamin, *Interactive Research and Development on Schooling, Report IV: Summary of Team Progress Reports* (New York: Teachers College, Columbia University, 1980).

Part Three
CONCLUSIONS

CHAPTER X

Toward a Conceptual Framework for Staff Development

GARY A. GRIFFIN

This chapter advances a set of related propositions regarding the elements of staff development programs that are believed to be essential considerations for planning, implementing, and inquiring about staff development. The principal argument is that consideration of these principles and elements as conceptually related, thereby forming a whole, will promote both comprehensiveness and clarity for those people who do the work of staff development and for those people who try to understand better that work and its effects.

Three influences on the content and form of this chapter should be acknowledged. First, the potential value of a conceptualization of often apparently disparate phenomena for better understanding and acting upon matters of schooling was made dramatically present to me more than fifteen years ago when Goodlad and Richter published the final report of a set of deliberations aimed at describing curricular and instructional decision making.[1] This slender volume, at the time and subsequently, appeared to have a significant effect upon the way curriculum scholars and practitioners "saw" their specialized field of study and interest. In fact, thirteen years after its publication, a more detailed and comprehensive book appeared which presented research findings and propositions that had their origins in the ideas put forth in the original monograph.[2] My professional attraction to the possibilities inherent in bringing order, often tentative, to complex and often ill-understood phenomena stems, in large measure, from the ideas in those works.

Second, the content of the preceding chapters in this yearbook was

228

deliberately selected to illustrate the array of considerations that many of us believe are necessary to successful implementation of staff development programs and research. This is a departure from many of the recent books on staff development that have had a single ideological or practical focus.[3] The Yearbook Committee was concerned that a unitary perspective would be unnecessarily limiting to the utility of the book. The comprehensiveness that has emerged, in terms of both theoretical and practical issues, demonstrates the need expressed by people who *do* staff development for a conceptual map of the territory they expect to cover.

Third, the impetus to engage in school improvement, often through staff development, has resulted in a set of apparently disparate research findings, propositions, and proposals for action.[4] The perceived differences between and among these ideas and practices are often consequences of giving incomplete attention to potentially complementary perspectives and/or logically related and influential but unattended phenomena. This chapter proposes a framework that can capture and draw attention to these phenomena without promoting them as prescriptions for thinking or acting.

In the remainder of the chapter, I present as a conceptual framework the basic and secondary elements believed to be important considerations in staff development practice and inquiry with illustrations of their interactive nature, and I propose data sources appropriate to the elements.

Basic Elements of a Conceptual Framework

The guiding assumption upon which much of this discussion rests is that staff development efforts involve *people* in *interaction* with one another in particular *contexts* to accomplish professional growth and school improvement goals. This assumption, by definition, identifies the first three elements of the framework. Other elements to be discussed are purposes, activities, evaluation, and data sources.

PEOPLE

It is axiomatic that staff development is people-centered. That is, the work of the school is seen as being carried out by people rather than by machines, abstract conceptions of practice, ideologies, or theories. This, of course, is not to say that people are practice-free, ideologically or theoretically mindless, or ignorant of the power of technology to advance their work. The specific emphasis given to the persons in the process is intended to focus attention on the possibilities and problems encountered by working with human groups in schools.[5]

To note only that staff development is people-focused is insufficient to guide staff development practices. It is important to acknowledge that the people inhabit different roles, carry contrasting responsibilities, and bring to their work sometimes unrelated and often conflicting points of view. These basic differences, when unaccounted for, have strong potential for building failure into a staff development program.[6]

Role differences are the most obvious people considerations and are most often acknowledged in school improvement efforts. The differences between teachers, principals, assistant superintendents, and so forth are typically the stuff of which staff development is made. Principals work with teachers to improve classroom interaction. System officials work with principals to solve building problems. Curriculum specialists work with teachers and school administrators to alter plans for instruction. And so on. It appears to be assumed by many concerned with staff development that these role descriptors have common meanings across settings.

It is clear from many of the chapters in this yearbook that within-role differences can be influential upon the success of an improvement activity. Goodlad points out the discrepancies in terms of the school principal. Schlechty and Whitford imply the need for greater role clarity at the system level. Tikunoff and Mergendoller acknowledge the effects of role perceptions of teachers on the conduct of interactive research and development. Sprinthall and Thies-Sprinthall, while not attending directly to role, remind us that adults, regardless of role, are different entities and that the differences will have some bearing on the outcomes of our staff development efforts.

Part and parcel of role difference is the disparate nature of responsibilities that accrue to the roles, both across and within roles. It is sharply apparent in the chapter by Lanier that classroom life is viewed differently by teachers and teacher educators. This across-role difference accounts for many of the communication problems experienced by persons with basically complementary professional interests. In like fashion, the differences within roles can be observed when one compares, for example, teachers in inner-city settings with teachers in suburban settings.

It can be hypothesized that these differences have much to do with the responsibilities that these professionals assume in their worklives. Lanier makes it clear that the sense of responsibility for conducting instruction (by teachers) and the acceptance of the obligations associated with teaching teachers (by teacher educators) prompt different conceptions of what classrooms and schools are all about. For teachers, it is reasonable to assume that the pressing needs arising from the daily activities of classrooms will cause them to seek answers to immediate questions. For teacher educators, the concern for developing alternate means to deal with both process and product classroom dilemmas will cause them to resist single responses to complex problems. The tensions that result, to a degree, have their origins in the view of the classroom world and the demands upon role which that view reveals. One's view is in large measure a reflection of how one conceives of his or her responsibilities.

This is also true for persons who have, in conventional terms, the same roles. The view of teaching and learning that derives from participation in a setting characterized by poverty, harsh interpersonal relationships, inadequate instructional materials, and the like will be much different from the view that emerges from teaching in a more receptive environment. These different views are, in large part, shaped by the responsibilities that teachers infer from their environments. (See also the discussion of context later in this section.) At the heart of every helping profession is the obligation to respond to the client in understanding and meaningful ways. This notion of derived responsibility can be considered a major influence upon teachers and, in like fashion, can be hypothesized as one of the forces shaping the identification and enactment of responsible professional behavior, which in turn accounts for teacher-to-teacher differences.

Also, although there are points of view suggesting that teachers become teachers because of similar orientations to work and to life, it is possible to identify clearcut differences among teachers regarding philosophic positions as to the good life, beliefs about the relation of school to society, perspectives on growing up in a culture, and other value positions. These differences, as do the ones noted above, define school people as individuals even though their roles may be either complementary or the same. Further, the differences influence how participants act out their roles, how they move through schooling tasks.

Recent times have seen a resurgence of interest in what might be called conservative views of schooling.[7] Whether the focus of attention is competency testing of students, performance ratings of teachers, basic skills as the heart of instruction, or the elimination of certain curriculum materials, there is an implicit set of values regarding the very nature of schooling. This set of values is in conflict with others that undergird a less restrictive view of teaching and learning. Characteristic of the latter orientation are such practices as open education, values clarification, social problem solving, inquiry methods in the social sciences, and others. To suggest that these contrasts regarding schooling practice, and the beliefs that promote or hinder them, exist only *outside* the schoolhouse doors is to deny the variability of humankind.

Debates regarding what schooling ought to be do take place in schools. The nature of the arguments advanced in those debates, to a degree, shapes the practices of schools. And the kind of schooling offered by teachers and administrators varies from state to state, district to district, school to school, and classroom to classroom.

In sum, the inclusion of people as the central element of this conceptual framework is less simplistic than some proponents of "person-centered staff development" have acknowledged explicitly. Educators are not all alike. They do not perceive their responsibilities in carbon-copy-like fashion. The people are not stamped from the same template. They do not move through life experiencing the same sets of sensations, thoughts, and stimuli. And, important to this discussion, they do not enter the educating profession with the same or necessarily similar expectations for acting out their roles even when the labels given to those roles are identical.[8]

INTERACTIONS

The first chapter of this yearbook attends to selected aspects of the work of staff development. Subsequent chapters report activities, propositions, outcomes, and conclusions regarding selected staff development programs and strategies. Several of the chapters give specific attention to the ways in which staff development work was accomplished in specific settings. All of these chapters imply the importance of human interactions in those accomplishments.

Much recent attention has been given in schooling literature to the complexity of classrooms and schools.[9] Likewise, scholars in the past two decades have produced convincing arguments regarding the complexities involved in attempts to change or improve teaching and learning situations.[10] What one begins to discern as a pattern is the constancy of interacting phenomena and the apparent differential effects those phenomena and interactions have upon school effectiveness. These interactions are essentially human ones. Although policy and practice are often seen as abstract concepts, especially in certain models, schema, and the like, the policies and practices are invented, carried forward, and enacted by people.

Human interactions regarding staff development occur across and within constituencies, institutions, and roles. These interactions, naturally, have different purposes, different central activities, and different outcomes. The character of the interactions, as suggested elsewhere in this chapter, is influenced by who is interacting with whom (person-oriented) and the contexts within which the interactions take place. The nature of the interactions, for our purposes, is defined by an intentional activity designed to promote professional growth of school people.

The participants in the interactions, it must be remembered, will often have different perceptions regarding that purposefulness. Some people will initiate an interaction, some will be the object of that initiation, some will become involved as a consequence of personal and professional intention, some will be unwilling participants, and some will be enthusiastic seekers of staff development opportunities.[11] This suggests that it is not only the nature of the interaction (for example, participation in a workshop) that is the predictor of outcomes but the nature of the participants (and their attendant values, beliefs, and predilections) in the interaction as well.

CONTEXT

Every author contributing to this volume attends in some fashion to the context or contexts of staff development. The school is described in terms of the ways in which its organizational properties can be marshalled for improvement purposes. The school system's characteristics are noted as a means toward better understanding of why staff development programs are only variously successful in accomplishing their goals. It is acknowledged that institutions of higher education differ along certain organizational lines from public elementary and secondary schools. The normative structures of the typical educational institutions clearly are influential upon the enactment of staff development opportunities.

There is a growing literature, propositional and research-derived, that suggests the power of context in relation to accomplishing schooling goals.[12] There is every reason to believe that the arguments advanced in that literature, usually concerned with school effectiveness in terms of pupil outcomes, are at least equivalently related to the success of staff development strategies and programs. Certain context features are selected for inclusion here because of their logical relationship to the promotion of professional growth. They are certainly not all-inclusive.

Mission. School organizations have been described as having vague and often conflicting goals. Although it is rare to find a school system *without* a set of goals formulated as a means to guide instruction, it is equally rare to find that the goals are in fact influential upon policy or practice. Most often a public and logical relationship between system (or, for that matter, school) goals is difficult to discern.

Although conventional wisdom holds that schools have a well-understood purpose (for example, promoting active participation of citizens in a democracy, developing verbal and numerical literacy), the goal statements tend to lack specificity and thereby lose their power to influence decisions about means. Also, schools in the United States increasingly serve diverse populations of students and patrons. Recognition of this diversity, typically the result of pressures brought to bear by vocal self-interest groups, prompts school people to develop, for the sake of expediency, system or school goals that are not compatible.

A companion to the problem of responding to multiple client groups is the fact that schools have accepted (or have been coerced into accepting) the responsibility for providing guidance to students in an ever increasing array of instructional and social arenas. The period of history from World War II to the present has witnessed the adoption by the school of an almost bewildering array of offerings. Such contrasting issues as driver education, bilingual education, mainstreaming, family studies, computer science, values education, and the like have found their way into schools. Considering the finite nature of time and energy, it is not surprising to find that the plethora of issues to which the school is expected to give attention appears to have drained school people of much of their willingness to be responsive to subsequent attempts at innovation. And, again not surprisingly, it is clear that the goal statements that are believed to influence schooling cannot encompass all that schools are expected to accomplish.

This condition of conflicting goals and lack of goal clarity works against the staff development enterprise when it cannot be well ascertained that a school mission *requires* certain teacher or administrator capabilities. Although direct ends-means relationships are often difficult to establish in human service organizations, the vague or invisible mission statement is less than desirable when organizing for work. Too often the result of this condition is a scattering of effort driven largely by immediate perceived problems rather than well orchestrated and sustained set of attempts to accomplish a carefully formulated, important school goal.

Rewards. In every organization, including schools, an important feature is its reward structure. Rewards, as has been demonstrated in psychological studies, can be classified as intrinsic and extrinsic. Rewards can also be looked upon as formal and informal. The latter distinction will receive attention here.

Formal rewards in educational settings are often obvious to the participant and to the observer. Salaries, study leaves, health benefits, and the like are formal rewards. They are distributed according to a conception of the value of a person's work to the organization. In schools and particularly with teachers, these formal rewards are most often distributed equally with differentiation present only according to a uniform set of criteria. For example, teachers in a system typically receive the same salary when they have very similar years of experience and/or graduate education. It is rare for a teacher to be paid more than his or her colleagues because of observed excellence, the assumption of extra responsibilities, or for teaching in difficult situations. Generally, teachers are rewarded through the formal structure with little consideration for these differences in performance, task accomplishment, or teaching assignment.

Because of the static nature of the formal reward structure of schools, the informal rewards become more powerful than they would in a setting with a differentiated structure. Informal rewards for school people, particularly teachers, appear to emerge from two sources: interactions with students and alterations in conditions of work made available by authorities in the system.

Research findings and craft knowledge support the conclusion that teachers, in general, look to their work for "satisfaction."[13] This often undefined outcome of teaching is expressed in such phrases as "I feel good when a child learns in my class," "I am happy when I can reach just one student," "When I look back on where these students were ten months ago I feel that I've accomplished something," and so on. In a relatively uniform organization, as schools tend to be, the real differences appear to be in the character of the client groups. And the degrees of those differences, when perceived positively, constitute rewards for teachers.

A powerful, but often unrealized, component of the informal reward structure in schools is the modification of working conditions for teachers. Teaching is characteristically viewed only as meeting with students. Very seldom are the activities of planning, evaluating, reflecting, or engaging in professional and intellectual pursuits noted in definitions of teaching, although these and other sets of behaviors are considered essential to the maintenance of effective teaching-learning situations. Consequently, teachers and others in schools become preoccupied with the adult-child relationship at the expense of the potential power of adult-adult relationships.

When a teacher is provided with opportunities to engage in teaching-related experiences (as opposed to direct teaching experience), it is often necessary to alter the character of the workplace. The clients of schools are present in schools for a mandated and compulsory number of hours each year. It is assumed that teachers will be present and responsible for students during those same hours. In order to accommodate a view of teaching that values and accounts for professional behavior which is largely noninstructional, the students' time and the community's expectations must be taken into consideration. Some school systems arrange for students to be released early on regularly scheduled days of the week, month, or semester. Some schools provide substitute teachers so that adults in schools can plan or reflect or assess together. Some individual administrators move into classrooms and provide instruction in order to release teachers. Certain of these practices can be considered part of a formal structure but most often they are informal and rooted more in an administrator's perception of valued activity for teachers than in a system norm. This is especially true in a period of declining resources.

Other manifestations of the informal reward structure for elementary and secondary school educators include providing differential access to instructional materials, opportunities to receive public praise, special considerations in the placement of students, allocation of scarce resources, grade level and/or subject assignments, placement on decision-making bodies, and the like. Although each of these may be associated with a formal organizational property (for example, resources), it is through the informal system of rewards that they are typically distributed.

The reward structures, formal and informal, continue to be powerful organizational variables and should be a major focus of attention when planning and implementing staff development programs.

Authority. The issue of authority in organizations is a troublesome one in that it is usually readily evident to an observer where the *vested* authority is located but it is often less clear where the *informal* authority is located. Vested authority refers to the legitimate power given by an organization to an individual. The most common formal authorities in school settings are superintendents, directors of secondary education, principals, and so forth. It is possible to trace the location of formal authority through observation of behavior as well as through analyses of organization charts.

Informal authority, however, is less obvious in that its presence may or may not coincide with formal authority. That is, although the principal has nominal power of decision making, the decisions may really be made (or subverted) by another influential member of the school community. This is not to say that principals and other formal authority figures may not redistribute the authority vested in them by the organization. (The phrase "delegation of responsibility" often carries with it the delegation of authority as well.) But, in most complex organizations such as schools there is a network of authority that is influential upon practice although not represented in or publicly acknowledged by the formal institution.

An example of the exercise of informal authority is the veteran teacher in a building who has "seen principals come and seen principals go" and manages to maintain and even encourage pedagogical or curricular practices which, at least according to institutional policy, would appear to be out of favor. Another example is the curriculum worker in the central office who, partly as a consequence of visiting numbers of schools and the attendant possibility of being more aware of the larger system, creates a circle of interest around a particular issue such that perceptions and practice change without any formal agreement to the changes.

Authority as an organizational variable is influential upon staff development formally and informally. Policy decisions regarding the purposes, activities, and outcomes of staff development programs typically emerge from the formal authority structure. The degree of maintenance of the program, the persistence of participants in it, and the perceptions of its worth can usually be traced to the influence of the informal authority structure. Both should be considerations when doing staff development.

Support systems. Even the simplest of human organizations usually find the need for internal mechanisms, resources, and technologies to carry their work forward. Schools are not different. Human and material resources are necessary to advance effective teaching and learning. Among a school's resources are teachers and administrators, materials of instruction, secretarial and clerical assistance, machines, buildings, time, space and, of course, money.

When the resources are organized to accomplish particular tasks, a support system has been established. In schools it is not uncommon for innovative activities to be supported by a system specifically designed for the innovation. In the introduction of a new curriculum segment, for example, the support system may be a planned amalgam of new materials, availability of expert consultation, released time for teachers to meet together, and auxiliary study materials for participating teachers' use. The key word here is "planned." It is the purposeful distribution of resources toward some desired end that is the hallmark of a support system.

The attention given to support systems by persons engaged in staff development is essential. This attention is characterized by an acknowledgement of both availability and accessibility as well as by a receptivity to the notion of redistribution of resources.

Leadership. A great deal of attention has been given to the issue of school leadership.[14] Research and proposition regarding "effective" leadership in schools are easily found in the educational literature. The research reports and proposals for action, however, are rarely in agreement as to precise definition of leadership and, certainly, are often contradictory regarding what leadership behaviors are most appropriate for what situations. It is, perhaps, unwise to expect that leadership, as a behavioral construct, *can* be observed with accuracy, promoted with predictability, or assessed objectively across settings.

It is possible to hypothesize that leadership is situation-specific. That is, certain school settings, because of their formal and informal organizational properties, either cause or call for certain leadership characteristics. Certainly, the demands of some settings on leaders are different from the demands of others. To confound the problem of "effective leadership," there are some hypotheses that center on the assumption that specific situations change with such frequent unpredictability that a given set of leader behaviors, desirable in one mix of problems and prospects but not in another, simply will not serve over time even if the general setting remains constant.

It is important to acknowledge that leadership need not be in line with conventional conceptions regarding its public place in organizations. As was noted above in terms of authority, leadership need *not* be vested only in persons whose titles suggest that its presence is necessary. Informal leadership is observed in most settings. Many teachers, for example, assume leadership according to the perceived relationships between their interests and knowledge or skills and the needs of the school at a given time. This may be the result of some formal arrangement whereby the organization sanctions the teacher's decision and action or of a sense of the need for expediency.

To state that leadership is not a well-understood or clearly defined phenomenon in organizations is not to suggest that therefore it need not be considered in bringing about staff development programs. There is a clear need for staff developers to both exercise leadership and recognize its potential for influence upon programs.

Five organizational variables have been proposed here as necessary considerations for thinking about and carrying forward staff development programs: mission, rewards, authority, support systems, and leadership. Although their inclusion at the expense of others can be argued, it is believed that these institutional phenomena impact upon staff development work to a degree that prohibits their exclusion from any conceptual framework that attempts to clarify staff development as a school-related activity.

The three basic elements of the proposed framework are seen as interactive and influential upon one another. The people are influenced by the nature and content of their interactions with others, the context influences where and how interactions take place, and the people in the context are mutually (if unequally) influential upon one another.

Secondary Elements of a Conceptual Framework

In addition to the three elements discussed above, a set of practice-related elements is proposed for inclusion in the framework: purpose, activity, and evaluation. These elements are either directly or indirectly included in many conceptions of staff development and are present in the case studies presented in the preceding chapters by Lanier, Tikunoff and Mergendoller, Romberg and Price, and Courter and Ward.

It can be argued that the inclusion of these elements directs the framework toward a positivist stance. That is, the inclusion of purpose, for instance, by definition puts the framework in the rational, behaviorist mode. The potential for criticism is that the framework, then, is far from value-free. But, as Goodlad has stated, although a conceptualization of a set of interacting phenomena can be *relatively* unencumbered by values, it is probably not possible for it to be completely uninfluenced by them.[15] It could be argued, though, that the framework demands that some attention be given to the role of purpose in a staff development program but that the attention may result in a decision to abandon purpose (in the positivist sense) as a consequence.

The inclusion of activities and evaluation is also subject to the same criticism as that noted for purpose. Obviously, the purpose-activity-evaluation paradigm, when followed prescriptively, rests on an assumption about the value of empiricism. That assumption is not denied here; rational empiricism is believed to be a means of viewing staff development that "fits" the reality of schooling, despite recurring criticism of its impact on human organizations. The fit is observed in the relation of policy to practice, the quite reasonable expectations that school persons be accountable for their actions, the beliefs about schooling held by patrons and clients, and the typical conventions of curriculum and instruction as they are present in elementary and secondary schools. Although one could argue that there should be some alterations in these relationships, they are imbedded in public schools in the United States and to ignore them is to ignore powerful influences upon school (and staff development) practice.

PURPOSE

Schools are, in the main, purposeful institutions. That is, they promote the acquisition and demonstration of knowledge, skill, and belief by students. The corpus of what is to be transmitted by schools (and, conversely, to be learned by students) is selected from a vast array of what might be selected. As noted earlier, the schools may appear to act irrationally or quixotically but whatever the label one gives to the decision-making process, decisions *are* made about content and process of schooling.

The same is true for staff development efforts. Although one can certainly point with disdain to programs that appear to be relatively free-floating, unguided by intention or by intentions only vaguely articulated, it is rare to find a program without any built-in purpose-fulness. What is important for this discussion is that the question "Toward what end are we engaging in staff development?" be addressed by persons charged with planning and implementing profes-sional growth opportunities for school people.

As noted above, the answer to the question may not be a set of precisely articulated behavioral objectives as found in some of the more rationalistic curriculum materials, but may, in fact, be that the purposes will emerge out of the activities or that the purposes will be differentially expressed by participants. In an extreme case, the purpose question may be answered by the response, "After consider-ing purpose, we cannot at this time be clear about that but believe that what is planned is of enough value in and of itself that we are moving ahead."

Attention to purpose can be a focusing mechanism. It helps to clarify values about an activity ("Why are we doing this?"), the relative power of an activity ("Are these purposes ones that are widely influential?"), the potential impact of a program ("Are others interested in accomplishing these goals to the degree that we are?"), and guides for reflection ("Are we 'on course'?").

ACTIVITIES

Not surprisingly, the principal focus of planning and implementation activities related to staff development is upon what participants will *do* in a given program. The list of possible activities for staff development is a long one. Planners of staff development strategies can select from familiar learning opportunities (such as the workshop) or less familiar ones (such as "coaching").[16] One way to classify staff development activities is to examine them in terms of their ideological and temporal distance from the school phenomena they are meant to influence.

The staff development activities that are probably farthest removed from the problems they are intended to address, at least temporally and often theoretically and practically, are the typically broad-based and relatively comprehensive programs exemplified by advanced degree courses of study in higher education institutions. These sets of graduate degree programs may be given such titles as "elementary education, science education, special education" and the like and tend most often to be planned and executed by professors and instructors whose orientations to professional growth of educators are both comprehensive in scope and quasi-theoretical in nature. The comprehensiveness is manifested in the inclusion of offerings such as sociology and philosophy of education, testing and measurement, and second-level developmental psychology courses. Theory (or, in some instances, proposition as a substitute for accepted theory) is attended to in addition to practice. These dimensions of conventional programs more often than not substitute for clinical education, largely as a consequence of the influence of the expectations and beliefs about the appropriate nature of graduate education as evidenced by the norms of higher education institutions.

A mid-level set of staff development activities is composed of problem- or issued-focused learning opportunities planned and put in place by school system administrators and/or teachers. Workshops, institutes, and other group strategies generally have a system issue as the object of attention (for example, the teaching of reading, means to diagnose and act upon learning difficulties, informal evaluation procedures). The activities are usually acted out in groups with primary attention given to the generalized issue and, in some instances, secondary attention given to the specific manifestations of that issue in particular teaching-learning settings. Such programs are dependent for success on the participants' abilities to receive, process, and act upon the information received. Usually, little attention is given to the impact of the activities beyond the perceptions of participants regarding the value they place upon the experience of participation in them.

The third level of staff development activities is made up of those strategies that emerge from and are acted out in the actual environments upon which an effect is expected to be demonstrated. In the case of teachers, this set of growth opportunities is classroom-bound and instruction-oriented. An example would be the observation of one teacher by another with attendant requirements that the teachers discuss the observation in terms of its specific contribution to the improvement of teaching and learning. Another example would be the in-class participation of a staff developer working with a teacher on an agreed upon problem or issue. In other words, this set of activities is sharply situation-specific in terms of intention and is implemented within the boundaries of the situation.

For the purposes of this chapter, it is neither necessary nor appropriate to argue the merits and demerits of these levels of activities. It is important, however, to acknowledge the structural differences among them so that decisions about staff development programs and procedures can be more fully informed. Certain perspectives would promote activities at one level over another (for example, the belief that a teacher with a well-established philosophical orientation is more effective than a teacher who has a tested set of instructional strategies would lead to participation in a graduate degree program). Other perspectives would lead to a systematic and carefully designed mix of activities drawn from all three levels of impact. The recognition of the relation of the perspective one holds regarding professional development and the activities one plans or engages in is the important issue for this discussion.

EVALUATION

The issue of the evaluation of staff development programs is one that plagues scholars and practitioners alike. There have been few proposals for evaluating the impact of these programs beyond the level of some immediate perception of worth of the experience, as noted above. The effects of programs at several levels of inference (for example, teacher behavior to pupil behavior to pupil outcome) have received little attention because of the conceptual and methodological difficulties associated with having confidence in the findings. These difficulties are not radically different from the ones experienced by researchers concerned with the relation of teaching behavior and pupil outcomes.[17]

The proposition advanced here is that evaluation of staff development programs be attentive to three interacting phenomena: perceptions of participants, effects upon participants, and the apparent influence upon the organization.

Of the evaluation foci noted immediately above, the most commonly observed in practice is the elicitation of the perceptions of participants. This usually takes the form of a brief questionnaire distributed to those persons in attendance at a workshop, institute, or other group activity. The value of these perception data is obvious and the utility is relatively immediate. That is, the worth of the experience (as opposed to the effect of that experience upon participants' behavior) is judged and subsequent decisions regarding format, presenters, and so on can be made in light of this information.

The most difficult evaluation issue is the determination of the effects of the staff development strategy or program upon the practices of participants. This is hardest to accomplish for activities that are generalized or in some other sense removed from actual professional experience. Less difficult, but certainly not easy, is gaining a sense of whether or not a situation-specific, person-focused staff development activity has made a difference in school life. In general, the effects of staff development interventions are more easily identified when the interventions are precisely purposeful, focused on particulars of educational activity, and bounded by an observable situation.

If the proposal that staff development is a purposeful activity is accepted, the third focus for evaluation, the organization, becomes more meaningful. Every organization, as the discussion of context is meant to illustrate, is a complex combination of interacting properties. These structural properties are also influential upon and affected by staff development programs. It is unlikely that a school or system's mission, governance structure, reward systems, support mechanisms, and the like exist independently of attempts to promote professional growth of members. Evaluation of staff development programs that does not account for the interaction of the programs and the properties of the organization is incomplete at best.[18]

Data Sources

Clearly, staff development efforts are accomplished, in part, as a consequence of using appropriate data to inform decisions about those efforts. This section proposes five data sources that observation and experience have shown to be necessary and reasonable ones. Each will be discussed briefly.

FUNDED KNOWLEDGE

In the best of all possible scientific worlds, decisions would be made on the basis of funded knowledge. Facts would inform. Reality would be the reflector of practice. And "truth" would guide.

This potential for certitude, however, is so far a distant illusion. We are not sanguine about the predictive validity of our efforts nor are we positive about the relation of our efforts to observed outcomes. In short, the available store of funded knowledge regarding teaching, learning, and other social science phenomena is extremely limited.

There *is* a growing body of information that can be counted on to be accurate, given certain situational configurations, but it is extremely limited. This, of course, is one of the principal differences between the eclectic amalgam of orientations that has been adopted by educators and the more mature sciences. Decision making for purposes of staff development is, more often than not, hampered by the incompleteness of this data source. And the staff developer who limits his or her decisions regarding program because of this incompleteness is, in large measure, forced to engage in efforts that are narrow and shallow.

Although the available funded knowledge can be brought to bear on problems of staff development, other data sources have proven to be effective options.

CRAFT KNOWLEDGE

In the absence of funded knowledge, it is proposed that an appropriate data source is craft knowledge. Craft knowledge is the body of information that practitioners can agree to as central to or influential upon the work in which they engage. Consequently, craft knowledge might be characterized as being a set of agreements about practice, consensus regarding effects of that practice, and beliefs associated with the reaching of consensus.

Examples of craft knowledge include the recognition that certain materials of instruction are appropriately matched with certain pupil groups (in the absence of research findings to support that match), the acceptance of the principle that learning takes place best when the instruction moves from concrete to abstract (generally true but disproven in specific cases), and the conclusion that certain teaching behaviors are consistently linked to certain pupil outcomes (although the nature of that linkage is largely unknown). The recent findings of correlational studies of teaching can be considered as craft-derived knowledge. In short, although there is both objective and testimonial evidence to support the positions embedded in craft knowledge, the evidence is yet insufficient to move the positions into the arena of funded knowledge.

A staff development program that ignores the potential role of craft knowledge in planning, implementation, and evaluation stages is incomplete. (It should be noted that *most* staff development programs are almost completely dependent upon craft knowledge.) The purpose of including this data source here is to offer it some legitimacy. Naturally, that legitimacy will accrue to craft knowledge in scientific circles only if it has been subjected to rigorous scrutiny and systematic inquiry. This has been true of the studies of teaching noted above and is true of many of the ongoing studies of schools as organizations.

PERCEPTIONS

An important data source for informing development of professional growth opportunities is composed of the perceptions of planners, participants, and clients and patrons. As is true for craft knowledge, perception data are subject to lack of completeness, nonuniversality, and idiosyncracy. In contrast to craft knowledge, however, perception data are persistently interactive with staff development programs in that they influence not only receptivity to program elements but, in large measure, shape subsequent activities of participants.

It is a truism that one's perceptions may not be verifiable but, despite that conclusion, they are present and active. If one believes something to be so, that belief will have an impact upon related phenomena. For staff developers, it may be inconsequential in the grand scheme of things that a number of teachers believe that the findings of research on teaching are inaccurate or otherwise flawed but, in terms of program operation, it is important to acknowledge the perceptions and act upon them toward some desired end. It may be important, for instance, to delay certain staff development activities until the perceptions of the participants regarding those activities have been changed toward a more positive stance than was originally observed.

The usefulness of perceptions as a data source far outweighs their limitations. Staff development here, it will be recalled, is seen as a purposeful activity involving people in interaction within an educational context. It is not a set of events pure in scope and pristine in nature. The systematic collection, formal or informal, of data regarding perceptions of the program from planning through implementation and evaluation will allow the staff developer to move with caution when necessary, boldness when appropriate, and will inform the decision-making process more comprehensively than is usually the case.

HISTORY OF THE ORGANIZATION

Every organization has a history. That history may be success-laden or marked by numbers of failed attempts at improvement. Schools, in like fashion, have histories and those histories are usually influential upon current practice and plans for change.

The history of a school setting is a legitimate and valuable data source for decisions regarding staff development. Most of us have encountered one or both of the following comments: "We've already tried that and it didn't work." "We've never done this." Those comments are usually early warnings that the effort being discussed is in some danger. Unfortunately, because organizational history is most often neglected by decision makers, the warning signals are not heeded and the change effort falters.

This is not to suggest that a planned or in-progress effort should be abandoned in light of the past. What should occur is a careful examination of the historical data to draw inferences about why perceptions are as they are, why earlier work was successful or not, and what groundwork needs to be undertaken in order to pave the way for current or future success. For example, when plans for a staff development program aimed at increasing the sensitivity of teachers and administrators to the characteristics of special learners ignore the set of events through which a similar program was abandoned five years ago, successful implementation is likely to be difficult. More positively, when a set of program format characteristics (for example, school-based problem solving, teacher-teacher interactions) has been consistently related to participant satisfaction and program success, it would be foolhardy to ignore, even unintentionally, the characteristics when planning new ventures for the same setting.

Using the history of an organization as a data source is seen, at the simplest level, as a means to avoid making the same mistakes over and over again, on the one hand, and as a strategy to borrow and adapt successful mechanisms on the other. More dramatically, knowledge of organizational history may influence the staff developer to postpone or abandon plans for professional growth programs and attack organizational problems directly and in advance of attempts to act upon individuals.

POLICIES AND PRACTICES OF THE ORGANIZATION

Closely related to the argument above is the proposal that staff development activities be conceived of within an understanding of the prevailing policies and practices of an ongoing institution. Certain well-intentioned and, at least propositionally, sound staff development efforts are in line with these policies and practices and certain others are not. In the event of a conflict, it is reasonable to predict that the staff development proposal will meet opposition during implementation.

Consider, for example, the introduction of new curricula during the innovation-laden decade of the 1960s. In far too many instances, new programs were introduced as a consequence of a school officer's individual decision—innovation by fiat, as it were. Without considerations of where the new program might mesh with ongoing ones, what resources would have to be redirected to the innovative effort, what policies regarding teaching and learning would be impacted, and so on, the change attempt is in some jeopardy from the start.

Clearly, this framework promotes the importance of the role played by the organization in which staff development is to take place.

Considerable attention is given to this issue through the inclusion of context as a primary consideration and by the attention given to organizational history, policy, and practice as data sources for decisions. As with the other sections of the framework, however, it is important to recognize the interaction of the organizational variables with the other elements selected for attention, in this case data sources. There are no hard and fast rules about examining this interaction except to signal the apparent (and observed) utility of basing staff development decisions upon data from funded knowledge, craft knowledge, perceptions of participants, and the history, policies, and practices of the organization.

Summary

This chapter has suggested primary and secondary elements of a tentative conceptual framework for planning, implementing, and inquiring about staff development programs. Data sources that are logically consistent with the elements have also been proposed. The interactive nature of the elements and the data sources has been pointed out.

What has been proposed is one way to think about and enact staff development. The elements to be considered in this particular view emerge in large measure from the material prepared for and presented in this yearbook. Certainly, there are other ways, based upon different assumptions and different conceptions of practice, which could be used to understand a very complex and often misunderstood schooling phenomenon. Other views, because of different propositions regarding what is most central to the staff development enterprise, would result in observations and practices different from the ones that would come about as a consequence of using this orientation. This is seen as desirable. Accumulated information from conceptually different but not unrelated vantage points will result in stronger possibilities for the positive re-creation of school places. This proposal may be helpful toward that end.

FOOTNOTES

1. John I. Goodlad and Maurice N. Richter, Jr., *The Development of a Conceptual System for Dealing with Problems of Curriculum and Instruction* (Los Angeles: University of California, Los Angeles, and Institute for Development of Educational Activities, 1966).

2. John I. Goodlad and Associates, *Curriculum Inquiry* (New York: McGraw-Hill Book Co., 1979).

3. Elizabeth Dillon-Peterson, ed., *Staff Development/Organization Development* (Alexandria, Va.: Association for Supervision and Curriculum Development, 1981).

4. Gary A. Griffin, "Staff Development" (Paper presented at the Implications of Research on Teaching for Practice Conference, Airlie House, Virginia, February 25-27, 1982).

5. Seymour B. Sarason, *The Culture of the School and the Problem of Change* (New York: Allyn and Bacon, 1971); idem, *The Creation of Settings and the Future Society* (New York: Allyn and Bacon, 1974).

6. Neal Gross, Joseph B. Giacquinta, and Marilyn Bernstein, *Implementing Organizational Innovations: A Sociological Analysis of Planned Educational Change* (New York: Basic Books, 1971).

7. Ben Brodinsky, "The New Right: The Movement and Its Impact," *Phi Delta Kappan* 64 (October 1982): 87-94.

8. Gene E. Hall, "The Concerns-Based Approach to Facilitating Change," *Educational Horizons* 57 (Summer 1979): 202-8.

9. Ann Lieberman and Lynne Miller, eds., *Staff Development: New Demands, New Realities, New Perspectives* (New York: Teachers College Press, 1978).

10. M. Maxine Bentzen, *Changing Schools: The Magic Feather Principle* (New York: McGraw-Hill Book Co., 1974).

11. Judith Warren Little, *School Success and Staff Development: The Role of Staff Development in Urban Desegrated Schools, Final Report* (Boulder, Colo.: Center for Action Research, 1981).

12. Gary A. Griffin, Ann Lieberman, Joann Jacullo-Noto, *Interactive Research and Development on Schooling: Final Report* (New York: Teachers College, Columbia University, 1982).

13. Gary A. Griffin, Susan Barnes, Robert Hughes, Jr., Maria Defino, Sharon O'Neal, Hobart Hukill, and Sara Edwards, *Preservice Clinical Teacher Education: Final Report of a Descriptive Study* (Austin, Tex.: The Research and Development Center for Teacher Education, The University of Texas at Austin, 1982).

14. William Rutherford, Shirley Hord, and Leslie Huling, *A Review and Critique of the Literature: In Search of Understanding the Facilitation of Change* (Austin, Tex.: The Research and Development Center for Teacher Education, The University of Texas at Austin, 1982).

15. Goodlad and Richter, *The Development of a Conceptual System for Dealing with the Problems of Curriculum and Instruction*.

16. Bruce R. Joyce and Beverly Showers, "Transfer of Training: The Contribution of 'Coaching,' " *Journal of Education* 163 (Spring 1981): 163-72.

17. Thomas L. Good, *Research on Teaching: What We Know and What We Need to Know* (Austin, Tex.: The Research and Development Center for Teacher Education, The University of Texas at Austin, 1981).

18. Gary A. Griffin, "Guidelines for the Evaluation of Staff Development Programs," in *Staff Development*, ed. Lieberman and Miller, pp. 126-39.

CHAPTER XI

A View from the Schools

STUART C. RANKIN

The separation of theoreticians and practitioners is becoming narrower, thankfully. Each one is now having a greater impact on the other than in earlier years. Some theoreticians are first-rate practitioners, and I know some school people who are welcome, effective, and comfortable as researchers.

Even so, we in the schools are often asked to react to research, scholarship, and theory about education. Such is my assignment for this yearbook—to consider the utility of the ideas in the preceding chapters for school improvement involving staff development. What does all this mean for people in schools?

First, a review is given to the ideas presented by others on staff development; these reactions deal largely with the participants, the content, and the processes. Second, some concerns about staff development are identified that are important for school people, and a guide for school improvement is presented that fits with the ideas on staff development in earlier chapters and with the concerns of practitioners.

Reactions

For this analysis the ideas given in earlier chapters are grouped into four categories. Who should be involved in staff development and where should it occur? What should the content be? What processes should be used? What is the state of the art of staff development, how important is it, and what needs to happen next? Such categorization risks serious reduction of others' ideas, but depicts fairly well the process repeatedly used by practitioners to make sense out of theory.

The point is that school people have the problems now; they cannot wait for certainty; they must go forward with the best hunch, using available information.

WHO AND WHERE

In this yearbook, the teacher is seen as the primary target of staff development. Although research can do little as yet to connect staff development efforts causally with pupil attainment of learning objectives, teaching behavior is seen both as modifiable through staff development and as a key variant in student achievement.

Less attention is given to principals, assistant principals, department heads, counselors, and paraprofessionals as participants in staff development except indirectly by Goodlad, who emphasizes that the improvement unit (and thus the staff development unit) must be the total faculty of a school. However, district-level support staff, principals, and higher education faculty are seen not only as central to any successful staff development effort as trainers, but also as persons who can and do learn from teachers what works, what does not work, and what problems need attention. A similar role is given to persons from teacher centers, research and development centers, and regional educational laboratories. But state departments of education and county intermediate offices of education are given little attention, although school districts in many states work closely with them in staff development and are seriously influenced by statewide objectives, tests, guidelines, and directives.

Several models describe collaboration between higher education staff and school staff. The Lanier four-party connection shows all parties as learners, tension as a catalyst, and a nonthreatening, joint focus as beneficial. The Sprinthalls, Schlechty and Whitford, and others point to the importance of strengthening collaboration between theorists and practitioners. The collaboration for program design and evaluation was effective for the San Diego project. The interactive research and development units described by Tikunoff and Mergendoller worked well in different settings. For persons working in a school system, such collaborations are impressive, but experience has taught us two important cautions. The first lesson is that all parties to a collaborative effort must know exactly what each party expects to give and expects to get from the other collaborators. The idea that each party is a learner is necessary but not sufficient to answer those questions. The second lesson that school people in large systems have learned is that to be helpful, solutions should be generalizable to many schools. The existence of a few small collaborative groups may help a higher education organization to achieve its purposes, but may not be a major, direct force in improving the school or schools participating.

In my view, the most correct statement about who the participants in staff development should be is made by Goodlad. He identifies the total staff of the single school as the participant group. Observations of effective schools reinforce the notion that the single school staff is the best unit of change—not the district, not the principal, not the teacher, not the child, but the total school. Most staff development efforts are aimed at individuals even if they are put into groups for training. If ownership matters, if school culture matters, if a school has an identifiable learning climate or an ethos, if the school can be a satisfying place for persons who work there, then efforts to improve the school are perhaps best focused on the whole school, its problems and its strengths. The best schools in Detroit are generally those where the faculty as a unit frequently works together on problems, on needs, and on self-development.

There seems to be increasing understanding or at least belief among researchers on school effectiveness that the most effective staff development efforts occur at the school site. Continuing education programs may occur at other locations, but such choices are usually based on the convenience of the developer rather than the participant.

CONTENT

Howey and Vaughan, as well as other writers of earlier chapters, appear to agree that trends in staff development efforts point away from remedying deficiencies in teacher skills and toward developmental experiences. The concept of the collaboration unit of researchers and practitioners and the Goodlad whole-school participant group also favor a developmental rather than a deficiency approach. As Schlechty and Whitford point out, however, there always will be efforts by districts to maintain procedures or to establish new programs where the content is prescribed almost in the sense of fixing a deficiency in the knowledge or performance of teachers. When the content is drawn from the new research on effective schools or effective classrooms, it can probably be argued to be of a developmental or a deficiency nature, depending on the process.

The most powerful, long-range impact of staff development will come from content designed to improve the cognitive development and inquiry skills of the participants, according to the Sprinthalls, Tikunoff and Mergendoller, and Schlechty and Whitford. Lanier and Goodlad also appear to support such content when it grows out of joint planning for instructional improvement. If school people can raise their thinking, learning, and inquiring skills, they will be better able to analyze the teaching and learning processes and to consider alternative methods and materials. They may also improve their communication and interpersonal skills. One new innovation is nice but innovative, reflective, and evaluative skills can produce self-renewal and a continuing flow of innovations.

Several specific kinds of content are highlighted in earlier chapters. The Romberg and Price example focuses on new systemwide learning objectives for all subjects and grade levels in a school district. Howey and Vaughan recommended the effective schools research as content for staff development. Courter and Ward's San Diego program drew heavily from the effective schools research but also from effective teaching research, such as that done on direct instruction, time-on-task, and classroom management.

If the school staff selects its own content, it should and often will focus first on school climate, according to Goodlad. Later, the staff will be able to concentrate on promising practices, ideas from recent research, and even its own inquiry capability and teaching skills for staff development content.

Large school systems have a wide variety of content in staff development efforts ranging from carefully prescribed systemwide procedures to near autonomy at the school level. In my view, substantial improvements in staff performance will accrue when the content for staff development is defined by a single school staff with itself as the unit for change. In order to support such emphases, the school district must be ready to provide training support in cognitive development, inquiry skills, and research on effective schools and classrooms so that schools can receive such training when they are ready. In addition, school districts will need to communicate their capability to provide assistance so that a school staff will be aware of the options and the assistance.

PROCESS

Most staff development efforts can be grouped roughly into one of two processes. Either the objectives of the staff development are determined in advance or the development is part of a combined school improvement-planning-training effort and the staff development evolves as a natural part of the inquiry, design, and implementation planning.

Earlier chapters identify a number of desirable conditions or procedures that ought to attend most objective-based staff development efforts. The Sprinthall paper describes conditions needed for educators to advance from one cognitive developmental stage to the next. Included among the conditions are conflict, readiness, support, practice, concentration, continuity, reflection, and feedback—a list well known to students of the learning process. Lanier's emphasis on tensions and Romberg and Price's recommendation that traditions to be challenged should be identified publicly, both reinforce the importance of conflict in change and self-renewal. The crucial ingredients of system support and commitment from the top are highlighted in the Berea and San Diego illustrations and are quickly recognized as important by school district staff, as are involvement of everyone, extensive support materials, a dissemination plan, and close monitoring of implementation and progress as emphasized by Romberg and Price, and by Courter and Ward.

When the staff development is not objective-based, but a part of a school improvement planning effort, the process focuses more on communication and the problem-solving model. Problem identification and analysis, evaluation of alternative solutions, planning steps, consensus models, and evaluation become the process considerations. Howey and Vaughan report teachers talking about teaching, observing teaching, designing instruction together, and teaching each other. Goodlad recommends autonomy in planning at each school; rewards for group problem solving, not individual training; preservice emphasis on group planning; and whole-staff participation. He recommends a process that focuses first on improving the quality of the workplace with emphasis on local problems, with the understanding that attention can shift later to excellence in education and improved teaching methods.

Most school people have plenty of experience with objective-based staff development. Their major plea is that such efforts recognize all of the other things that are going on in the school and be properly coordinated. "Here comes another program from central office and we haven't even installed the last one yet. Oh well, this too shall pass."

It may have been Coombs who first said, "We need to stop giving teachers the answers to questions they don't have." Or was it students? School people are tired of new programs; they have seen too many failures and false starts. They sometimes resist participation in training even though it is superior, because they have been let down before. Most of them are hardworking, dedicated, unthanked, and increasingly maligned professionals. My hunch is that, if the goal is better teaching and learning, school improvement efforts that feature participant-designed or participant-requested staff development programs are more promising than continued dependence on top-down, systemwide, objective-based in-service education.

OTHER CONSIDERATIONS

The general state of the art in staff development receives some attention in earlier chapters. Howey and Vaughan point to its importance at a time of declining resources and increasing demands for quality and equity. Schlechty and Whitford state without qualification that continuing education has produced very little change in schools. The Sprinthalls and others recognize the great need for more research and theory on staff development; we know too little about it and have too few competent staff developers. My hunch is that it is like many other things in education. We know a lot more than we use, and there is a lot more to know.

Problems in using what we know are apparent to writers in this yearbook and to practitioners. Traditionally we are without methods of rewarding educators for improved performance. Group problem solving is often more difficult in large schools than in smaller ones because of the more extensive communication required. Small collaborative inquiry units are not widely implementable. The extensive resources used in San Diego and Berea are not available in districts like Detroit where nearly every class has thirty-five students, program offerings are seriously curtailed, high school students can have only five classes, the deficit is enormous, and precious few funds can be used for staff development or to provide access to teacher time for in-service education. This last—finding time for school staff to meet and learn—is the toughest problem of all.

Implications

School systems in many places throughout the country are hiring no new teachers and are promoting few persons to leadership positions. Both regular education funds and special project funds are shrinking, and enrollment is down, providing less state support. At the same time pressures for higher test scores and other indicators of improved quality are increasing from parents, legislators, and the general community. Under such conditions the quality and the cost of staff development programs receive increased attention.

During the last two decades, school systems generally, and urban districts in particular, have had the benefit and the burden of a large number of new programs. At times it has seemed that everyone inside or outside the field of education is an expert in education, or thinks himself or herself so, or at least has one great idea. School staff members are weary of the proliferation of programs and leery of any new innovation or training effort. They have tried new materials, new methods of presentation, new grouping procedures, new promotion guidelines, and new assessment devices. They have received training of every kind imaginable. They will keep trying, but they need some victories or at least greater control of their professional lives.

In response to this situation, the public school system in Detroit has instituted two school improvement programs, each of which is generally consistent with a number of the ideas presented in this yearbook.

The first program is operated jointly by the Institute for Research on Teaching at Michigan State University and the Detroit Public Schools. Participants are the faculties of three elementary schools, two middle schools, and one high school. Each faculty is its own improvement team and has a planning team that is a subset of itself. The project is supported by a small research dissemination grant from the National Institute of Education. These grant funds are used mainly to buy staff meeting time, to publish summaries of research findings used by the schools, and to document the program.

The second school improvement program is funded by the Ford

Foundation, takes place at eight senior high schools, and is patterned after the six-school project. Both programs provide some research, evaluation, training, and general curriculum support service to meet with the school planning teams.

A planning guide has been developed for the two school improvement projects based on a research-based, planned-change model. The mission is to improve all schools, working with the individual school as the unit for improvement. Underlying assumptions emphasize that educators and schools are both capable of self-renewal, that improvement from within is more lasting than exogenous change, and that useful, proven knowledge about better practice is available. Effective schools are defined as places where all students master fundamental skills.

The Detroit guide describes the major steps in the recommended improvement process beginning with definitions of principal readiness and staff readiness that require knowledge of the process and the consequences of agreement to participate. Project schools each have a planning team representative of the total staff. The planning team must be willing to give some extra effort and to check frequently with the total staff at decision points to ensure understanding and support. The planning team uses an approach that begins with problem identification and problem analysis, including a study of indicators of success and any shortcomings in these desired outcomes. When the selection of one or more problem areas is made, it must include agreement by the total faculty.

Research findings and a search for promising practices are focused on the problem areas. Many school staffs will want to select a "quick fix" to improve school climate as an initial strategy. Such decisions should not only be tolerated but supported, even though we know that improved learning is not likely to occur except as a result of changes in teaching practices. The staff can begin with climate and move later to a look at classroom activities and teaching skills. Whatever the change, staff ownership is the key.

A school improvement plan is developed specifying objectives, strategies, resources, staff training, orientation of students and community, calendar, budget, and evaluation.

With experience, the problem-solving process will become more effective and staff will become increasingly aware that what they do makes a difference in school outcomes, that they can change and improve as professionals, and that the quality of the school is largely a function of their actions.

The two Detroit projects are already producing better school climates and better staff attitudes. It is too early to expect major improvements in achievement as yet, but initial signs provide us with cautious optimism.

Name Index

Subject Index

INFORMATION ABOUT MEMBERSHIP IN THE SOCIETY

From its small beginnings in the early 1900s, the National Society for the Study of Education has grown to a major educational organization with more than 3,000 members in the United States, Canada, and overseas. Members include professors, researchers, graduate students, and administrators in colleges and universities; teachers, supervisors, curriculum specialists, and administrators in elementary and secondary schools; and a considerable number of persons who are not formally connected with an educational institution. Membership in the Society is open to all persons who desire to receive its publications.

Since its establishment the Society has sought to promote its central purpose—the stimulation of investigations and discussions of important educational issues—through regular publication of a two-volume yearbook that is sent to all members. Many of these volumes have been so well received throughout the profession that they have gone into several printings. A recently inaugurated series of substantial paperbacks on Contemporary Educational Issues supplements the series of yearbooks and allows for treatment of a wider range of educational topics than can be addressed each year through the yearbooks alone.

Through membership in the Society one can add regularly to one's professional library at a very reasonable cost. Members also help to sustain a publication program that is widely recognized for its unique contributions to the literature of education.

The categories of membership, and the current dues in each category, are as follows:

Regular. The member receives a clothbound copy of each part of the two-volume yearbook (approximately 300 pages per volume). Annual dues, $20.

Comprehensive. The member receives clothbound copies of the two-volume yearbook and the two volumes in the current paperback series. Annual dues, $35.

Retirees and Graduate Students. Reduced dues—Regular, $16; Comprehensive, $31.
The above reduced dues are available to (a) those who have retired or are over sixty-five years of age and who have been members of the Society for at least ten years, and (b) graduate students in their first year of membership.

Life Membership. Persons sixty years of age or over may hold a Regular Membership for life upon payment of a lump sum based upon the life expectancy for their age group. Consult the Secretary-Treasurer for further details.

New members are required to pay an entrance fee of $1, in addition to the dues, in their first year of membership.

Membership is for the calendar year and dues are payable on or before January 1. A reinstatement fee of $.50 must be added to dues payments made after January 1.

In addition to receiving the publications of the Society as described above, members participate in the nomination and election of the six-member Board of Directors, which is responsible for managing the business and affairs of the Society, including the authorization of volumes to appear in the yearbook series. Two members of the Board are elected each year for three-year terms. Members of the Society who have contributed to its publications and who indicate a willingness to serve are eligible for election to the Board.

Members are urged to attend the one or more meetings of the Society that are arranged each year in conjunction with the annual meetings of major educational organizations. The purpose of such meetings is to present, discuss, and critique volumes in the current yearbook series. Announcements of meetings for the ensuing year are sent to members in December.

Upon written request from a member, the Secretary-Treasurer will send the current directory of members, synopses of meetings of the Board of Directors, and the annual financial report.

Persons desiring further information about membership may write to

KENNETH J. REHAGE, Secretary-Treasurer
National Society for the Study of Education

5835 Kimbark Ave.
Chicago, Ill. 60637

PUBLICATIONS OF THE NATIONAL SOCIETY FOR THE STUDY OF EDUCATION

1. The Yearbooks

NOTICE: Many of the early yearbooks of this series are now out of print. In the following list, those titles to which an asterisk is prefixed are not available for purchase.

*First Yearbook, 1902, Part I—*Some Principles in the Teaching of History.* Lucy M. Salmon.
*First Yearbook, 1902, Part II—*The Progress of Geography in the Schools.* W. M. Davis and H. M. Wilson.
*Second Yearbook, 1903, Part I—*The Course of Study in History in the Common School.* Isabel Lawrence, C. A. McMurray, Frank McMurry, E. C. Page, and E. J. Rice.
*Second Yearbook, 1903, Part II—*The Relation of Theory to Practice in Education.* M. J. Holmes, J. A. Keith, and Levi Seeley.
*Third Yearbook, 1904, Part I—*The Relation of Theory to Practice in the Education of Teachers.* John Dewey, Sarah C. Brooks, F. M. McMurry, et al.
*Third Yearbook, 1904, Part II—*Nature Study.* W. S. Jackman.
*Fourth Yearbook, 1905, Part I—*The Education and Training of Secondary Teachers.* E. C. Elliott, E. G. Dexter, M. J. Holmes, et al.
*Fourth Yearbook, 1905, Part II—*The Place of Vocational Subjects in the High-School Curriculum.* J. S. Brown, G. B. Morrison, and Ellen Richards.
*Fifth Yearbook, 1906, Part I—*On the Teaching of English in Elementary and High Schools.* G. P. Brown and Emerson Davis.
*Fifth Yearbook, 1906, Part II—*The Certification of Teachers.* E. P. Cubberley.
*Sixth Yearbook, 1907, Part I—*Vocational Studies for College Entrance.* C. A. Herrick, H. W. Holmes, T. deLaguna, V. Prettyman, and W. J. S. Bryan.
*Sixth Yearbook, 1907, Part II—*The Kindergarten and Its Relation to Elementary Education.* Ada Van Stone Harris, E. A. Kirkpatrick, Marie Kraus-Boelté, Patty S. Hill, Harriette M. Mills, and Nina Vandewalker.
*Seventh Yearbook, 1908, Part I—*The Relation of Superintendents and Principals to the Training and Professional Improvement of Their Teachers.* Charles D. Lowry.
*Seventh Yearbook, 1908, Part II—*The Co-ordination of the Kindergarten and the Elementary School.* B. J. Gregory, Jennie B. Merrill, Bertha Payne, and Margaret Giddings.
*Eighth Yearbook, 1909, Part I—*Education with Reference to Sex: Pathological, Economic, and Social Aspects.* C. R. Henderson.
*Eighth Yearbook, 1909, Part II—*Education with Reference to Sex: Agencies and Methods.* C. R. Henderson and Helen C. Putnam.
*Ninth Yearbook, 1910, Part I—*Health and Education.* T. D. Wood.
*Ninth Yearbook, 1910, Part II—*The Nurses in Education.* T. D. Wood, et al.
*Tenth Yearbook, 1911, Part I—*The City School as a Community Center.* H. C. Leipziger, Sarah E. Hyre, R. D. Warden, C. Ward Crampton, E. W. Stitt, E. J. Ward, Mrs. T. C. Grice, and C. A. Perry.
*Tenth Yearbook, 1911, Part II—*The Rural School as a Community Center.* B. H. Crocheron, Jessie Field, F. W. Howe, E. C. Bishop, A. B. Graham, O. J. Kern, M. T. Scudder, and B. M. Davis.
*Eleventh Yearbook, 1912, Part I—*Industrial Education: Typical Experiments Described and Interpreted.* J. F. Barker, M. Bloomfield, B. W. Johnson, P. Johnson, L. M. Leavitt, G. A. Mirick, M. W. Murray, C. F. Perry, A. L. Stafford, and H. B. Wilson.
*Eleventh Yearbook, 1912, Part II—*Agricultural Education in Secondary Schools.* A. C. Monahan, R. W. Stimson, D. J. Crosby, W. H. French, H. F. Button, F. R. Crane, W. R. Hart, and G. F. Warren.
*Twelfth Yearbook, 1913, Part I—*The Supervision of City Schools.* Franklin Bobbitt, J. W. Hall, and J. D. Wolcott.
*Twelfth Yearbook, 1913, Part II—*The Supervision of Rural Schools.* A. C. Monahan, L. J. Hanifan, J. E. Warren, Wallace Lund, U. J. Hoffman, A. S. Cook, E. M. Rapp, Jackson Davis, J. D. Wolcott.
*Thirteenth Yearbook, 1914, Part I—*Some Aspects of High-School Instruction and Administration.* H. C. Morrison, E. R. Breslich, W. A. Jessup, and L. D. Coffman.
*Thirteenth Yearbook, 1914, Part II—*Plans for Organizing School Surveys, with a Summary of Typical School Surveys.* Charles H. Judd and Henry L. Smith.
*Fourteenth Yearbook, 1915, Part I—*Minimum Essentials in Elementary School Subjects—Standards and Current Practices.* H. B. Wilson, H. W. Holmes, F. E. Thompson, R. G. Jones, S. A. Courtis, W. S. Gray, F. N. Freeman, H. C. Pryor, J. F. Hosic, W. A. Jessup, and W. C. Bagley.
*Fourteenth Yearbook, 1915, Part II—*Methods for Measuring Teachers' Efficiency.* Arthur C. Boyce.
*Fifteenth Yearbook, 1916, Part I—*Standards and Tests for the Measurement of the Efficiency of Schools and School Systems.* G. D. Strayer, Bird T. Baldwin, B. R. Buckingham, F. W. Ballou, D. C. Bliss, H. G. Childs, S. A. Courtis, E. P. Cubberley, C. H. Judd, George Melcher, E. E. Oberholtzer, J. B. Sears, Daniel Starch, M. R. Trabue, and G. M. Whipple.

270

*Fifteenth Yearbook, 1916, Part II—*The Relationship between Persistence in School and Home Conditions.* Charles E. Holley.
*Fifteenth Yearbook, 1916, Part III—*The Junior High School.* Aubrey A. Douglass.
*Sixteenth Yearbook, 1917, Part I—*Second Report of the Committee on Minimum Essentials in Elementary-School Subjects.* W. C. Bagley, W. W. Charters, F. N. Freeman, W. S. Gray, Ernest Horn, J. H. Hoskinson, W. S. Monroe, C. F. Munson, H. C. Pryor, L. W. Rapeer, G. M. Wilson, and H. B. Wilson.
*Sixteenth Yearbook, 1917, Part II—*The Efficiency of College Students as Conditioned by Age at Entrance and Size of High School.* B. F. Pittenger.
*Seventeenth Yearbook, 1918, Part I—*Third Report of the Committee on Economy of Time in Education.* W. C. Bagley, B. B. Bassett, M. E. Branom, Alice Camerer, J. E. Dealey, C. A. Ellwood, E. B. Greene, A. B. Hart, J. F. Hosic, E. T. Housh, W. H. Mace, L. R. Marston, H. C. McKown, H. E. Mitchell, W. V. Reavis, D. Snedden, and H. B. Wilson.
*Seventeenth Yearbook, 1918, Part II—*The Measurement of Educational Products.* E. J. Ashbaugh, W. A. Averill, L. P. Ayers, F. W. Ballou, Edna Bryner, B. R. Buckingham, S. A. Courtis, M. E. Haggerty, C. H. Judd, George Melcher, W. S. Monroe, E. A. Nifenecker, and E. L. Thorndike.
*Eighteenth Yearbook, 1919, Part I—*The Professional Preparation of High-School Teachers.* G. N. Cade, S. S. Colvin, Charles Fordyce, H. H. Foster, T. S. Gosling, W. S. Gray, L. V. Koos, A. R. Mead, H. L. Miller, F. C. Whitcomb, and Clifford Woody.
*Eighteenth Yearbook, 1919, Part II—*Fourth Report of Committee on Economy of Time in Education.* F. C. Ayer, F. N. Freeman, W. S. Gray, Ernest Horn, W. S. Monroe, and C. E. Seashore.
*Nineteenth Yearbook, 1920, Part I—*New Materials of Instruction.* Prepared by the Society's Committee on Materials of Instruction.
*Nineteenth Yearbook, 1920, Part II—*Classroom Problems in the Education of Gifted Children.* T. S. Henry.
*Twentieth Yearbook, 1921, Part I—*New Materials of Instruction.* Second Report by Society's Committee.
*Twentieth Yearbook, 1921, Part II—*Report of the Society's Committee on Silent Reading.* M. A. Burgess, S. A. Courtis, C. E. Germane, W. S. Gray, H. A. Greene, Regina R. Heller, J. H. Hoover, J. A. O'Brien, J. L. Packer, Daniel Starch, W. W. Theisen, G. A. Yoakam, and representatives of other school systems.
*Twenty-first Yearbook, 1922, Parts I and II—*Intelligence Tests and Their Use,* Part I—*The Nature, History, and General Principles of Intelligence Testing.* E. L. Thorndike, S. S. Colvin, Harold Rugg, G. M. Whipple, Part II—*The Administrative Use of Intelligence Tests.* H. W. Holmes, W. K. Layton, Helen Davis, Agnes L. Rogers, Rudolf Pintner, M. R. Trabue, W. S. Miller, Bessie L. Gambrill, and others. The two parts are bound together.
*Twenty-second Yearbook, 1923, Part I—*English Composition: Its Aims, Methods and Measurements.* Earl Hudelson.
*Twenty-second Yearbook, 1923, Part II—*The Social Studies in the Elementary and Secondary School.* A. S. Barr, J. J. Coss, Henry Harap, R. W. Hatch, H. C. Hill, Ernest Horn, C. H. Judd, L. C. Marshall, F. M. McMurry, Earle Rugg, H. O. Rugg, Emma Schweppe, Mabel Snedaker, and C. W. Washburne.
*Twenty-third Yearbook, 1924, Part I—*The Education of Gifted Children.* Report of the Society's Committee. Guy M. Whipple, Chairman.
*Twenty-third Yearbook, 1924, Part II—*Vocational Guidance and Vocational Education for Industries.* A. H. Edgerton and others.
*Twenty-fourth Yearbook, 1925, Part I—*Report of the National Committee on Reading.* W. S. Gray, Chairman, F. W. Ballou, Rose L. Hardy, Ernest Horn, Francis Jenkins, S. A. Leonard, Estaline Wilson, and Laura Zirbes.
*Twenty-fourth Yearbook, 1925, Part II—*Adapting the Schools to Individual Differences.* Report of the Society's Committee. Carleton W. Washburne, Chairman.
*Twenty-fifth Yearbook, 1926, Part I—*The Present Status of Safety Education.* Report of the Society's Committee. Guy M. Whipple, Chairman.
*Twenty-fifth Yearbook, 1926, Part II—*Extra-Curricular Activities.* Report of the Society's Committee. Leonard V. Koos, Chairman.
*Twenty-sixth Yearbook, 1927, Part I—*Curriculum-making: Past and Present.* Report of the Society's Committee. Harold O. Rugg, Chairman.
*Twenty-sixth Yearbook, 1927, Part II—*The Foundations of Curriculum-making.* Prepared by individual members of the Society's Committee. Harold O. Rugg, Chairman.
*Twenty-seventh Yearbook, 1928, Part I—*Nature and Nurture: Their Influence upon Intelligence.* Prepared by the Society's Committee. Lewis M. Terman. Chairman.
*Twenty-seventh Yearbook, 1928, Part II—*Nature and Nurture: Their Influence upon Achievement.* Prepared by the Society's Committee. Lewis M. Terman, Chairman.
*Twenty-eighth Yearbook, 1929, Parts I and II—*Preschool and Parental Education.* Part I—*Organization and Development.* Part II—*Research and Method.* Prepared by the Society's Committee. Lois H. Meek, Chairman. Bound in one volume. Cloth.
*Twenty-ninth Yearbook, 1930, Parts I and II—*Report of the Society's Committee on Arithmetic.* Part I—*Some Aspects of Modern Thought on Arithmetic.* Part II—*Research in Arithmetic.* Prepared by the Society's Committee. F. B. Knight, Chairman. Bound in one volume.
*Thirtieth Yearbook, 1931, Part I—*The Status of Rural Education.* First Report of the Society's Committee on Rural Education. Orville G. Brim, Chairman.
Thirtieth Yearbook, 1931, Part II—*The Textbook in American Education.* Report of the Society's Committee on the Textbook. J. B. Edmonson, Chairman. Cloth, Paper.

*Thirty-first Yearbook, 1932, Part I—*A Program for Teaching Science.* Prepared by the Society's Committee on the Teaching of Science. S. Ralph Powers, Chairman.
*Thirty-first Yearbook, 1932, Part II—*Changes and Experiments in Liberal-Arts Education.* Prepared by Kathryn McHale, with numerous collaborators.
*Thirty-second Yearbook, 1933—*The Teaching of Geography.* Prepared by the Society's Committee on the Teaching of Geography. A. E. Parkins, Chairman.
*Thirty-third Yearbook, 1934, Part I—*The Planning and Construction of School Buildings.* Prepared by the Society's Committee on School Buildings. N. L. Engelhardt, Chairman.
*Thirty-third Yearbook, 1934, Part II—*The Activity Movement.* Prepared by the Society's Committee on the Activity Movement. Lois Coffey Mossman, Chairman.
Thirty-fourth Yearbook, 1935—*Educational Diagnosis.* Prepared by the Society's Committee on Educational Diagnosis. L. J. Brueckner, Chairman. Paper.
*Thirty-fifth Yearbook, 1936, Part I—*The Grouping of Pupils.* Prepared by the Society's Committee. W. W. Coxe, Chairman.
*Thirty-fifth Yearbook, 1936, Part II—*Music Education.* Prepared by the Society's Committee. W. L. Uhl, Chairman.
*Thirty-sixth Yearbook, 1937, Part I—*The Teaching of Reading.* Prepared by the Society's Committee. W. S. Gray, Chairman.
*Thirty-sixth Yearbook, 1937, Part II—*International Understanding through the Public-School Curriculum.* Prepared by the Society's Committee. I. L. Kandel, Chairman.
*Thirty-seventh Yearbook, 1938, Part I—*Guidance in Educational Institutions.* Prepared by the Society's Committee. G. N. Kefauver, Chairman.
*Thirty-seventh Yearbook, 1938, Part II—*The Scientific Movement in Education.* Prepared by the Society's Committee. F. N. Freeman, Chairman.
*Thirty-eighth Yearbook, 1939, Part I—*Child Development and the Curriculum.* Prepared by the Society's Committee. Carleton Washburne, Chairman.
*Thirty-eighth Yearbook, 1939, Part II—*General Education in the American College.* Prepared by the Society's Committee. Alvin Eurich, Chairman. Cloth.
*Thirty-ninth Yearbook, 1940, Part I—*Intelligence: Its Nature and Nurture. Comparative and Critical Exposition.* Prepared by the Society's Committee. G. D. Stoddard, Chairman.
*Thirty-ninth Yearbook, 1940, Part II—*Intelligence: Its Nature and Nurture. Original Studies and Experiments.* Prepared by the Society's Committee. G. D. Stoddard, Chairman.
*Fortieth Yearbook, 1941—*Art in American Life and Education.* Prepared by the Society's Committee. Thomas Munro, Chairman.
Forty-first Yearbook, 1942, Part I—*Philosophies of Education.* Prepared by the Society's Committee. John S. Brubacher, Chairman. Paper.
Forty-first Yearbook, 1942, Part II—*The Psychology of Learning.* Prepared by the Society's Committee. T. R. McConnell, Chairman. Cloth.
*Forty-second Yearbook, 1943, Part I—*Vocational Education.* Prepared by the Society's Committee. F. J. Keller, Chairman.
*Forty-second Yearbook, 1943, Part II—*The Library in General Education.* Prepared by the Society's Committee. L. R. Wilson, Chairman.
Forty-third Yearbook, 1944, Part I—*Adolescence.* Prepared by the Society's Committee. Harold E. Jones, Chairman. Paper.
*Forty-third Yearbook, 1944, Part II—*Teaching Language in the Elementary School.* Prepared by the Society's Committee. M. R. Trabue, Chairman.
*Forty-fourth Yearbook, 1945, Part I—*American Education in the Postwar Period: Curriculum Reconstruction.* Prepared by the Society's Committee. Ralph W. Tyler, Chairman.
*Forty-fourth Yearbook, 1945, Part II—*American Education in the Postwar Period: Structural Reorganization.* Prepared by the Society's Committee. Bess Goodykoontz, Chairman. Paper.
*Forty-fifth Yearbook, 1946, Part I—*The Measurement of Understanding.* Prepared by the Society's Committee. William A. Brownell, Chairman.
*Forty-fifth Yearbook, 1946, Part II—*Changing Conceptions in Educational Administration.* Prepared by the Society's Committee. Alonzo G. Grace, Chairman.
*Forty-sixth Yearbook, 1947, Part I—*Science Education in American Schools.* Prepared by the Society's Committee. Victor H. Noll, Chairman.
*Forty-sixth Yearbook, 1947, Part II—*Early Childhood Education.* Prepared by the Society's Committee. N. Searle Light, Chairman. Paper.
Forty-seventh Yearbook, 1948, Part I—*Juvenile Delinquency and the Schools.* Prepared by the Society's Committee. Ruth Strang, Chairman. Cloth.
Forty-seventh Yearbook, 1948, Part II—*Reading in the High School and College.* Prepared by the Society's Committee. William S. Gray. Chairman. Cloth. Paper.
*Forty-eighth Yearbook, 1949, Part I—*Audio-visual Materials of Instruction.* Prepared by the Society's Committee. Stephen M. Corey, Chairman. Cloth.
*Forty-eighth Yearbook, 1949, Part II—*Reading in the Elementary School.* Prepared by the Society's Committee. Arthur I. Gates, Chairman.
*Forty-ninth Yearbook, 1950, Part I—*Learning and Instruction.* Prepared by the Society's Committee. G. Lester Anderson, Chairman.
*Forty-ninth Yearbook, 1950, Part II—*The Education of Exceptional Children.* Prepared by the Society's Committee. Samuel A. Kirk, Chairman.
Fiftieth Yearbook, 1951, Part I—*Graduate Study in Education.* Prepared by the Society's Board of Directors. Ralph W. Tyler, Chairman. Paper.
Fiftieth Yearbook, 1951, Part II—*The Teaching of Arithmetic.* Prepared by the Society's Committee. G. T. Buswell, Chairman. Cloth, Paper.
Fifty-first Yearbook, 1952, Part I—*General Education.* Prepared by the Society's Committee. T. R. McConnell, Chairman. Cloth, Paper.

Fifty-first Yearbook, 1952, Part II—*Education in Rural Communities.* Prepared by the Society's Committee. Ruth Strang, Chairman. Cloth, Paper.

*Fifty-second Yearbook, 1953, Part I—*Adapting the Secondary-School Program to the Needs of Youth.* Prepared by the Society's Committee: William G. Brink, Chairman.

Fifty-second Yearbook, 1953, Part II—*The Community School.* Prepared by the Society's Committee. Maurice F. Seay, Chairman. Cloth.

Fifty-third Yearbook, 1954, Part I—*Citizen Cooperation for Better Public Schools.* Prepared by the Society's Committee. Edgar L. Morphet, Chairman.

*Fifty-third Yearbook, 1954, Part II—*Mass Media and Education.* Prepared by the Society's Committee. Edgar Dale, Chairman.

*Fifty-fourth Yearbook, 1955, Part I—*Modern Philosophies and Education.* Prepared by the Society's Committee. John S. Brubacher, Chairman.

Fifty-fourth Yearbook, 1955, Part II—*Mental Health in Modern Education.* Prepared by the Society's Committee. Paul A. Witty, Chairman. Paper.

*Fifty-fifth Yearbook, 1956, Part I—*The Public Junior College.* Prepared by the Society's Committee. B. Lamar Johnson, Chairman.

*Fifty-fifth Yearbook, 1956, Part II—*Adult Reading.* Prepared by the Society's Committee. David H. Clift, Chairman.

*Fifty-sixth Yearbook, 1957, Part I—*In-service Education of Teachers, Supervisors, and Administrators.* Prepared by the Society's Committee. Stephen M. Corey, Chairman. Cloth.

Fifty-sixth Yearbook, 1957, Part II—*Social Studies in the Elementary School.* Prepared by the Society's Committee. Ralph C. Preston, Chairman. Cloth, Paper.

*Fifty-seventh Yearbook, 1958, Part I—*Basic Concepts in Music Education.* Prepared by the Society's Committee. Thurber H. Madison, Chairman. Cloth.

*Fifty-seventh Yearbook, 1958, Part II—*Education for the Gifted.* Prepared by the Society's Committee. Robert J. Havighurst, Chairman.

*Fifty-seventh Yearbook, 1958, Part III—*The Integration of Educational Experiences.* Prepared by the Society's Committee. Paul L. Dressel, Chairman. Cloth.

Fifty-eighth Yearbook, 1959, Part I—*Community Education: Principles and Practices from World-wide Experience.* Prepared by the Society's Committee. C. O. Arndt, Chairman. Paper.

Fifty-eighth Yearbook, 1959, Part II—*Personal Services in Education.* Prepared by the Society's Committee. Melvene D. Hardee, Chairman.

*Fifty-ninth Yearbook, 1960, Part I—*Rethinking Science Education.* Prepared by the Society's Committee. J. Darrell Barnard, Chairman.

*Fifty-ninth Yearbook, 1960, Part II—*The Dynamics of Instructional Groups.* Prepared by the Society's Committee. Gale E. Jensen, Chairman.

Sixtieth Yearbook, 1961, Part I—*Development in and through Reading.* Prepared by the Society's Committee. Paul A. Witty, Chairman. Cloth.

Sixtieth Yearbook, 1961, Part II—*Social Forces Influencing American Education.* Prepared by the Society's Committee. Ralph W. Tyler, Chairman. Cloth, Paper.

Sixty-first Yearbook, 1962, Part I—*Individualizing Instruction.* Prepared by the Society's Committee. Fred T. Tyler, Chairman. Cloth.

Sixty-first Yearbook, 1962, Part II—*Education for the Professions.* Prepared by the Society's Committee. G. Lester Anderson, Chairman. Cloth.

Sixty-second Yearbook, 1963, Part I—*Child Psychology.* Prepared by the Society's Committee. Harold W. Stevenson, Editor. Cloth.

Sixty-second Yearbook, 1963, Part II—*The Impact and Improvement of School Testing Programs.* Prepared by the Society's Committee. Warren G. Findley, Editor. Cloth.

Sixty-third Yearbook, 1964, Part I—*Theories of Learning and Instruction.* Prepared by the Society's Committee. Ernest R. Hilgard, Editor. Paper, Cloth.

Sixty-third Yearbook, 1964, Part II—*Behavioral Science and Educational Administration.* Prepared by the Society's Committee. Daniel E. Griffiths, Editor. Paper.

Sixty-fourth Yearbook, 1965, Part I—*Vocational Education.* Prepared by the Society's Committee. Melvin L. Barlow, Editor. Cloth.

*Sixty-fourth Yearbook, 1965, Part II—*Art Education.* Prepared by the Society's Committee. W. Reid Hastie, Editor.

Sixty-fifth Yearbook, 1966, Part I—*Social Deviancy among Youth.* Prepared by the Society's Committee. William W. Wattenberg, Editor. Cloth.

Sixty-fifth Yearbook, 1966, Part II—*The Changing American School.* Prepared by the Society's Committee. John I. Goodlad, Editor. Cloth.

Sixty-sixth Yearbook, 1967, Part I—*The Educationally Retarded and Disadvantaged.* Prepared by the Society's Committee. Paul A. Witty, Editor. Cloth.

*Sixty-sixth Yearbook, 1967, Part II—*Programed Instruction.* Prepared by the Society's Committee. Phil C. Lange, Editor. Cloth.

Sixty-seventh Yearbook, 1968, Part I—*Metropolitanism: Its Challenge to Education.* Prepared by the Society's Committee. Robert J. Havighurst, Editor. Cloth.

Sixty-seventh Yearbook, 1968, Part II—*Innovation and Change in Reading Instruction.* Prepared by the Society's Committee. Helen M. Robinson, Editor. Cloth.

Sixty-eighth Yearbook, 1969, Part I—*The United States and International Education.* Prepared by the Society's Committee. Harold G. Shane, Editor. Cloth.

Sixty-eighth Yearbook, 1969, Part II—*Educational Evaluation: New Roles, New Means.* Prepared by the Society's Committee. Ralph W. Tyler, Editor. Paper.

*Sixty-ninth Yearbook, 1970, Part I—*Mathematics Education.* Prepared by the Society's Committee. Edward G. Begle, Editor. Cloth.

Sixty-ninth Yearbook, 1970, Part II—*Linguistics in School Programs.* Prepared by the Society's Committee. Albert H. Marckwardt, Editor. Cloth.

Seventieth Yearbook, 1971, Part I—*The Curriculum: Retrospect and Prospect.* Prepared by the Society's Committee. Robert M. McClure, Editor. Paper.

Seventieth Yearbook, 1971, Part II—*Leaders in American Education.* Prepared by the Society's Committee. Robert J. Havighurst, Editor. Cloth.

Seventy-first Yearbook, 1972, Part I—*Philosophical Redirection of Educational Research.* Prepared by the Society's Committee. Lawrence G. Thomas, Editor. Cloth.

Seventy-first Yearbook, 1972, Part II—*Early Childhood Education.* Prepared by the Society's Committee. Ira J. Gordon, Editor. Paper.

Seventy-second Yearbook, 1973, Part I—*Behavior Modification in Education.* Prepared by the Society's Committee. Carl E. Thoresen, Editor. Cloth.

Seventy-second Yearbook, 1973, Part II—*The Elementary School in the United States.* Prepared by the Society's Committee. John I. Goodlad and Harold G. Shane, Editors. Cloth.

Seventy-third Yearbook, 1974, Part I—*Media and Symbols: The Forms of Expression, Communication, and Education.* Prepared by the Society's Committee. David R. Olson, Editor. Cloth.

Seventy-third Yearbook, 1974, Part II—*Uses of the Sociology of Education.* Prepared by the Society's Committee. C. Wayne Gordon, Editor. Cloth.

Seventy-fourth Yearbook, 1975, Part I—*Youth.* Prepared by the Society's Committee. Robert J. Havighurst and Philip H. Dreyer, Editors. Cloth.

Seventy-fourth Yearbook, 1975, Part II—*Teacher Education.* Prepared by the Society's Committee. Kevin Ryan, Editor. Cloth.

Seventy-fifth Yearbook, 1976, Part I—*Psychology of Teaching Methods.* Prepared by the Society's Committee. N. L. Gage, Editor. Paper.

*Seventy-fifth Yearbook, 1976, Part II—*Issues in Secondary Education.* Prepared by the Society's Committee. William Van Til, Editor. Cloth.

Seventy-sixth Yearbook, 1977, Part I—*The Teaching of English.* Prepared by the Society's Committee. James R. Squire, Editor. Cloth.

Seventy-sixth Yearbook, 1977, Part II—*The Politics of Education.* Prepared by the Society's Committee. Jay D. Scribner, Editor. Paper.

Seventy-seventh Yearbook, 1978, Part I—*The Courts and Education,* Clifford P. Hooker, Editor. Cloth.

Seventy-seventh Yearbook, 1978, Part II—*Education and the Brain,* Jeanne Chall and Allan F. Mirsky, Editors. Cloth.

Seventy-eighth Yearbook, 1979, Part I—*The Gifted and the Talented: Their Education and Development,* A. Harry Passow. Editor. Cloth.

Seventy-eighth Yearbook, 1979, Part II—*Classroom Management,* Daniel L. Duke, Editor. Paper.

Seventy-ninth Yearbook, 1980, Part I—*Toward Adolescence: The Middle School Years,* Mauritz Johnson, Editor. Cloth.

Seventy-ninth Yearbook, 1980, Part II—*Learning a Second Language,* Frank M. Grittner, Editor. Cloth.

Eightieth Yearbook, 1981, Part I—*Philosophy and Education,* Jonas F. Soltis, Editor. Cloth.

Eightieth Yearbook, 1981, Part II—*The Social Studies,* Howard D. Mehlinger and O. L. Davis, Jr., Editors. Cloth.

Eighty-first Yearbook, 1982, Part I—*Policy Making in Education,* Ann Lieberman and Milbrey W. McLaughlin, Editors. Cloth.

Eighty-first Yearbook, 1982, Part II—*Education and Work,* Harry F. Silberman, Editor. Cloth.

Eighty-second Yearbook, 1983, Part I—*Individual Differences and the Common Curriculum,* Gary D Fenstermacher and John I. Goodlad, Editors. Cloth.

Eighty-second Yearbook, 1983, Part II—*Staff Development,* Gary Griffin, Editor. Cloth.

Yearbooks of the National Society are distributed by

UNIVERSITY OF CHICAGO PRESS, 5801 ELLIS AVE.,
CHICAGO, ILLINOIS 60637

Please direct inquiries regarding prices of volumes still available to the University of Chicago Press. Orders for these volumes should be sent to the University of Chicago Press, not to the offices of the National Society.

2. The Series on Contemporary Educational Issues

In addition to its Yearbooks the Society now publishes volumes in a series on Contemporary Educational Issues. These volumes are prepared under the supervision of the Society's Commission on an Expanded Publication Program.

The 1983 Titles

The Hidden Curriculum and Moral Education (Henry A. Giroux and David Purpel, eds.)

The Dynamics of Organizational Change in Education (J. Victor Baldridge and Terrance Deal, eds.)

The 1982 Titles

Improving Educational Standards and Productivity: The Research Basis for Policy (Herbert J. Walberg, ed.)

Schools in Conflict: The Politics of Education (Frederick M. Wirt and Michael W. Kirst)

The 1981 Titles

Psychology and Education: The State of the Union (Frank H. Farley and Neal J. Gordon, eds.)

Selected Issues in Mathematics Education (Mary M. Lindquist, ed.)

The 1980 Titles

Minimum Competency Achievement Testing: Motives, Models, Measures, and Consequences (Richard M. Jaeger and Carol K. Tittle, eds.)

Collective Bargaining in Public Education (Anthony M. Cresswell, Michael J. Murphy, with Charles T. Kerchner)

The 1979 Titles

Educational Environments and Effects: Evaluation, Policy, and Productivity (Herbert J. Walberg, ed.)

Research on Teaching: Concepts, Findings, and Implications (Penelope L. Peterson and Herbert J. Walberg, eds.)

The Principal in Metropolitan Schools (Donald A. Erickson and Theodore L. Reller, eds.)

The 1978 Titles

Aspects of Reading Education (Susanna Pflaum-Connor, ed.)

History, Education, and Public Policy: Recovering the American Educational Past (Donald R. Warren, ed.)

From Youth to Constructive Adult Life: The Role of the Public School (Ralph W. Tyler, ed.)

The 1977 Titles

Early Childhood Education: Issues and Insights (Bernard Spodek and Herbert J. Walberg, eds.)

The Future of Big City Schools: Desegregation Policies and Magnet Alternatives (Daniel U. Levine and Robert J. Havighurst, eds.)

Educational Administration: The Developing Decades (Luvern L. Cunningham, Walter G. Hack, and Raphael O. Nystrand, eds.)

The 1976 Titles

Prospects for Research and Development in Education (Ralph W. Tyler, ed.)

Public Testimony on Public Schools (Commission on Educational Governance)

Counseling Children and Adolescents (William M. Walsh, ed.)

The 1975 Titles

Schooling and the Rights of Children (Vernon Haubrich and Michael Apple, eds.)

Systems of Individualized Education (Harriet Talmage, ed.)

Educational Policy and International Assessment: Implications of the IEA Assessment of Achievement (Alan Purves and Daniel U. Levine, eds.)

The 1974 Titles

Crucial Issues in Testing (Ralph W. Tyler and Richard M. Wolf, eds.)

Conflicting Conceptions of Curriculum (Elliott Eisner and Elizabeth Vallance, eds.)

Cultural Pluralism (Edgar G. Epps, ed.)

Rethinking Educational Equality (Andrew T. Kopan and Herbert J. Walberg, eds.)

All of the preceding volumes may be ordered from

McCutchan Publishing Corporation
2526 Grove Street
Berkeley, California 94704

The 1972 Titles

Black Students in White Schools (Edgar G. Epps, ed.)

Flexibility in School Programs (W. J. Congreve and G. L. Rinehart, eds.)

Performance Contracting—1969–1971 (J. A. Mecklenburger)

The Potential of Educational Futures (Michael Marien and W. L. Ziegler, eds.)

Sex Differences and Discrimination in Education (Scarvia Anderson, ed.)

The 1971 Titles

Accountability in Education (Leon M. Lessinger and Ralph W. Tyler, eds.)

Farewell to Schools??? (D. U. Levine and R. J. Havighurst, eds.)

Models for Integrated Education (D. U. Levine, ed.)

PYGMALION *Reconsidered* (J. D. Elashoff and R. E. Snow)

Reactions to Silberman's CRISIS IN THE CLASSROOM (A. Harry Passow, ed.)

The 1971 and 1972 titles in this series are now out of print.